Physical
Perspectives • Inquiry • Applications

Cohen

Physical Education
Perspectives • Inquiry • Applications
Second Edition

Robert E. Gensemer
The University of Denver

 Wm. C. Brown Publishers

Book Team

Editor *Chris Rogers*
Developmental Editor *Sue Pulvermacher-Alt*
Production Coordinator *Carla D. Arnold*
Photo Editor *Carrie Burger*

 Wm. C. Brown Publishers

President *G. Franklin Lewis*
Vice President, Publisher *George Wm. Bergquist*
Vice President, Publisher *Thomas E. Doran*
Vice President, Operations and Production *Beverly Kolz*
National Sales Manager *Virginia S. Moffat*
Senior Marketing Manager *Kathy Law Laube*
Marketing Manager *George H. Chapin*
Executive Editor *Edgar J. Laube*
Managing Editor, Production *Colleen A. Yonda*
Production Editorial Manager *Julie A. Kennedy*
Production Editorial Manager *Ann Fuerste*
Publishing Services Manager *Karen J. Slaght*
Manager of Visuals and Design *Faye M. Schilling*

Part Opener One: © Library of Congress/Photo Researchers, Inc.
Part Opener Two: © James L. Shaffer
Part Opener Three: © Spencer Grant/Photo Researchers, Inc.

Copyright © 1985 CBS College Publishing

Copyright © 1991 by Wm. C. Brown Publishers. All rights reserved

Library of Congress Catalog Card Number: 90–80347

ISBN 0-697-10691-8

No part of this publication may be reproduced, stored in a retrieval system, or transmitted, in any form or by any means, electronic, mechanical, photocopying, recording, or otherwise, without the prior written permission of the publisher.

Printed in the United States of America by Wm. C. Brown Publishers, 2460 Kerper Boulevard, Dubuque, IA 52001

10 9 8 7 6 5 4 3 2 1

Contents

Preface *xi*

Part I
Perspectives *3*

Chapter 1
Physical Education: An Emergent Profession *5*
    A Description of Physical Education *7*
    A Name Game *7*
    The Body as a Place for the Mind *8*
    Common Ground: An Enrichment of Being *9*
    Who Should Enter the Profession? *10*
    Personality Traits of Physical Educators *12*
    The Influence of Interests *13*
    Summary *13*
    To the Reader *14*
    Suggested Projects *14*
    References *15*

Chapter 2
Dimensions of the Field: Variations on a Theme *19*
    Related Areas *20*
    Academic Expansion *22*
    From School Programs to Adult Business *24*
    Into the Medical and Technological Marketplaces *26*
    Six Meanings for Physical Education *27*
    Summary *28*
    To the Reader *29*
    Suggested Projects *29*
    References *30*

Chapter 3
Heritage of the Profession: Past Events with Modern Meanings *31*
  Legacy of a Greek Ideal *33*
  Thoughts of Greek Philosophers *35*
  The Rise of Athletic Competition *36*
  End of a Golden Era *38*
  The Roman Empire: Suppression of the Ideal *38*
  Physical Education in Europe *39*
  Early Programs in America *42*
  Civil War to the Turn of the Century *43*
  Twentieth Century Physical Education *44*
  Summary *47*
  To the Reader *48*
  Suggested Projects *49*
  References *50*

Part II
Inquiry *53*

Chapter 4
Research: The Enterprise of Discovery *55*
  A Science of Curiosity *56*
  The Characteristics of Research *57*
  A Search for Facts *58*
  The Value of Scientific Inquiry *59*
  Is All Research Meaningful? *61*
  Developing an Analytical Attitude *61*
  The Impact of Research in Physical Education *62*
  Summary *65*
  To the Reader *66*
  Suggested Projects *66*
  References *67*

Chapter 5
Exercise Physiology: Improving Physical Capacity *69*
  The Heart of the Matter *70*
  Muscle in Motion *72*
  Energy for Physical Activity *73*
  Science and Medicine Together *75*
  In the Subcellular World *76*
  Wellness: Good for Everyone *77*
  The Benefits of Regular Exercise *79*
  Cardiac Risk Factors *80*

Exercise Prescription *84*
Summary *86*
To the Reader *87*
Suggested Projects *88*
References *89*

Chapter 6
Biomechanics: The Science of Human Motion *93*
The Relationship to Kinesiology *95*
The Influence of Science *95*
Descriptions of Movement *97*
Qualitative Analysis: The Eyes Have It *98*
Quantitative Analysis: Computers Tell the Truth *99*
Kinematics, Kinetics, and Optimization *100*
The Absolute Essentials of Performance *101*
Implications for the Real World *103*
Summary *104*
To the Reader *105*
Suggested Projects *106*
References *106*

Chapter 7
Motor Learning and Control: The Mind in Action *109*
Learning and Performance *110*
Learning in Stages *113*
Practice Makes Perfect and Other Myths *114*
Brain in Thought: Information Processing *115*
Motor Programs *116*
Neuromotor Integration *117*
Sensory Feedback *119*
Thinking about the Brain *120*
Summary *120*
To the Reader *121*
Suggested Projects *122*
References *122*

Chapter 8
Sociology of Sport: Society in a Capsule *125*
Description without Prescription *126*
Sport and Social Values *127*
Sport as a Socializing Process *128*
Socialization through Physical Education *130*
Sports in Educational Settings *131*
Equity and Discrimination in Sport *133*
The Future of Sport *134*

Sport Sociology in the Future *136*
Summary *136*
To the Reader *137*
Suggested Projects *137*
References *138*

Chapter 9
Sport Psychology: Inside the Mind of the Athlete *141*
The Final Frontier *142*
Brain in Emotion *143*
The Activation of Arousal *144*
Intervention Strategies *147*
Who's in Control Here? *149*
Go See the Movie in Your Head *151*
The Transcendent Mind *153*
Summary *154*
To the Reader *154*
Suggested Projects *155*
References *156*

Chapter 10
Sports Medicine: Keeping Active People Active *159*
A Synthesis of Many Fields *160*
Preparation of the Human Machinery *161*
What the Outside Can Do to the Inside *163*
The Critical Role of the Athletic Trainer *165*
Duties of the Trainer *166*
The Realm of Physical Therapy *167*
Other Therapeutic Modalities *169*
Summary *170*
To the Reader *171*
Suggested Projects *171*
References *172*

Part III
Applications *175*

Chapter 11
Teaching: Art and Science Together *177*
Components of the Job *178*
A Managerial Manifesto *181*
Profile of an Effective Teacher *182*
A Matter of Method *185*

Why Teach? *186*
The Matter of Money *188*
The State of the Market *189*
Summary *191*
To the Reader *191*
Suggested Projects *193*
References *193*

Chapter 12
Coaching: Seasonal Challenges, Lifetime Rewards *199*
A Typical Working Day *200*
The Multiple Roles of a Coach *201*
What Makes a Coach Successful? *204*
Reasons for Coaching *206*
Why Coaches Quit *208*
The Teaching and Coaching Challenge *209*
Evaluating Your Potential as a Coach *211*
Summary *213*
To the Reader *214*
Suggested Projects *214*
References *215*

Chapter 13
Special Populations: Considerations
for the Handicapped *219*
Who Are the Handicapped? *220*
The Legislation for Handicapped Students *221*
Mainstreaming *223*
The Least Restrictive Environment *224*
The Individualized Education Program *225*
Inclusion or Exclusion? *226*
The Clumsy Child *228*
Summary *229*
To the Reader *230*
Suggested Projects *231*
References *231*

Chapter 14
Careers: Jobs Worth Doing *235*
Careers in Education *237*
Careers in Sport *240*
Careers in the Health and Leisure Industries *242*
Careers in Sports Medicine *245*

Other Options *249*
Summary *251*
To the Reader *251*
Suggested Projects *252*
References *253*

Chapter 15
Career Development: Getting Ready for the Real World *255*
The Academic World and the Vocational World *256*
Narrowing the Focus *257*
Vocational Values *259*
General Vocational Themes *260*
Specific Job Requirements *263*
The Value of Field Experiences *265*
Summary *265*
To the Reader *266*
Suggested Projects *267*
References *268*

Chapter 16
The Future: Not Exactly Like the Present *271*
The Changing Marketplace *272*
Providing a Better Product *275*
New Preparation Needs *277*
Readiness for Tomorrow *277*
Summary *278*
To the Reader *278*
Suggested Projects *279*
References *279*

Glossary *281*
Index *285*

Preface

This book is for anyone who is considering a career that originates from a study of human physical movement.

The range of these careers includes helping people to gain or improve upon their physical skill, to restore lost function, to generate self-management of personal and mental well-being, or to improve the quality of people's lives by promoting healthy life-styles, physical and mental integrity, and enjoyable leisure.

A long-standing name has been associated with these careers: physical education. Affiliated terms have included health, recreation, and leisure. Now there are new terms: exercise science, kinesiology, sport science, human movement science, sports medicine, and a profusion of others. All still attend to the central focus of developing and improving people's personal welfare. And all have foundational concerns and clustered areas of study that support any of the careers that branch from this general objective.

This book describes the professional enterprise that has traditionally been given the umbrella term *physical education,* which now includes a number of associated interests. It provides discussion of the position ideals and issues confronting the profession. It details the supporting areas of academic involvement and informational content. And it gives counsel concerning the vocational applications of each area of study. Thus, the writings herein describe what the profession is, what its study areas are, and where the jobs can be found.

Sixteen chapters follow. Each is somewhat independent and could be read separately, although the book is organized around three central themes. The first three chapters, presented in Part I, are an excursion through the patterns of thought and values, past and present, that guide the profession. Part II includes chapters 4 through 10, wherein attention is given to the substantive areas of academic focus that provide the informational content of the profession. The last six chapters, comprising Part III, describe how the profession comes alive in career settings.

Two new chapters are included in this second edition: chapter 9, Sport Psychology, and chapter 10, Sports Medicine. The entire text has been restyled, in effect having been completely rewritten. New material has been added throughout, and updated references support each chapter. A continual thread of vocational applications carries through the text, with particular attention being given to thoughtful career preparation. In sum, the topics are contemporary, with foresight toward the future.

Each chapter begins with four brief statements of content, which lead into the discussions that follow. At the end of every chapter, a "To the Reader" synopsis addresses the real-world considerations of the material. In addition, a "Suggested Projects" section offers ways to further expand on the topical content. In all, each chapter gives the reader information, explains what that information means, and suggests ways to find out more about the topic.

The narrative is not excessively detailed; yet the content is exacting and provides ample substance. The information is presented in such a way that the reader will become informed, enlightened, entertained, and encouraged to go beyond the limits of length and words in this book.

Special acknowledgment is extended to M. Gene Lee, Metropolitan State College; Michael R. Griffin, Valdosta State College; and Bob Pearson, Berry College for their in-depth reviews of this second edition. Their comments helped to shape this textbook.

Finally, it is customary for authors to dedicate their books to someone who, without their help, the book probably would have been written anyhow. Instead, this book is dedicated to you, the reader, without whom it definitely would not have been written. If in some small way the words that follow help you to form clear decisions about these important years of your life, then the major objective of this written communication has been accomplished.

Physical Education
Perspectives • Inquiry • Applications

Part I

Perspectives

Chapter 1   **Physical Education: An Emergent Profession**
Chapter 2   **Dimensions of the Field: Variations on a Theme**
Chapter 3   **Heritage of the Profession: Past Events with Modern Meanings**

Chapter 1

Physical Education: An Emergent Profession

A Description of Physical Education

A Name Game

The Body as a Place for the Mind

Common Ground: An Enrichment of Being

Who Should Enter the Profession?

Personality Traits of Physical Educators

The Influence of Interests

Summary

To the Reader

Suggested Projects

References

As an enduring profession, physical education has focused its attention on the dimensions of human physical activity.

In its most acknowledged application, the profession has delivered organized programs designed to facilitate people's control of their own movement capabilities.

Since the mind and the body function as an integrated whole, enhancement of the physical self is seen to also elicit positive outcomes in mental states.

The profession has now expanded these endeavors into a wide range of vocational settings, with a consequent increase in the variety of career options.

Perspectives

EVERY mind has a body.
No startling revelation, that. But not so long ago, as it seems in retrospect, the body was considered to be merely a biological housing for the mind. A subordinate chauffeur. Now it is widely appreciated that the mind and the body are in collaboration, each one inexorably affecting the other. So the human mind, which has come to comprehend the infinity of the cosmos and the multiple potentials of the atom, has realized that it is in dependent communication with its own body; a collective whole of mental and physical alliance.

Plenty of people recognize this connection, as evidenced by the multitudes who take themselves out for a jog, or to the bike paths, or to the courts, or to fitness centers. On any given day, 15 to 20 percent of the adult population could be participating in some form of vigorous physical activity (Shephard, 1988). In America, 20 million people jog (Thornberry, Wilson, and Golden, 1986), 20 million play tennis, 40 million walk regularly, 42 million play basketball, and 44 million do aerobics (Stephens, 1987). Add the numbers who swim, weight train, ski, play racketball, softball, and other sports, and perhaps six of every ten Americans engage in some type of physical activity (Ellis, 1988).

It's a natural. Our bodies were made for motion, whether for long, purposeful strides across a backcourt, or for the free, expressive creations of a dance. There is something magnetic and totally captivating

Our bodies were made for motion.
Photo by Tom Cherrey.

about activity. It challenges and it satisfies. It excites and it calms. It wins our allegiance with a compelling urge that may be an answer to some fundamental human need. We are enlivened and rejuvenated by the pure joy of movement.

In response to this appeal, a long-standing profession has focused on human physical activity. It has built a scientific and philosophical collection of information about people in motion and has made a descriptive analysis of the benefits of regular exercise. Its most-often-used name is *physical education*.

A DESCRIPTION OF PHYSICAL EDUCATION

In the traditional sense, physical education may be thought of as *the sum of all the physical, mental, emotional, and social outcomes of an organized program that focuses on physical activity as the means to the ends.*

Also in a traditional sense, physical education has been considered to be primarily an enterprise for youths in school programs. These programs, properly administered, involve the conscious employment of exercise, sport, play, and other organized activities to enhance the physical and mental qualities of the participants and to provide aptitudes of skill that can be recreationally used for a lifetime. The means of delivery for these objectives is *movement*—human physical activity designed to foster definite ends, whether they be increased levels of physical fitness or specific sports skills. Furthermore, the outcomes of movement are not limited to the physical, but have effects on the mind as well. It is generally acknowledged that activity produces heightened mental alertness, or at least that the two are related. Thus, physical education is a means for eliciting positive states, through movement, in both mind and body.

A NAME GAME

Within recent times, the profession of physical education has greatly expanded beyond its original realm. As a result, the field is often misinterpreted, sometimes by definitions that confine its meaning rather than providing a true description. When someone hears the words *physical education,* the person may think only of experiences remembered from school activity classes. But with the now enlarged domain of physical education, the term is often found to be too limiting, and there has been a resulting trend away from its use. In fact, some have predicted that by the year 2000 the name will have disappeared completely (Lucas, 1986).

What terms will replace it? One survey of departmental titles in university and college settings found fifty-eight different names for the units assigned to the area traditionally called physical education (Brassie and Razor, 1989). Another discovered that since 1986 a dramatic increase in departmental name changes has occurred, yet more than 50 percent of the changes still included the term physical education, most often linked with denominations of health, leisure studies, or sport studies (Janz, Cottle, Mahaffey, and Phillips, 1989). Otherwise, when physical education is not included in a department's name, the most common designations are *kinesiology, human performance, sport studies,* and *sport sciences.*

The major reasons given for name changes are to more accurately describe the department's area of specialization and curricular content, and to enhance the image of the program in the academic community (Janz et al., 1989). But physical education remains by far the most commonly included moniker in a departmental title. In one survey of 318 schools that offered a major in what is traditionally called physical education, only 30 did not include the term in their departmental name (Brassie and Razor, 1989). Thus, physical education is still the most widely used title. The profession has adopted new terminologies intended to overcome the restricted connotations of the label physical education; nonetheless, physical education remains the most intuitively understood term and is therefore the name that will be used (to signify all its variants) throughout this text.

THE BODY AS A PLACE FOR THE MIND

As an organized unit, physical education may include a wide variety of professional functions ranging from basic skill instruction to the realms of the health enhancement and leisure industries. The expansion of the field has been indeed phenomenal (as discussed in the next chapter), penetrating as it has into medical areas and incorporating concerns that were originally those of physics, engineering, chemistry, biology, and other sciences.

The expansion of physical education has sprung from the basic concept that physical activity offers experiences that are not otherwise obtainable. Programs of physical education have been founded on the ideal that the mind can be educated *through* physical movement and that movement can be a conscious *expression* of things that the mind already knows. In this way, physical activity offers people distinct behavioral, developmental, and educational experiences whereby the body is a medium. Information comes into the mind *from* the body, and the mind

Physical activity offers unique experiences for the mind and the body.
University of Denver file photo.

in turn transmits learned information *to* the body for direct improvements in its prowess. This twofold perspective has been a basic endowment of the profession of physical education.

Within this context, if the word *physical* is accented in physical education, we can view it as a form of education in its own right: that in which the body is being educated. If we emphasize *education,* we can see physical education as a distinctive kind of learning in which the body is the medium through which the education takes place. Both viewpoints have validity, and both represent physical education in traditional (refer to Williams, 1954) and contemporary applications.

What distinguishes physical education from other professions is its regard for the physical—or more accurately, the *movement* of the physical—as the reference point. By no means does the profession isolate movement as its only interest, but it is the basis of the multidimensional areas of study that characterize physical education today.

COMMON GROUND: AN ENRICHMENT OF BEING

This is a time of diversity in physical education, with branches of inquiry that not too many years ago didn't even have names. Now a curriculum of the field looks like a menu at an Oriental restaurant.

Yet, in every aspect of present-day physical education, a common goal exists: to make life more vibrant, more enjoyable, and more complete. The goal is the same for all those whom the profession touches, from the youngster trying to coordinate all body parts in order to dribble a soccer ball to the debilitated individual reclaiming an injured limb. It is a profession that serves all who have come to know, or are coming to know, the extension of the self that is possible through such acts as sending a ball to a predetermined spot, or sending the body through articulate movements, or sensing the sheer pleasure of bringing the mind to life through a physical medium.

The body is a vehicle of consciousness that goes beyond the dimensions possible by thought alone. The body supplies an energy for the mind, and the mind energizes the body. Activity brings one into an extensive world of feeling, of knowing, of experiencing, of being. It is a way to self-completion.

What physical education adds to life is an amplitude that can be thought of as "being in the body" (Ulrich, 1982). It is a special kind of *awareness* of the qualities of one's physical self and a certain fluid understanding about how one can, through the physical self, become finitely dynamic, unbounded by the constraints and contingencies that are part of the more conventional aspects of life. At times, physical activity inspires ecstasy, joy, and bliss in movements called "peak experiences" (Maslow, 1968). Activity stimulates the agreeable sensation of knowing the mind and the physical self as one total, reciprocating being. It may be the best available path to enrichment of life (Leonard, 1974).

WHO SHOULD ENTER THE PROFESSION?

Activity *is* compelling. It *does* epitomize a certain purity of human existence. Therefore, a profession that centers on human physical activity should be gratifying. And surveys of physical education majors indicate that a love of sport is a general enticement for entry into the profession (Gilbert, 1988).

Other research shows that socially derived motives often attract students to potential careers in physical education, for the profession is perceived as providing opportunities to work with and help others, with the return of a rewarding and satisfying life (Templin, Woodford, and Mulling, 1982). On a less altruistic basis, some students have entered physical education because they think it to be one of the few university programs in which they can realistically hope to achieve academic success (Dewar and Lawson, 1984). But in these days of academically demanding programs, such a view is no longer common.

Being a physical educator offers an opportunity to work with and help others.
Camp Kingsmont, West Stockbridge, Massachusetts.

The dominant view of physical education, held by the majority of students in preparation programs, is that the profession is largely skill and sport oriented, centering on teaching. Accordingly, the most influential attractor to the field is a past affiliation with sport and a perceived opportunity to reproduce previous successes, or at least a chance to continue an active lifestyle via one's career (Dewar, 1989). Often, this general motive has grown from contact with physical education teachers or coaches who were seen as admirable, and a vocational choice is made on the basis of matching oneself with this image (Goc-Karp, Kim, and Skinner, 1985).

Students in physical education major programs who do not want to teach or coach view the curriculum as a prerequisite to careers in fields such as physical therapy, athletic training, rehabilitation, medicine, and other diverse interests such as architecture and business administration (Dewar, 1989). Indeed, one might argue (and some evidence supports a belief) that a degree in anything gives one a better opportunity for employment in any profession than no degree at all (Tracey, 1988).

In general, then, one may have a certain aptitude for physical education by virtue of past experiences in sports and physical activity. And one may have an ability for the profession because of talents in physical performance. Such developed aptitudes and abilities are at least reference points of important information about one's suitability for the profession. They are not the only determinants, but if one has an interest in the dimensions of human physical activity, then an automatic practical beginning is already in effect.

PERSONALITY TRAITS OF PHYSICAL EDUCATORS

It has often been assumed that there are certain personality characteristics that incline one toward the selection of physical education as a career. As such, a stereotype has developed that is founded in part on some early research that showed physical education students to be authoritarian, socially competitive, and aggressive (Hendry, 1973). Followup studies described physical education majors to be enthusiastic, adventuresome, self-assured, self-sufficient, emotionally stable, practical, extroverted, tough-minded, conservative, and imaginative (Clark, 1986; Gruber and Perkins, 1978; Ruffer, 1976; and Widdop and Widdop, 1975).

Such investigations do not produce much more than descriptions of the "typical" physical education major. They are not deterministic in the same regard that, for example, one needs an extraordinary gift of skill to become a world-class athlete. No personality traits automatically predispose or disqualify one from potential success in the profession. Accomplished coaches, for instance, tend to have similar personalities, but not *all* successful coaches have the *same* traits (Eitzen and Sage, 1986). However, some argument might be made for the need to have a sensitivity for working with people. This is in fact a common characteristic of physical education majors (Petrakis, 1981) and probably is related to the often-given description of physical education as a "people-oriented" profession.

Physical educators are often "people-oriented."
University of Denver file photo.

THE INFLUENCE OF INTERESTS

In the final analysis, career choices are generally based on interests: a person's likes and dislikes. Perhaps interests are the most logical of all reasons for making career decisions. A person's interests and values, when properly matched with a career, may be the most important factors in determining success and job satisfaction (Minton and Schneider, 1985).

Interests and values are among the most investigated variables in career development (Stankiewicz, 1986). Theory and research support the idea that people tend to be more productive and happier if their work roles and the organizational environment synchronize with their personalities, interests, and values (Eseem, 1986). Moreover, people who choose careers based on their interests and values tend to have a longer and more contented tenure in their chosen vocations (Kiefer and Neumann, 1989).

In many professions, decisions about entry are made on the basis of limited or fragmentary information. Often, the potential for high income is the overwhelming consideration, thereby narrowing the perspective and increasing the possibilities for a mismatch between a person's psyche and the job atmosphere. The results can be high levels of stress, failing health, and an abbreviated time in the career (London, 1988). Such a mismatch would seem less likely in physical education, however. Everyone has at least a fundamental grasp that the profession centers on human physical activity, and everyone knows clearly of their own interests in activity. Therefore, a projected job/interest correlation can be made with a reasonable degree of predictive reliance. And in summation, an interest in physical activity may be the only necessary prerequisite for a beginning consideration of physical education as a career.

SUMMARY

Physical education is a widening profession that focuses on human movement. Its customary applications have had the major objective of providing people with increasing control over their own performance capabilities. Within this process, the mind also becomes disciplined to the requirements and aptitudes of its body. Thus, the mind can guide the body, and the body in turn can give alertness and expression to the mind. In the end, physical education seeks to achieve an optimal functioning of all systems of the body in harmonic convergence with a discerning mind.

An increasing variety of professional services hold to this objective. In addition to programs delivered in school settings, the vocational field has expanded into public, private, and corporate endeavors that attend to instructing, maximizing, and reconstructing human movement potentials. In all cases, the common thread is the goal of eliciting positive states in both mind and body.

To the Reader

Ideally, this first chapter would conclude by providing the reader with a clear and definitive statement about why physical education is a fitting career choice. Given the limitations of the written word, however, that goal is beyond the reach of this text. In fact, such a statement would be misleading in disregarding the general theme of the profession as one of extraordinary diversity in application. There is no unidirectional end to which the degree leads. Whereas the degree was originally a ticket to (and virtual guarantee of) a teaching position, that potential is only one of the multitude of vocational avenues that are now possible.

The basic appeal of physical education could be oversimplified. It readily falls into a logic known as a syllogism: two beliefs or assumptions followed by a conclusion. First, physical activitiy is captivating; second, the profession of physical education focuses on physical activity; therefore, physical education is a captivating profession. This does make some sense but may not be the most appropriate way to confirm a career choice.

It is not of debate that having an intrigue with the dimensions of human physical activity is a magnet that attracts many to physical education as a profession. Teaching, coaching, athletic training, and other sporting careers all offer professional extensions of personal values that may be so enthralling and ingrained that they persuasively impel one into a choice that is not really a decision but rather a submission. If that be the case, then interests and values have simply had their effect.

But a final principle, and perhaps the most telling of all, is that the field integrates a diversified collection of academic interests. Those interests have given definitive strength to a degree that represents induction into a range of workplace settings that only yesterday was relatively narrow but today seems unlimited and still growing. In the next chapter, we'll examine the expanded market for these interests, and in the ensuing chapters, we'll have a look at the academic foundations that support this emergent profession.

Suggested Projects

1. It is probably safe to assume that you, the reader, have an intrinsic interest in physical education because of your previous experiences with activity. This may have come from participation on organized

athletic teams, in recreational pursuits, or both. Reflect on those experiences, trying to describe what it was that captured your attention to the point that you are now considering a career that focuses on activity.
2. Relatedly, what were the positive outcomes you gained from participation in sporting events? Were there any negative ones? How much influence did coaches, friends, or parents have on your enjoyment (or lack thereof) in participation?
3. Discuss how movement is a multidimensional aspect of human beings. How can it affect, and be affected by, various states of mind? Describe some experiences in which your athletic performance and your mental alertness were operating simultaneously at high levels.
4. Interview someone who is involved in a career directly connected with human physical activity. Ask for both the benefits and shortcomings of the profession. Compare your notes with other class members who have also conducted an interiew. Do commonalities exist among the professions?
5. Write down all the things you know about physical education. Then list the unknown factors that might cloud your career decisions. Ask for classroom discussion of the issues that are of most concern to you.

References

Brassie, P. S., and Razor, J. E. (1989). *A National Survey of the Changing Structure and Names of HPERD in Higher Education.* Reston, VA: American Alliance for Health, Physical Education, Recreation and Dance.

Clark, P. T. (1986). A Longitudinal Analysis of Physical Educators in Training. In J. Watkins, T. Reilly, and L. Burwitz (Eds.), *Sports Science* (pp. 315–320). London: E. & F. N. Spon Ltd.

Dewar, A. M. (1989). Recruitment into Physical Education Teaching: Toward a Critical Approach. In T. J. Templin and P. G. Schempp (Eds.), *Socialization into Physical Education: Learning to Teach* (pp. 39–58). Indianapolis: Benchmark Press.

Dewar, A. M., and Lawson, H. A. (1984). The Subjective Warrant and Recruitment into Physical Education. *Quest, 36,* 15–25.

Eitzen, D. S., and Sage, G. H. (1986). *Sociology of North American Sport* (3rd ed.). Dubuque, IA: Wm. C. Brown Publishers.

Ellis, M. J. (1988). *The Business of Physical Education: Future of the Profession.* Champaign, IL: Human Kinetics Books.

Eseem, E. L. (1986). *Low Tec Education in a High Tec World.* New York: Free Press.

Gilbert, K. (1988). Recruits to the Physical Education Profession: A Cross-Cultural Analysis. *The Physical Educator, 45,* 163–168.

Goc-Karp, G., Kim, D. W., and Skinner, P. C. (1985). Professor and Student Perceptions and Beliefs about Physical Education. *The Physical Educator, 43,* 115–120.

Gruber, J., and Perkins, S. (1978). Personality Traits of Women Physical Education Majors and Non-majors at Various Levels of Athletic Competition. *International Journal of Sport Psychology, 9,* 40–52.

Hendry, L. B. (1973). The Physical Educationist Stereotype. In H. T. A. Whiting, K. Hardman, L. B. Hendry, and M. G. Jones (Eds.), *Personality and Performance in Physical Education and Sport.* London: Henry Kimpton.

Janz, K. F., Cottle, S. L., Mahaffey, C. R. and Phillips, D. A. (1989). Current Name Trends in Physical Education. *Journal of Physical Education, Recreation and Dance, 60,* 85–92.

Kiefer, N. M., and Neumann, G. R. (1989). *Search Models and Applied Labor Economics.* Cambridge, England: Cambridge University Press.

Leonard, G. (1974). *The Ultimate Athlete.* New York: Viking Press.

London, M. (1988). Career Planning and Development. In S. Gael, *The Job Analysis Handbook for Business, Industry, and Government.* New York: John Wiley & Sons.

Lucas, J. A. (1986). Open Forum. *The American Academy of Physical Education News, 6,* 8.

Maslow, A. (1968). *Toward a Psychology of Being.* New York: Van Nostrand Reinhold.

Minton, H. L., and Schneider, F. W. (1985). *Differential Psychology* (2nd ed.). Monterey, CA: Brooks/Cole Publishing.

Petrakis, E. (1981). Cognitive Styles of Physical Education Majors. *Perceptual and Motor Skills, 53,* 574.

Ruffer, W. A. (1976). Multivariate Analyses of Physical Education Student Personality Profiles. *Perceptual and Motor Skills, 43,* 1242.

Shephard, R. J. (1988). Fitness Boom or Bust: A Canadian Perspective. *Research Quarterly for Exercise and Sport, 59,* 265–269.

Stankiewicz, R. (1986). *Academics and Entrepreneurs.* New York: St. Martin's Press.

Stephens, T. (1987). Secular Trends in Adult Physical Activity: Exercise Boom or Bust? *Research Quarterly for Exercise and Sport, 58,* 94–105.

Templin, T. J., Woodford, R., and Mulling, C. (1982). On Becoming a Physical Educator: Occupational Choice and the Anticipatory Socialization Process. *Quest, 34,* 119–133.

Thornberry, O. T., Wilson, R. W., and Golden, P. (1986). *Vital and Health Statistics* (DHHS Publication No. 86-1250). Hyattsville, MD: National Center for Health Statistics.

Tracey, W. R. (1988). *Critical Skills: The Guide to Top Performance for Human Resources Managers.* New York: American Management Association.

Ulrich, C. (1982). Body Being: The "Now" Physical Education. In C. Ulrich (Ed.), *Education in the 80s: Physical Education* (pp.12–17). Washington, DC: National Education Association.

Widdop, J. H., and Widdop, V. A. (1975). Comparison of the Personality Traits of Female Teacher Education and Physical Education Students. *Research Quarterly, 46,* 274–281.

Williams, J. F. (1954). *Principles of Physical Education.* Philadelphia: W. B. Saunders.

Chapter 2

Dimensions of the Field: Variations on a Theme

Related Areas

Academic Expansion

From School Programs to Adult Business

Into the Medical and Technological Marketplaces

Six Meanings for Physical Education

Summary

To the Reader

Suggested Projects

References

Physical education, as a total profession, can be viewed as attending to two encompassing goals: health enhancement and enjoyable leisure.

In recent decades the profession has employed a scholarly approach and has accumulated a growing body of scientific information to support its goals and the many dimensions of the field.

This disciplined information has taken the profession into new avenues of the health and leisure industries, and into the workplaces of technological enterprise and medical support systems.

As a result, the lasting vocational applications of the profession that are evident in educational settings are now being supplemented by new job opportunities in areas not previously available.

PHYSICAL education, as a professional enterprise in the total marketplace, is most commonly affiliated with the use of organized physical activity to promote healthy life-styles and enjoyable recreation. The programs are given most noticeably in educational settings, but also in public, private, and corporate establishments. In broad perspective, the central focuses of the programs are health enhancement and active leisure.

To the extent that it achieves these objectives, physical education offers a positive contribution that is both personal and societal. It directly affects individuals in organized programs through improvements in physical welfare and the acquisition of recreational skills. And it more diversely affects society by the provision for a healthy citizenry.

Curiously, the academic fields of physical education, health, and recreation have increasingly developed separation from one another. With the phenomenal growth of information accumulation, each area has become more specifically concerned with interests that are confined to its own assumed territory. Previously, the terms *health, physical education, and recreation* could describe professional preparation curriculums like vanilla, chocolate, and strawberry. But now we can find at least thirty-one flavors of academic concentration, albeit every one is a variant of the original three. Furthermore, the diversified interests remain interchangeably linked because they are all part of the larger concern for human health and the constructive use of leisure. So the academic boundaries that have been drawn are in reality only those of curricular content. The common concern for human welfare still ties everything together.

RELATED AREAS

The term *physical education* is often liberally used as an umbrella label to include a variety of interests. Some of the areas that are associated with physical education are as follows:

Sport. A sport is generally defined as a type of competitive physical activity that involves specific administrative organization and that has limits set in explicit and formal rules governing the behavior of the participants.

Athletics. This term denotes organized, competitive, vigorous sports, usually meaning interscholastic, intercollegiate, and professional sports, but sometimes also including intramurals.

All areas of physical education, including its activities, have become technical.
University of Denver file photo.

Play. Activities that are spontaneous, with no predetermined ending and no tangible outcome, victory, or reward. The rules of play, if there are any, are generally also spontaneous.

Recreation. The identifiable activities of a sportlike nature that one does when one is not required to work. Recreation is undertaken voluntarily, is generally in keeping with personal interests, and should provide enjoyment and satisfaction by virtue of the participation alone.

Dance. A rhythmical and patterned succession of bodily movements, usually to the accompaniment of music. Traditionally considered a performing art, dance also includes variations that promote fitness and expressive enjoyment.

Physical Fitness. This wide-ranging term usually refers to organic vigor, strength, muscular endurance, and cardiovascular endurance. The definition, however, can refer to a general state of biological function or to highly specific measures of organic capacity.

Health. The general condition of the body, often expressed as a three-dimensional physical, mental, and social makeup, but usually meaning a physical "soundness" that enables one to function in a state of well-being.

Wellness. Whereas *health* refers to a state of being, *wellness* means an active approach to life management, including attention to nutrition, stress management, alcohol and drug control, smoking cessation, physical fitness, and other matters of comprehensive life-style conduct.

Athletic Training. A discipline that implements prevention-of-injury programs and provides immmediate treatment of injuries and rehabilitation of injured athletes.

Physical Therapy. The methodological designing and/or implementing of programs for rehabilitation of injuries, usually to athletes. A physical therapist does not diagnose or evaluate injuries, or provide immediate care-of-injuries, as the athletic trainer does.

Sports Medicine. Originally referring to the application of medicine to the diagnosis, treatment, rehabilitation, and prevention of sports-related ills and injuries. In principle, it is most closely associated with athletic training and physical therapy, but it has become a loosely used term to include any science dealing with human physical performance.

ACADEMIC EXPANSION

Physical education was once a loose conglomerate of interests that began and ended with sportlike activities. Now its study areas incorporate a wide range of decentralized fields of inquiry that seem limited only by the number of credits a preparing institution can cram into its curriculum. The core of attention remains on human physical activity, but the realms of study have branched into avenues that are ordinarily thought of as the territories of science, technology, and medicine.

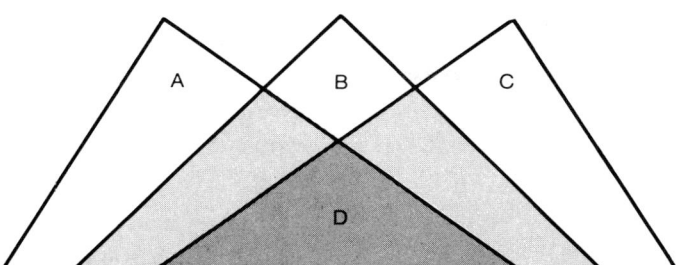

Figure 2.1 The interdisciplinary nature of physical education is represented here where A is physiology, B is psychology, C is sociology, and D is physical education. A and B interrelate, as do B and C. D has incorporated elements of all three.

To a large extent, the expanding inclusiveness of new interest areas is an outgrowth of the scholarly maturation that has taken place within physical education. It began in the 1960s (Crase, 1978) and was heavily influenced by a compelling writing by Franklin Henry (1964), who implored physical educators to generate their own internal body of knowledge. For a long time, physical education had relied almost entirely on information supplied from other fields of study, particularly from physiology, psychology, and sociology. Physical education therefore was considered to be an "interdisciplinary" field. And in fact, these other disciplines still contribute to its collection of information (see figure 2.1).

A notable change has taken place in recent times in that physical education no longer depends on other disciplines for its most relevant information. Instead, these outside areas of study have become springboards for the internal development of a body of knowledge that is self-supporting. Thus, the pure science of physiology—as a science dealing with living organisms—became channeled into a dynamic study area that focuses on human systems under the effort of exercise, called *exercise physiology*. Likewise, the science of physics (the study of the properties of matter and energy) contributed to *biomechanics,* whereby the mechanical principles of motion previously applied only to machines are now used to study humans in motion. Psychology provided a foundation for *motor learning and control,* which attends to the psychological dimensions (and affiliated neurological factors) involved in the learning and performance of movement skills. Further expansion of the area led to the *psychology of sport,* which probes the human mind to find psychodynamic ways to help athletes achieve their best performances. Sociology supplied the basis of technique for the *sociology of sport,* where the world of sport is examined for its structure and its effects on the participants. And the medical profession became an impulse for *sports medicine,* which attends to the techniques of preparing athletes for competition and the rehabilitation of injuries sustained in sport.

Other specialized areas of concentrated study have developed within physical education, but the above six are perhaps most representative of the scientific attitude that is now common in the profession. Each will be examined in a separate chapter in this text.

The very existence of these disciplined study areas illustrates that science has entered physical education. In the main, "science" relates to the investigation of events that may be described as certain or absolute. There is no guesswork or speculation about what *seems* to be happening, but rather a reliance on what the facts of the situation show to be true. Science makes use of instrumentation that does not provide misleading information—cameras, computers, and other electronic devices. In physical education, these instruments are used to record human movement and to show exactly what happens, without bias. This approach has extracted precise information about the dynamics of human function and has taken physical education into new domains. In particular, it has added a broad expanse to the health and leisure industries, and has penetrated a wide array of professional workplaces that are considered technological and medical.

FROM SCHOOL PROGRAMS TO ADULT BUSINESS

Everyone knows that physical education takes place in the schools, serving the youth of the nation with organized programs that are assigned to generate life-style habits of attention to physical and mental welfare. Perhaps these programs are having an effect, for increasing numbers of adults are now actively observing healthy behaviors.

Several large social forces also have brought the adult population's attention to how we treat ourselves. One major influence is more free time. Since the Second World War, a steady decline in the workweek has brought the average down to about thirty-eight hours per week (Gerson, Ibrahim, DeVries, and Eisen, 1988). Relatedly, daily household chores are requiring less time (because of such conveniences as microwave ovens, for example), so that today the average worker has 70 percent more free time than at the turn of the century (Veal, 1987).

In general, people have more free time and disposable income to use in leisure pursuits.
Photo by Bob Gensemer.

In addition, the mass media has alerted the public to the benefits of healthy habits with substantive accounts of medical reasons for attending to one's own well-being. Moreover, people now have more money to spend on such affairs. Americans today have a greater percentage of "disposable income," which is what's left from the paycheck after all the normal living expenses and assorted bills are paid. Disposable income has increased by an average of more than 1 percent a year since 1973 (Sommers, 1988). Likewise, the amount of money being spent on recreation has shown a similar increment (Earl, 1986). And perhaps because of these factors, nearly every incorporated community of 10,000 or more in the United States now has a municipal recreation department (Sessoms, 1987).

Two enterprises serve the public's interest in active and healthy lifestyles—health enhancement organizations and the leisure industry. The health industry seeks to improve the basic functional state of people's health. The leisure industry has the objective of offering more enjoyable self-directed activities. The two overlap, for a person can achieve both enjoyment in the pursuit of a sporting endeavor and improvements in health at the same time.

The result of these trends has been the growth of entrepreneur organizations that have made health and leisure services available to the public. And the translation of all this for physical educators is: more jobs.

INTO THE MEDICAL AND TECHNOLOGICAL MARKETPLACES

The study of humans in motion has a product unto itself. That product is an understanding of human movement phenomena, regardless of the context of the performance. When human motion is comprehended as a functional whole, that understanding has application in any situation where movement is a foundational part of an objective, however subtle the objective may be.

In any situation, the objectives of movement are very direct, focusing on an individual's gaining acceptable or refined control of movement patterns, usually for use in sportlike settings. In other, more indirect applications, knowledge about human movement has been used, for instance, in the design and manufacture of sports equipment. Clothing, especially footwear, has been patterned on the basis of how the human body moves. Other equipment has been changed to provide for the best performance. Notable examples are the evolving configurations and construction materials used in striking implements such as golf clubs and tennis rackets, which are fashioned to produce more power and accuracy for the user.

And the functional understanding of human movement carries into applications that either do not have sport themes or are not associated with skilled performance in sports. Consider, for example, the need to understand movement phenomena to formulate programs of physical therapy, or in athletic training, where the rehabilitation of an injured person can be facilitated or hindered by the plan of the movement patterning. Even further, the design of personally fitted artificial limbs or mechanical devices that aid rehabilitation must be based on an appreciation of how the human body moves.

Furthermore, a comprehensive knowledge of how the systems of the body function is vital in medical support professions such as exercise technology and cardiac rehabilitation. New vocational opportunities are

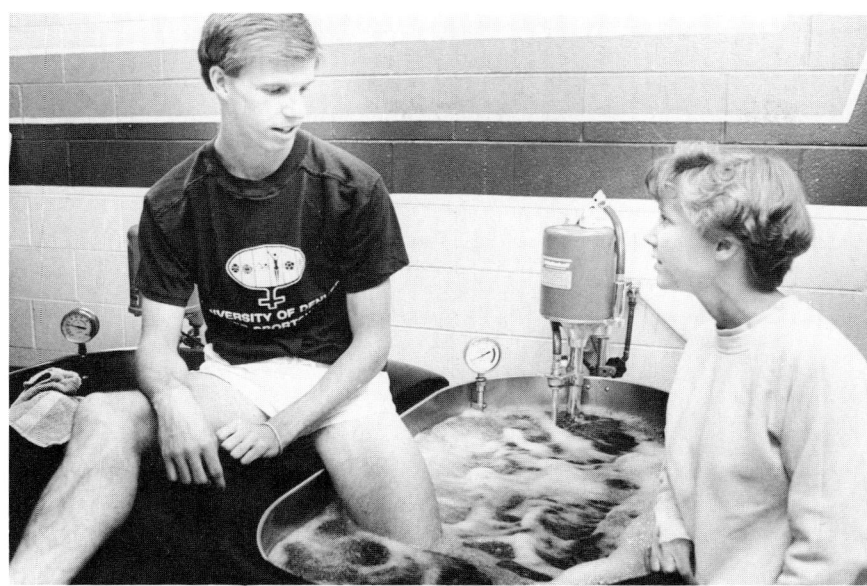

A functional understanding of human movement is essential for developing quality physical therapy programs.
Photo by Tom Cherrey.

now available in hospitals, clinics, institutions, and private practice. Jobs that were previously filled by medically trained personnel are now being taken by those with appropriate background in the human movement sciences. And in wellness and fitness centers, unqualified persons are being replaced by physical educators who are prepared to conduct sound and safe programs. Even management positions are most effectively secured by persons who have a comprehensive knowledge of human movement. In short, wherever there is a setting in which humans move, there is cause to study and apply information on how to arrange for the most productive outcomes of that movement.

SIX MEANINGS FOR PHYSICAL EDUCATION

In summary, physical education may be seen as an enterprise that has six components (Zeigler, 1981), as follows:

1. *The subject matter.* The first component is what the field is *about,* or what it attends to. Essentially, this is found in human movement. More specifically, it exists on the contention that movement can be defined, analyzed, understood, and changed. And while some of the interests of physical education are less discernible, such as psychological states of mind, they still emanate from activity.

2. *The occupation.* Next is what people in the profession *do*. It's a diverse list. They are employed in educational settings as teachers, coaches, or researchers. They may work as fitness leaders or exercise technicians in colleges, private clubs, clinics, recreation centers, or business and industry. Or they may be involved with athletic training programs or therapy in schools, hospitals, institutions, or rehabilitation clinics. Some get involved in sports product design or sales. Others acquire management positions in athletic or fitness locations.
3. *The process.* This refers to the *means* whereby the subject matter of physical education is dispersed. In general it is affiliated with organized programs of physical activity designed to achieve various objectives.
4. *The product.* The *result* of the process could broadly be conceived of as health enhancement and enjoyable leisure for those who are the consumers.
5. *The discipline.* This is the *field of inquiry,* which is the collection of identifiable information unique to physical education. In effect, it is all that is currently known about human physical movement and its inclusive ramifications.
6. *The profession.* In a larger sense, physical education is an enterprise that is composed of people who use (1) *the subject matter* through (2) *the occupations* of the profession by organizing (3) *the process* to optimally achieve (4) *the desired products,* and then to appraise and alter the effects based on the acquired knowledge of (5) *the discipline.*

SUMMARY

The most emphatic change that has occurred in physical education in recent times has been the shift to a scientific attitude. In this venture the profession has taken on a new way of seeing things. It resembles a whole industry retooling for new production. The new attitude understands perfectly the messages of the past but has added the dimension of systematizing information from careful study and exacting scrutiny.

This concept has broadened to where the spirit of science, as well as its methods, is applied to understanding human movement. Technology has given its powers to physical education by verifying much of what was once only conjecture about movement. And most compelling of all, this scientific approach has opened vocational doors that are providing opportunities not previously available.

In reality, many if not most of the new careers now accessible to physical educators are not really new. Rather, they had formerly been taken by persons with other backgrounds. But as the study of human motion has become more sophisticated, the applications of the investigations have broadened to include areas of employment that are technological, managerial, curative, and preventative. Health enhancement and enjoyable leisure continue to be the foremost objectives, and educational settings continue to provide a notable delivery system, but the worksite deployment of the profession has expanded into newly acquired and widely diverse settings.

To the Reader

One way to acquire familiarity with a profession is to read the journals that are associated with the field. For physical education, this list could potentially include at least thirty publications, but four in particular will provide a broad perspective of the profession. The *Journal of Physical Education, Recreation and Dance,* and the *Physical Educator* will offer reading of general interest, with emphasis on articles for teachers and coaches. The *Research Quarterly for Exercise and Sport* contains original research reports, review articles, and discussions dealing with a diversity of scientific interests regarding human movement. And *Quest* publishes scholarly manuscripts of a mostly theoretical and philosophical nature. Collectively, these journals present reflective issues, research endeavors, and the applications of the profession.

Suggested Projects

1. Secure recent issues of the above-named journals. Read a selection of articles, and try to sense the scholarly "flavor" of the profession. Offer your reactions to the other members of your class.
2. Have a brainstorming session in class about all the possible areas of employment where one can utilize a knowledge of human movement. Think of every setting in which motion is a factor in the objective of the job, and share your thoughts about how that motion could be analyzed and its effects improved.
3. Spend one entire day noting all the facets of your routine that are dependent on movement or are affected by information about human motion. Include not only items such as getting from here to there but also such items as athletic equipment design and the arrangement of your physical environment.

4. Make a list of study areas in physical education that you believe are commonly good for all students, regardless of their career aspirations. Compare the lists of everyone in class, and on that basis, construct a hypothetically perfect "core" of courses that all students in the field should take.

References

Crase, D. (1978). Has Physical Education Achieved a Scholarly Dimension? *Journal of Physical Education and Recreation, 49,* 21–24.

Earl, P. (1986). *Lifestyle Economics: Consumer Behavior in a Turbulent World.* New York: St. Martin's Press.

Gerson, G. J., Ibrahim, H. M., DeVries, J., and Eisen, G. (1988). *Understanding Leisure: An Interdisciplinary Approach.* Dubuque, IA: Kendall/Hunt Publishing.

Henry, F. M. (1964). Physical Education: An Academic Discipline. *Journal of Health, Physical Education and Recreation, 37,* 32–33ff.

Sessoms, H. D. (1987). Reassessing the Role of Public Leisure Services. In J. J. Bannon (Ed.), *Current Issues in Leisure Services: Looking Ahead in a Time of Transition* (pp. 168–177). Washington, DC: International City Management.

Sommers, A. T., with Blau, L. R. (1988). *The U.S. Economy Demystified: What the Major Economic Statistics Mean and Their Significance for Business.* Lexington, MA: Lexington Books.

Veal, A. J. (1987). *Leisure and the Future.* London: Allen & Unwin.

Zeigler, E. F. (1981). Physical Education and Sport Philosophy: Foundations and Definitions. In J. S. Bosco and M. A. Turner (Eds.), *Encyclopedia of Physical Education, Fitness, and Sports: Philosophy, Programs, and History* (pp. 25–40). Salt Lake City: Brighton Publishing.

Chapter 3

Heritage of the Profession: Past Events with Modern Meanings

Legacy of a Greek Ideal

Thoughts of Greek Philosophers

The Rise of Athletic Competition

End of a Golden Era

The Roman Empire: Suppression of the Ideal

Physical Education in Europe

Early Programs in America

Civil War to the Turn of the Century

Twentieth Century Physical Education

Summary

To the Reader

Suggested Projects

References

The fundamental ideal of utilizing physical activity to acquire strength of both body and mind can be traced to the ancient Greeks.

Since their time, the rise and fall of a panorama of nations, morals, religions, and technologies has alternately supported and suppressed physical education as a societal value.

In America, the evolution of programs in physical education can be paralleled to the change from a largely puritanical view of life to one of individualistic expression of the self and a high regard for recreational pursuits.

Today the profession once again sustains the concept of mind-body unity that permeated ancient Greece and that now strengthens society's acknowledgment of the worth of physical activity.

Perspectives

Modern physical education, like every area of study, has evolved through the years.
University of Denver file photo.

MOST of the time, nothing is happening.

From an evolutionary perspective, whether it be the formation of the universe, or the unfolding of life on earth, or the development of a culture, or any other natural process, long periods of daily repetition are interspersed by rare moments of activity. Focus on almost any given evolutionary moment, and not much is going on.

But evolution in all things does happen. And ultimately, the perspective of time provides a sufficient range of events to allow us to select some prominent moments of activity and then to link them together into a story. Thus, a history can be written, and by this selective process, a chronicle of physical education has been structured.

An early sporting moment occurred somewhere in ancient Greece, probably in the eighth century B.C. By today's standards, it was a bizarre scene. There had just been a funeral, yet rousing athletic contests were going on: foot racing, wrestling, javelin throwing, boxing, and chariot racing. And there were valuable prizes being offered: fine trophies, silver bowls, horses, oxen, skilled laborers, and gold. The contestants, many of whom were nobles, routinely asked for, and believed they got, divine help.

The games were being held to commemorate the memory of Patroclus, beloved friend of Achilles (he of the infamous heel). The account of the games comes to us from the Greek poet Homer, in his book the *Iliad.* With its companion, the *Odyssey,* it marks the beginning of Western literature. The *Iliad* also presents the very first written record of athletic competition. Centuries later, ancient Greece would represent perhaps the finest expression of mind and body unity the world has ever known. It is to those days of mental-muscle oneness that physical education, accurately or inaccurately, often assigns its origin.

In truth, to conclude that the roots of physical education are in ancient Greece is impractical. No single beginning of physical education exists. There are instead many sagas and assimilations from all periods of time. Basic themes have fallen in and out of favor, depending on the calendar of circumstances. But nowhere else did a provocative ideal of physical education become so worthy of emulation as that in ancient Greece. What matters is not so much that an early society developed an organized agenda of physical education; what is more important is that this particular culture converted introspection and extrospection into a clearly defined message—that real and lasting value accrues from conscientiously improving one's physical welfare. Twenty-three centuries later, contemporary physical education returns inevitably to the original philosophical soundness of ancient Greece.

LEGACY OF A GREEK IDEAL

Legend tells us that Homer was a blind poet who wandered from city to city. But he was no mere minstrel. To the Greeks of his time, he was their greatest philosopher.

In his *Iliad,* Homer describes the military exploits of Achilles,[1] and in the *Odyssey,* we read of the adventurous wanderings of Odysseus.[2] Both books offer vivid descriptions of athletic contests and thus supply evidence that sport was a common and important part of early Greek culture. Athletic prowess was valued, not only because "nothing makes a man so famous as what he can do with his hands and feet" (from the *Iliad*) but also because winning an athletic contest implied earning the favor of the gods.[3]

In time, mythology and illusion gave way to fact. The Greeks wanted to get to the bottom of things, to seek the irreducible ultimate of everything. What eventually emerged were wonderfully organized systems of philosophy, astronomy, physics, chemistry, physiology, medicine—and education.

By the fifth century B.C., two Greek cities had become prominent: Sparta, the size of Allentown, Pennsylvania (population about 100,000), and Athens (around 300,000), as large as Louisville, Kentucky (Payne, 1964). Both of these ancient cities supported educational systems, but in different packages.

In austere Sparta, citizens could pursue only one profession—the military. To this end, only the strong were permitted to survive. At birth, every child was examined by a council of elders, and unfit babies were cast to their deaths. When formal education began in Sparta, it was purely a systematic regimen of military training. Thus, physical education in its first days was preparation for war. Except for the reprieve of an occasional "ball game," the standard activities for boys were boxing, throwing

---

[1] One of the greatest warriors of early Greece, Achilles was reported to have led the capture of twenty-three cities and to have been a central figure in the Trojan War. But the best-known folklore about Achilles is that he was made invulnerable to harm from weapons by being completely submerged in the river Styx, save for one heel by which his mother held him; it was by piercing this heel that he was eventually slain.

[2] Odysseus, a hero of the Trojan War, masterminded the construction of a massive wooden horse inside which Greek soldiers hid to breach the gates of Troy and successfully besieged the city. The event reportedly marked the end of the war.

[3] The religious imagination of ancient Greece produced a lavish mythology. Every natural force in the sky or on the earth, every blessing or nuisance, and every human quality was believed to be either the presence or contrivance of gods. There were twelve major gods who lived on Mount Olympus, in northeastern Greece. They were called Olympians, and people believed that they whiled away their time sipping wine and eating fruit while whimsically plotting the fate of the world.

spears, running, wrestling, and other games designed to prepare one for combat. Girls trained in many of the same events, although their programs were a bit more "sporting" (Spears, 1984), but they were being prepared ultimately to bear strong children. Older boys competed in hand-to-hand fighting, sometimes with no holds barred, ending only when one of the rivals conceded defeat, which no honorable Spartan would do. It was, occasionally, a fight to the death (Osborne, 1987).

A hundred-and-forty miles away, Athens was generating a society never before seen, based on an idea called democracy. Athens flourished with magnificent new buildings, and with philosophers, poets, and artists. Athenians became cultural and gathered everywhere in the city to philosophize, to litigate, to harangue, to learn. Favorite gathering places were the city's three gymnasiums.

The body was as esteemed as the mind. Athenians scorned any man who was portly or who could not swim or wrestle. Sport was a pursuit equal to philosophy, music, literature, art, and sculpture. The athlete was a favorite subject for artisans, so we are left today with a fine and extensive illustrative record of athletic endeavors in ancient Greece.

At the gymnasium, the Greek male would disrobe (the word gymnasium means, literally, "a place for naked exercise"), anoint his body with oil, perhaps do a few sprints in the stade (a running track two hundred yards long), then find a partner for some wrestling or boxing, or join others for throwing the javelin or discus. Workout over, he would bathe and dress, then seek companionship for his other reason for coming to the gymnasium—conversation drenched with philosophy.

A historic turning point had preceded this scene. In 490 B.C., twenty thousand Persian infantry had assembled near the plain of Marathon, 25 miles north of Athens, intent on invading the city and overrunning Greece. An Athenian courier, Pheidippides, set out for Sparta to summon aid. He reputably covered the 140 miles on foot in two days but could not elicit help. So the Athenians quickly mobilized their own forces, went to Marathon, and repulsed the Persians. Pheidippides ran again, this time from Marathon to Athens, where he collapsed and died from exhaustion after announcing the victory.[4] Today we have named a race after the plain on which the battle was fought.

The victory at Marathon was a springboard for Athens to become one of the most influential cities ever. Ten years later, Athens entered its "Golden Age" (480–430 B.C.). It was a glorious time in history—a cul-

---

[4]There remains some question whether Pheidippides was actually the Athens-to-Sparta runner, although likely he was. For his run from Marathon to Athens, the distance covered was probably 24 miles rather than the 26-plus of today's marathon races, and there is general agreement that he did indeed fall dead after proclaiming the victory (Lloyd, 1973).

tural explosion for art and religion, science and philosophy, mind and body—a trance of enlightenment that flourished as never before or since, but that ended too soon.

THOUGHTS OF GREEK PHILOSOPHERS

Philosophy was an everyday pursuit in Athens, where great minds found freedom. Socrates, whose method of inquiry was his hallmark, was the earliest philosopher. He believed that seeking truth was a more important educational goal than the mere acquisition of information. He also believed that every person should maintain excellent physical condition through regular habits of exercise in order to serve the state in any capacity necessary, including as a warrior (Frede, 1987).

Later, Plato, a student of Socrates, held seminars in the Academy, which is correctly regarded as the first university. He considered education to be the most logical way to improve society, and he was probably the first to express the well-known statement: "A sound mind in a sound body" (Hooper, 1978), thus sanctioning the generalized benefits of exercise. When he wrote *The Republic*[5] he spoke freely of physical education:

> Neither are the two arts of music and gymnastic really designed, as is often supposed, the one for the training of the soul, and the other for the training of the body.
>
> I believe, I said, that the teachers of both have in view chiefly the improvement of the soul.
>
> And he who mingles music with gymnastic in the fairest proportions, and best attempts them to the soul, might be rightly called the true musician and harmonist in a far greater sense than the tuner of the strings.

Plato himself was an accomplished wrestler (Taylor, 1984) and emphatically promoted the ideal of the "whole person." He may have been the first to realize how much the mind could affect the body, and the body the mind.

Enter Aristotle. Naturalistic science and logic began with him and found their focus in him. He promoted practicality in all things, saying that sound health and a fit body were essentials for moral character and intellectual growth. He believed that physical education should be the first emphasis of education, even before academic training (Urmson, 1988).

---

[5]Plato wrote *The Republic* as a treatise on politics but also included a chapter on physical education, even calling it by that name. It was the first literary work to give such attention to the subject.

To a great extent, Athenian society shared in these thoughts, for the schools (the world's first) disciplined both mind and body. Physical exercise was assumed to have intrinsic value in itself, and movement was seen as an art form. Dance, gymnastics, and track and field were particularly regarded as ways not only to improve strength and athletic prowess but also to develop character, self-discipline, courage, humility, and sportsmanship.

In lighter moments, Athenian youngsters flew kites, spun tops, walked on stilts, and played jacks, blindman's buff, and hide-and-seek. Ball games were popular among older youths. One well-preserved stone relief shows what is thought to be a game of catch. Another shows what appears to be a form of field hockey. Yet another illustrates what could be an early version of rugby.

Physical education was part of every school day, as were music, math, writing, poetry, and philosophy. But alas, by age eighteen, in both Athens and Sparta, youths were graduated and were expected to assume their mandatory occupation of being soldiers.

THE RISE OF ATHLETIC COMPETITION

On an otherwise indistinct field in southwestern Greece are the toppled columns and weathered pediments of Olympia, site of the sacred and original Olympic Games. Every four years, starting in 776 B.C., Greeks from every part of the nation gathered for the week-long festival. For one month before and one month afterward, a truce was observed throughout the land as citizens of rival city-states stood side by side at the contests. All war was postponed in recognition of the games, in stark contrast to modern times when the Olympic Games have twice been cancelled and three times boycotted because of war.

Today, only grey crumbling stones lie in the cove where athletes took an oath of honesty, and only foundations remain of the statues to the gods that dishonest athletes were compelled to pay for. But one can still walk the hallowed archway entrance to the stadium, an area two football fields long enclosed by grass-covered slopes. Here an all-male crowd of forty thousand stood (there were seats only for dignitaries) and probably behaved the way forty thousand fans do today.

The most important contests of the Olympic Games were grouped together as the pentathlon, consisting of five events: a running broad jump, discus throw, javelin throw, wrestling, and a sprint of usually two hundred yards. Ancient writing tells us that winning distances in the broad jump exceeded fifty feet (Harris, 1964), although their version was

A Chariot race in Ancient Greece.
© Antman Archives/The Image Works

probably more of a hop-step-jump event. Other accounts are less exact, saying only that a runner, for example, could "outdistance a hare."

The culminating events of the Olympic Games were the chariot races, with two- or four-horse teams. Like auto races today, they were sometimes a spectacle of accidents. In one race of forty chariots, only one racer finished (Durant, 1966).

At the end of five days of competition, the victors received their reward: a crown of wild olive plucked from a sacred tree on the grounds of Olympia. It was the only prize given, but like the medallion in today's Olympic Games, it represented other potential rewards. Victorious athletes were welcomed back into their cities as heroes; sometimes a section of the city wall would be torn down so that the athlete could enter the city as no other had before ("With sons like these, who needs walls?" a town magistrate once said). Usually, a statue of the athlete would be erected; some cities made their heroes generals; often they were given free meals for life and front row seats at the theater; and frequently they received gifts of money (Drees, 1968).

In addition to the Olympic Games, in the off-years major athletic gatherings occurred at three other places (Delphi, Corinth, and Nemea). Each offered its own price: a crown of laurel, celery, or pine. Together with the Olympic Games, these events formed the Panhellenic festivals. The greatest ambition of an athlete was to win a crown at all four: the original grand slam of athletic competition.

In time, the Panhellenic Games also became celebrations for music, art, and oratory, thus mingling physical prowess with the expressive arts. The games were central to the growth of almost every art form—poetry, sculpture, painting, pottery, choral singing, oratory, and drama. It was a time when all manner of human performance was recognized and respected.

END OF A GOLDEN ERA

Maybe history never truly repeats itself, but the events that led to the decline of ancient Greece have been recast in other societies since. First there was a devastating civil war: Athens against Sparta. A period of ineffective national leadership followed. Ultimately, poverty, greed, and corruption infested government and business.

Relatedly, athletic ideals fell to familiar wanton influence. Athletes became hired hands, as sport became their livelihood. The concept of competition for its own sake disappeared. Winning became not only everything, but the only thing. Athletes experienced shortened careers, "allowed their minds to go stale in favor of their training" (Raschke, 1988), and sold their souls to any city-state willing to pay their price. Had television been invented then, they would have done commercials.

But amidst the tragedy was triumph. Socrates had said, "Life unexamined is not worth living." The attitude permeated athletics, as the human body was extensively studied for ways to optimize its capacities. The Greeks refined performance techniques, many of which are, at least in principle, still used today. They also developed effective training methods, studied the effects of diet on performance, and examined the mental preparation of athletes (Toombs, 1987). But most progressive of all was their original ideal of mind and body harmony, so nobly expressed in the Golden Age, which reverberates in the philosophy of physical education today. The essence of the finest hour of their thinking is with us still.

THE ROMAN EMPIRE: SUPPRESSION OF THE IDEAL

Exit Greece. Enter Rome. The Romans believed, and pillaged to prove, that they were the rightful inheritors of the Greek legacy. But they cared little for the Greek philosophy. The Greeks were thinkers; the Romans doers. The Greeks reveled in philosophy; the Romans built roads.

By 46 B.C. Caesar had captured the soul of Rome. He reaped the attention of the citizens with oratory genius, impressed them with military victories, and dazzled them, at the Colosseum, with theatrical presentations, gladitorial combats, and beast-versus-human brawls.

One reason for the eventual downfall of Rome was spectatorship. While the Romans were energetic, they never became active participants in games or recreation. They did not delight in exercise for its own sake. They preferred to be entertained.[6]

In the early days of the Roman Empire, there was no need for schools, since the only objective of youth was to prepare for war. But by the end of the first century, public education had become common. Also common was a complaint from the teachers: they claimed to be underpaid (Liverside, 1976).

For a brief moment, physical education was considered for inclusion in Roman schools. It never happened, mostly owing to the prevailing attitude that a Roman should always have dignity and that to exercise was undignified (Bonner, 1977).

But it was *not* undignified to be a spectator. So Rome spent increasing amounts of money on professional games and offered most events free to the citizens. Ninety thousand could cram into the Colosseum; a nearby racecourse could accommodate 260,000. But the rampant spending eventually led to financial exhaustion, a fate known in sports today.

The emphasis given to professional athletics did create a new profession—sports medicine. It was common for athletes to have a personal physician who supervised their training, and in turn the physicians developed a medical specialty of serving athletes. One of note, Claudius Galen (A.D. 120–200), may have been the first and remains the best known of the physicians who applied hard-core medicine to athletics. He even recognized the mind-body relationship: "There is no unimportant advantage of an exercise, if it can help both the body and the mind toward the perfection innate in each" (Siegel, 1968).

PHYSICAL EDUCATION IN EUROPE

According to the chronology of empires, Rome fell in A.D. 476. For the next five hundred years, cultural time stood still. Even the names often given to that stretch of time—the Middle Ages or the Dark Ages—suggest the general gloom of an insignificant bridge of history. It was marked

---

[6]Thanks largely to Hollywood, we may associate the festive games of Rome with a reckless sacrifice of human lives. While accidents and deadly combat did sometimes occur, far more commonly the events were staged for their spectacle alone, usually with slaves and professional actors as the performers (Scullard, 1980).

by widespread epidemics, mass poverty, and religious fanaticism. Ironically, these years also saw the emergence of universities.

And then an awakening occurred in a time called the Renaissance, literally translated as "to be born again." The period was a complex of literary and artistic movements that originated in fourteenth century Italy and spread throughout all of Europe. Archives mark it as the beginning of modern history. Much of what exists today as contemporary thought can be traced back to the Renaissance (Rosenthal, 1981).

Individualism flourished, even through recreational pursuits. Archery and fencing were revived from Greece. Golf and bowling-on-the-green were introduced, and by the seventeenth century, Paris alone had eighteen hundred tennis courts (Grimsley, 1971). Sports were a source of pleasure, but in the schools not one program of physical education was to be found anywhere.

Following the Renaissance, a "humanistic" impulse prevailed. The unique worth of each human being became valued, and as a result, individualized education was promoted. Relatedly, a philosophy of "realism" emerged that in concept tied education to life "as it really was." Together, humanism and realism enlivened the theoretical considerations of education during the seventeenth and eighteenth centuries.

Jean-Jacques Rousseau (1712–1788), who is often cited as having provoked the French Revolution, had provided a hypothetical plan of "naturalistic" learning for an imaginary child in his book *Emile*. He included education of the body as an important part of the learning. *Emile* became an insurgent statement against the still austere education of the times, but it roused enough contention to become a primary reason for Rousseau's expulsion from France and for the public burning of his book.

In Germany, Johann Basedow (1724–1790) became strongly influenced by Rousseau's work and founded a school designed on the principles in *Emile*. The curriculum included three daily hours of physical education and recreation. To implement the program, he hired Johann Simon, who might rightfully be recognized as the first full-time physical education teacher. Basedow's writings about the values of physical activity in the out-of-doors convey concepts that are remarkably similar to the approach taken in Outward Bound types of programs in existence today.

Basedow's school, though short-lived, inspired Christian Salzmann (1744–1811) to establish a similar school, also in Germany. He hired Johan Guts Muths (1759–1839) as his physical education teacher. Guts Muths (pronounced goots-mooths) would become one of the more influential leaders the field has known. He described an ingenuous series of gymnastic exercises (which allowed for differences in ages and abilities) in a heralded book *Gymnastics for the Young*. It became the basis for many modern practices in physical education implemented throughout Europe and the United States. He wrote:

> No one doubts the great influence of the body on the mind; the physical treatment of the body, therefore, particularly in childhood and in youth, must tend to determine the character of the man: and indeed affect it more deeply, than is commonly supposed (Guts Muths, 1800, p. 79).

Again the Greek ideal of mind-body harmony is seen. This theme repeats throughout history, ancient to modern, and will probably exist for as long as there is human physical activity.

Come the nineteenth century, and European physical education was embodied by Friedrich Ludwig Jahn (1778–1852), a German educator who is called the "father of gymnastics." Guts Muths had been an inspiration to Jahn. Patriotism was his passion. He believed gymnastics could be a common avenue that would unify Germany, which was then fractured into small kingdoms. To this end, he devised rather formal gymnastic routines that were performed in a "turnplatz," a playground-like area with heavy apparatus, and his program became known as the Turner movement. Gymnastic societies called turnvereins began to form. Their basis was patriotism, and Jahn's gymnastics was their bond.

The Turners eventually fell into political disfavor; they were viewed as rebel organizations, but Jahn's system of gymnastics had spread to the schools of Germany and had become the core of the physical education programs. Jahn's influence also penetrated the United States, where turnvereins sprouted in the East and Midwest, and still exist today in some larger cities.

Another German educator, Adolph Spiess (1810–1858), formalized Jahn's system of gymnastics, but eased its strength requirements for performance. He also included exercises designed for girls, one of the first programs to do so. The system found even more widespread acceptance in the German schools than Jahn's, and remnants of it remain in use today.

Other programs of physical education, as militaristic as the German systems of gynmastics but less complicated, were designed in Sweden by Per Henrick Ling (1776–1839) and in Denmark by Franz Nachtegall (1777–1847). In 1804 Nachtegall became the first director of the Military Gymnastic Institute, which today remains the oldest institution in Europe for the preparation of the physical education professions.

Throughout most of Europe, the programs of physical education that emerged in the schools were essentially reflections of the prevailing attitudes toward nationalism and fitness. Each system tended toward stylistic exercises and formal routines. Only in England could a more flamboyant attitude toward physical education be found. Athletic sport and games were deeply ingrained in the English system, flourishing in the great public schools like Eton, Harrow, and Rugby (where the game of the same name originated). This more "recreational" view of physical education would eventually become a cornerstone for the nontraditional programs that later arose in the United States.

EARLY PROGRAMS IN AMERICA

From the earliest settlements in America to the Revolutionary War (1775–1783)—a span of time called the colonial period—education took place mostly in the home. Fledgling America was inhabited by European immigrants who were basically conservative and religious. They saw little need for any formal preparation beyond home economics and religious training.

But slowly, schools began to appear. Overall, however, the purpose of the schools was almost exclusively religious. There was no sign of physical education, even though it had been suggested by the widely heeded Benjamin Franklin, who may have been the first American to propose that physical education be part of the educational curriculum (Van Dalen and Bennett, 1971).

There was, nevertheless, the beginning of sport. When the settlers became more organized in societal structure and occupational specialty, they gained a new element of free time. In some areas the religious climate dictated that the extra time be devoted to spiritual study, but in other areas the spirit of games began to fill the leisure hours.

At first the games were impromptu, but soon they became organized. Many of the early players were English, primarily because a flair for sport was in their blood and also because they were the only immigrants to have brought rule books with them. And so, the first organized games played in America were traditional English games: bowling,[7] rowing, boxing, running, horseback riding, and of course, the hunt. Even baseball, popularly regarded as of American origin, began as an adaptation of an English game called rounders.[8]

---

[7]The English game was bowling-on-the-green. In New York, Dutch settlers had established lane bowling, but the game quickly became tied with gambling interests and was banned. However, the original game included only nine pins, so the enthusiasts added another pin to the rack, making it a new and consequently legal game.

[8]A certain Abner Doubleday was an aspiring politician who, following the Civil War, needed a strong patriotic image, so his political cronies decided to give him credit for having invented baseball. But it's unlikely that Doubleday had ever been to Cooperstown, N.Y. (the supposed site of the beginning of the game), and most certainly he was not the inventor of the game.

Eventually the growing interest in recreational activities invaded the schools, although at first only in after-hours events (which could more accurately be considered as the beginnings of intramurals). When formal programs of physical education began to appear, they were largely reanimations of German gymnastics. Two are of particular note and are rightly recognized as the earliest significant incorporation of physical education into regular curriculums in America. In 1825 Dr. Charles Beck, a German refugee, established the first gymnasium in the country at Round Hill School in Northhampton, Massachusetts, and thereby became the first teacher of physical education in America (Lee, 1983). The Round Hill School, a college preparatory academy, was short-lived because it was, curiously, too successful. Its graduates gained the equivalence of three years of college education and were consequently considered to be "overprepared" for campus academics.

In 1826 Dr. Charles Follen, like Beck a political refugee from Germany, began the first college program of physical education at Harvard, the oldest university in America (founded in 1636). Both Beck and Follen were proponents of the Jahn system of gymnastics, but the inclusion of these ritualized exercises in other schools was only occasional.

Catherine Beecher, sister of Harriet Beecher Stowe, was director of the Hartford Seminary for Girls and believed in the value of exercise, but not the German system. So she devised her own program, less strenuous and more rhythmical, but it too met with only limited recognition.

Then came Dio Lewis, who was an early advocate of women's rights. He took certain ideas of Beecher's, combined them with the Swedish gymnastics devised by Per Ling, and developed a system of exercises that found wide acceptance in the public schools. In 1861 Lewis also began the first periodical devoted to physical education, the *Gymnastic Monthly and Journal of Physical Culture*. Physical education, it would seem, was finally gaining its place, only to be repressed by the Civil War.

CIVIL WAR TO THE TURN OF THE CENTURY

After the ruination of the Civil War, physical education gradually became endorsed as part of total education. In 1866, only one year after the war ended, California enacted the first legislation to require physical education in the schools. However, the second state to have such a regulation (Ohio) did not enact it until 1892.

Teachers in these early programs had diverse credentials ranging from medical backgrounds to merely having an interest in the field. Responding to this assortment, Dr. Dudley Sargent founded, at Boston College in 1881, a school to prepare teachers of physical education—the first of its kind. The Sargent School, as it was called, became one of the most prestigious institutions the field has ever known (Weston, 1962).

Nationally, there was a resurgent interest in German gymnastics. A growing debate ensued over whether physical education should return to the formal programs of European origin or should pursue the more liberal programs of American design. The dispute came to be known as the "battle of the systems." This argumentative state of affairs prompted William G. Anderson, a young medical doctor and instructor of physical education at Adelphi Academy in Brooklyn, to call a meeting of leaders in the field in an effort to resolve the issues. The assembled group founded, at their 1885 meeting at Adelphi, the Association for the Advancement of Physical Education, later to become the American Alliance for Health, Physical Education, Recreation and Dance (AAHPERD), today the largest professional association of physical educators in America.

In spite of Anderson's efforts, the conflicts between the systems remained unsettled. Subsequently, another meeting was called by Mary Hemenway in 1889 at the Massachusetts Institute of Technology. This gathering, known simply as the "Boston Conference," is considered the most important meeting in the history of physical education (Van Dalen and Bennett, 1971). The conference blended the thoughts of the acknowledged leaders and crystallized the direction of the profession.

In the world of sport, a significant event was the revival of the Olympic Games, which had declined during the Roman Empire and had ended somewhere around A.D. 400 (Drees, 1968). The modern Olympic Games were reborn from the efforts of Baron de Coubertin, who believed that they could stimulate international goodwill. He also thought the games would foster the growth of physical education programs in his native France, and this may in fact have been one of his main objectives (Mandell, 1984). The Olympic Games were reinstated on Easter Sunday, 1896, appropriately in Athens, in a gleaming white stadium, still in use today, that was a replica of an earlier stadium from ancient times.

TWENTIETH CENTURY PHYSICAL EDUCATION

In the twentieth century, schools became, in the truest sense, progressive. A turn-of-the century leader was John Dewey. He advocated the philosophy of "learning by doing," implying that students would learn best by direct involvement, and he considered physical education to be a fine example of how the technique worked.

Dewey's progressive ideas were adopted by Thomas Wood, who developed the "new physical education." Its program was to be as natural as possible, focusing on instinctive, wholistic movements. It rings of the philosophy inherent in contemporary "movement education" (explained in chapter 11)—a design that encourages self-discovery of motor skills. In 1910 Wood wrote,

> It is most desirable that mechanical uniformity should not be demanded, but that, with the observance of certain general principles of action, the pupil should be left free to express individuality in action. (Wood, 1910)

The new physical education ended forever the overwhelming emphasis on gymnastics and designated the first program of physical education that can be considered American. For the first time, the field began to show the broad perspective that characterizes the profession today.

However, the First World War narrowed the objectives of physical education to a fitness theme. That theme would be emphasized again during the Second World War and the Korean War, just as it always has been in wartime ever since the days of ancient Greece.

Following the First World War, physical education was able to return to the dimensions that Thomas Wood had advocated. A new voice was Clark Hetherington of the Teachers College of Columbia University, New York. The Columbia Teachers College was a center for experimentation and innovation, and was even considered somewhat radical (Lawrence, 1970). But it was a fitting locale for Hetherington, who had once worked for Wood and would carry on his ideals and express them in eloquent writings that would give him a national reputation and the unofficial title "father of modern physical education."

Also at Columbia, a young Jesse Feiring Williams was inspired by the concepts of Wood and Hetherington. Williams worked their ideas into his own philosophy, which came to be known as "education through the physical." It was in opposition to the long-prevalent thesis of "education *of* the physical," which meant that the primary intent of physical education was to develop the physical—in essence, to get stronger. But the *through* concept suggested that physical education could be the means for outcomes other than just biological ones. The contention was that the mind is directly influenced by what its own body does. Thus, physical education was seen as a *medium* for emotional, social, and intellectual growth—indeed, all the dimensions of development incorporated into one human endeavor. Activity was more than activity—it was a way of assimilating experiences which led to a certain kind of mental and spiritual "knowing" with a meaning all its own (Williams, 1954).

A related development was the evolution of free time. Industrial efficiency had, between the two world wars, given Americans more leisure, and one result was an upsurge in recreational pursuits. Golf courses multiplied: By 1930 there were seven hundred public and one thousand private courses in the country, whereas at the time of the First World War

An early 1900's basketball team.
University of Denver file photo.

there may have been as few as two dozen (Lee, 1980). Bowling became incredibly popular; tennis began its phenomenal growth; and softball fields appeared everywhere. Weekends and evenings, once a time of rest, became a time for play.

In the schools, physical education curriculums responded with programs of less formal and more playlike activities, and the number of schools offering physical education increased dramatically. Interscholastic competition also mushroomed, and intramurals became a welcome addition for those who could not qualify for their school teams. It was, in short, a time when America, and everything in it, was experiencing exponential growth.

As the Second World War ended, the nuclear age began. The atomic bomb seeded the cultural climate of vacillating fear and optimism, which is now thought of as normal. The war also occasioned the baby boom, which populated the schools and consequently focused the attention of professional physical education on teacher preparation. But with a later declining birthrate and subsequent drop in school populations, teacher preparation fell out of emphasis. Ecomomic constraints reduced school programs in the arts and physical education, and teaching salaries continued to flounder. Predictably, fewer people committed themselves to a career in teaching.

Responding to all this, physical education in recent years has rethought its directions and has emerged with expanded interests. Even more leisure added a new social force and real income increased throughout the postwar decades. Americans began to pay for recreational services, and corporations began fitness programs for their employees, recognizing that such investment would return greater worker productivity and lowered health care costs. Private clubs sprang up everywhere, and community recreational services expanded. Overall, the general population became conscious of the relationship between lifestyles and health. And so physical education expanded its interests in the health and leisure industries as the field moved to renew its concerns of providing healthy life-styles for all people. The reach expanded beyond the schools to include a new clientele of adults who were purchasing the professional services of wellness and recreation. There was a correlated shift to curative enterprises, such as physical therapy and cardiac rehabilitation, and a venture into new branches of sports medicine.

To view the recent developments in any historical perspective is difficult, for they are still too close to us in time to judge their influence. Moreover, what may seem to have been significant recent advancements may pale in comparison with what will happen tomorrow. Suffice to say, however, that the escalation of interests, applications, and academic foundations of physical education has been phenomenal beyond all previous accounts.

SUMMARY

The earliest physical education teachers in America were people with medical backgrounds who believed that they could make their most emphatic contributions in a field that promoted exercise. Later, as sport became more prominent in colleges, athletic coaches were hired and given faculty status as physical education instructors. Thus, physical education began in this country as an outgrowth of medical interest and also as somewhat of a "dumping ground" for coaches. Today the profession has maintained its affiliation with coaching, although on a much more creditable base, and the relationship with medicine, which once disappeared, is now becoming reestablished.

Moreover, at the turn of the century, American physical education was largely dualistic: The body was to be trained, and the mind, separately, was to be disciplined. Today, however, the philosophy echoes the Greek ideal of mind-body harmony. The ancient Greeks never tried to separate the two; nor does the profession today.

Greece is distant in time, and yet it is not. Much of what is seen as valuable today finds a beginning in ancient Greece. It might be that in those days the veneration of human movement found its first full expression. And today, under a similar philosophy, physical activity is once again recognized as an essential part of a complete life.

Events of the world have always had effects on physical education. Wars, cultural advances or regressions, free time, and religious fervor all have influenced the curricular structure and the very existence of the field. In general, the times when physical education was suppressed were also times now viewed as cultural lags. But at the start of the space age (triggered by Russia's launching of the first satellite, Sputnik, in 1957), schools in America reacted with an all-consuming emphasis on science, almost lynching physical education. However, in the long run, that shift to science gradually, then rapidly and now widely, contributed to the field's own spirit of scientific inquiry. The catalyst had been from outside sources, but the energy is now driven from within.

And yet, the attention to science has not supplanted the value of movement as an expressive art form. Nor has it lessened the recognition that physical education is, after all, education. When Williams spoke of *education through the physical,* he may not have envisioned how widely realized the concept would become. Contemporary programs are housed in the principle that the physical is a means for educating all the senses. We have rediscovered that the body has a brain.

To the Reader

Physical education and sport have a penchant for finding archives. But the study of history does not necessarily tell us how we got to the present. History can be a fascinatng trickster. Words and memory and images can easily displace actual events over the years. And the past is so indifferently full of circumstances that a plausible case for any conclusion could be made by careful selection of episodes. Additionally, there is a tendency to embellish or romanticize historical truths. Were the ancient Greeks, for example, really that convinced of the mind-body harmony? Or is it a yarn of idealized legend making? Are we applying rules of logic and laws of fact to our observations, or are we merely telling stories—narratives of good intrigue, but stories nevertheless.

Notwithstanding this danger, even the most distant and abstract considerations of history are ways of understanding and of confirming our present circumstances. They are perceptions of the processes that have created the foundations of our being. Every frame of time involves progress, pageant, scenarios of evolution, and most importantly, ceaseless motion. Even when nothing was happening, *something* was happening.

Heritage of the Profession: Past Events with Modern Meanings 49

During times of suppression of the soul and the body, at least the mind eventually realized this was not the finest expression of life.

So we put ourselves into the past via the present. In the process we understand the past, and we are actually comprehending the present. In these days when change is so imperative, to see into the future we can clear our vision by a study of the mirror image of previous events. History is inexorably linked to the future, for it presents a narrative of designs that have failed, and designs that have worked, and the time in between to know the difference.

Suggested Projects

1. Historians often argue that all cultural orders eventually repeat, by deterministic fatality, all those events that had occurred in previous societies. Assume this to be true, and on that basis, predict what future value American society will give to physical education.
2. History does repeat itself, at least in the larger picture. Outline the major events that have led to growth or suppression of physical education. Note any trends, then make projections of the events that are likely to repeat in the future.
3. Create an argument that there is no reason to believe the past has any influence on the future. Take a stand that physical education is entering into realms that have no relationship to its past. Debate your views with other class members who have charted the past trends of the profession.
4. History has shown that athletics has always been plagued by wrongdoings. Blatant rule violations and drug usage were known even during the ancient Olympics. Discuss why athletics, in any epoch of time, has tended to display both the best and the worst of human nature.
5. In ancient Greece, athletes eventually became so socially prominent that they pledged themselves to compete for whichever city-state would provide them with the greatest rewards. Whenever they can, athletes of today do the same, including playing in other countries. But the Olympic Games require that an athlete compete only for the country of their citizenship. Discuss the pros and cons of these arrangements.
6. What did Plato mean by "a sound mind in a sound body"? Discuss how this philosophy might be relative to one's occupation, or leisure-time habits, or being a student, or other activities.

7. The "battle of the systems" was a dispute of whether programs in physical education should be structured with stylized routines of prescribed exercises (with presumed known value) or allowances for free expressions of movement (with unknown value). Arrange teams for a contemporary version of this debate.
8. Read chapter 1 in Jesse Feiring Williams' book *Principles of Physical Education*. Expound on his theory of *education-through-the-physical*. How has this philosophy been incorporated into the curriculums of present-day physical education? State your own beliefs about how the body can be a medium for enhancement of the mind.

References

Bonner, S. F. (1977). *Education in Ancient Rome*. Berkeley: University of California Press.

Drees, L. (1968). *Olympia: Gods, Artists, and Athletes*. New York: Frederick A. Praeger.

Durant, W. (1966). *The Life of Greece*. New York: Simon and Schuster.

Frede, M. (1987). *Essays in Ancient Philosophy*. Minneapolis: University of Minnesota Press.

Grimsley, W. (1971). *Tennis: Its History, People, and Events*. Englewood Cliffs, NJ: Prentice-Hall.

Guts Muths, J. F. (1800). *Gymnastics for the Young*. London: J. Johnson.

Harris, H. A. (1964). *Greek Athletes and Athletics*. London: Hutchinson and Co., Ltd.

Hooper, F. (1978). *Greek Realities: Life and Thought in Ancient Greece*. Detroit: Wayne State University Press.

Lawrence, E. (1970). *The Origins and Growth of Modern Education*. Harmondsworth, England: Penguin Books.

Lee, M. (1980). Notable Events in Physical Education: 1830–1980. *Journal of Physical Education and Recreation, 51,* 24–25.

Lee, M. (1983). *A History of Physical Education and Sports in the USA* (5th ed.). New York: John Wiley.

Liverside, J. (1976). *Everyday Life in the Roman Empire*. London: B. T. Batsford, Ltd.

Lloyd, A. (1973). *Marathon*. New York: Random House.

Low, D. M. (1960). *The Decline and Fall of the Roman Empire, by Edward Gibbon; An Abridgement*. New York: Harcourt, Brace and Company.

Mandell, R. D. (1984). *Sport: A Cultural History*. New York: Columbia University Press.

Osborne, C. (1987). *Rethinking Early Greek Philosophy*. Ithaca, NY: Cornell University Press.

Payne, R. (1964). *Ancient Greece: The Triumph of a Culture.* New York: W. W. Norton & Co.

Raschke, W. J. (1988). *The Archeology of the Olympics: The Olympics and Other Festivals in Antiquity.* Madison: University of Wisconsin Press.

Rosenthal, J. T. (1981). Dark Age Education: Our Latest Survey. *History of Education Quarterly, 21,* 115–121.

Scullard, H. H. (1980). *A History of the Roman World.* New York: Methuen & Co., Ltd.

Siegel, R. E. (1968). *Galen's System of Physiology and Medicine.* Basel, Switzerland: S. Karger AG.

Spears, B. (1984). A Perspective of the History of Women's Sport in Ancient Greece. *Journal of Sport History, 11,* 32–47.

Taylor, T. (1984). *The Works of Plato.* New York: Garland Publishing.

Toombs, S. K. (1987). Medicine and Patient-Physician Relationship in Ancient Greece. In R. M. Baird, W. F. Cooper, E. H. Duncan, and S. E. Rosenbaum (Eds.), *Contemporary Essays on Greek Ideas: The Kilgore Festschrift.* Waco, TX: Baylor University Press.

Urmson, J. O. (1988). *Aristotle's Ethics.* Oxford, England: Basil Blackwell Ltd.

Van Dalen, D. B., and Bennett, B. L. (1971). *A World History of Physical Education: Cultural, Philosophical, Comparative* (2nd ed.). Englewood Cliffs, NJ: Prentice-Hall.

Weston, A. (1962). *The Making of American Physical Education.* New York: Appleton-Century-Crofts.

Williams, J. F. (1954). *Principles of Physical Education.* Philadelphia: W. B. Saunders.

Wood, T. D. (1910). Physical Education. In *The Ninth Yearbook of the National Society for the Study of Education* (Pt. 1). Chicago: University of Chicago Press.

Part II

Inquiry

Chapter 4   **Research: The Enterprise of Discovery**
Chapter 5   **Exercise Physiology: Improving Physical Capacity**
Chapter 6   **Biomechanics: The Science of Human Motion**
Chapter 7   **Motor Learning and Control: The Mind in Action**
Chapter 8   **Sociology of Sport: Society in a Capsule**
Chapter 9   **Sport Psychology: Inside the Mind of the Athlete**
Chapter 10   **Sports Medicine: Keeping Active People Active**

Chapter 4

Research: The Enterprise of Discovery

A Science of Curiosity

The Characteristics of Research

A Search for Facts

The Value of Scientific Inquiry

Is All Research Meaningful?

Developing an Analytical Attitude

The Impact of Research in Physical Education

Summary

To the Reader

Suggested Projects

References

The profession of physical education once survived on foundations that were mostly philosophical. The field's objectives were guided by assumed outcomes that were widely accepted, without much question about their substance.

In recent times, research has cross-examined the long-held beliefs of the profession and has stimulated new areas of inquiry.

Research is a process of discovery. Its major goal is to arrive at the truth of any situation by using the most objective and scientific techniques possible.

The final outcome is that the profession has now acquired an attitude of analytical investigation, seeking a more complete, more comprehensive, and more factual understanding of all aspects of human function.

HUMAN beings have inquiring minds. Ultimately, every thinking person ponders *what is,* then speculates about *what might be* if certain conditions were changed. Such basic questioning can lead to new discoveries, and often what is discovered is that old beliefs are unfounded and must be altered or sometimes even discarded.

Inquisitiveness is inevitable today, in part because of a simple geometrical fact: The more that is known about something, the more questions it often raises. Each new bit of information can open the door to other deliberations that may not have previously been considered. Thus, one fact leads to other facts as information builds upon itself. The outcome is the so-called "knowledge explosion," which is not only a growing accumulation of information but also a necessary refinement in the techniques for probing into the new, often more difficult questions that arise. The basic strategy for this information gathering is a questioning-discovering-questioning cycle, and this mode of operation fundamentally defines the domain of *research.*

A SCIENCE OF CURIOSITY

Research is *a systematic way of answering questions.* Its purpose is to obtain information about a given problem, using techniques that are as scientific and objective as possible. Always, the intent is to find out the *truth* relative to specific questions.

Sometimes our understanding of the term *research* is distorted because the term is loosely used. Commercial advertising will use the term to gain acceptance, with statements such as, "Research on this product shows . . ." or, "Tests at a leading university . . ." or, "Nine out of ten doctors recommend . . ." Such claims may not necessarily be untruthful, but they are certainly misleading. Unfortunately, they fail to provide standards against which to judge the *quality* of the research that one is being asked to accept, and to believe what one is hearing becomes too easy. Not all that is called "research" is true scientific inquiry.

Research is first of all an *attitude of mind*—a way of thinking that attempts to come as close as possible to the fundamental facts of a problem. It requires that controlled observations be recorded so the information may be analyzed and used to develop generalizations, principles, or theories. The final goal is to discover cause-and-effect relationships within a particular problem. It is an effort to uncover the absolute *reasons* why something happens. The results may lead to increased confidence in predicting or influencing the outcomes of given situations, and thereby can provide more effective guidelines for teachers, coaches, therapists, and anyone else who organizes programs designed to improve the performance capabilities of people.

THE CHARACTERISTICS OF RESEARCH

Any research that is applied in a methodological scientific fashion will have at least the following characteristics:

1. *Research begins with a question.* Inquiry begins with the identification of a question (usually called a "problem") in the mind of the researcher. It is, simply, something that is unknown.
2. *Formulation of a hypothesis.* Next, it is usual to establish a tentative answer to the problem. For example, suppose a cross-country coach would like to know whether runners would improve their performance by ingesting extra carbohydrates. To speculate that they should, is a *hypothesis*. The hypothesis is an educated guess, or even just a hunch, about the possible results of the investigation. It is a potential answer that provides some direction for investigating the question.
3. *Organization of the research design.* Then, an organized plan must be established to study the problem. Should the carbohydrate supplement be given on the day of a meet, the day before, or whenever the runners want it? How much should be given? In what form?

    The organization of the study determines the strategy for collecting the information needed to solve the problem. A key factor is *control*. Effective research requires control over *variables*, which are the conditions or characteristics of the study the researcher wants to regulate. In the example given, carbohydrate intake must be controlled. Only measured amounts would be given, and at predetermined times. Also, the total diet of the runners would need monitoring.

    In general, the more control over the variables the research design offers, the more dependable the results will be. This dependability is referred to as the *validity* of the study and often is the determining factor in evaluating the results.
4. *Collecting the data.* Then comes the search for facts, the performance of the experiment itself. Facts are called *data*, which is the evidence gathered from the administration of the research design.
5. *Analysis of the data.* The meaning of the data becomes apparent through its analysis. An appropriate set of statistics will be applied to analyze the information. Statistics are impartial; they directly describe what occurred in the study, without bias.
6. *Interpretation of the meaning of the data.* The implications of the statistical analysis of the data depend on the way this information is regarded. If the results of the carbohydrate study showed improved performance with supplementation, the conclusion would seem obvious. In other studies, however, the results may not offer a defined

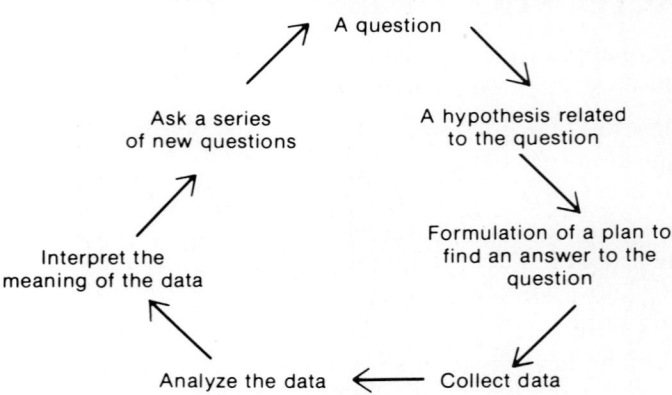

Figure 4.1

conclusion. Suppose, for example, a study found a relationship between regular exercise and sound mental health. Does this mean that regular exercise promotes healthy states of mind? Or does it suggest that mentally healthy people are more likely to exercise regularly?

7. *Development of further questions.* Often the completion of a study prompts further questions. If carbohydrates produced a positive effect, would increasing the dosage be even more beneficial? Is there a best time to give the supplementation? Generally, the more that is discovered about anything, the more questions the information raises. And this question-results-question cycle, represented in figure 4.1, exemplifies the continual generation of curiosity that research fosters.

A SEARCH FOR FACTS

There is a whimsical story about a psychologist who trained a grasshopper to jump at the verbal command "Jump." One day the psychologist pulled off a leg of the grasshopper, then said "Jump," and the grasshopper still did so. One by one, the psychologist yanked off all the grasshopper's legs and then said "Jump," but this time the grasshopper did not budge. So the psychologist concluded that when a grasshopper loses all of its legs, it becomes deaf.

Absurd, of course. Yet we are all guilty of sometimes arriving at erroneous conclusions. In everyday life, these mistakes are often based on inadequate information, but in research they are based on faulty interpretation of the data. Sometimes, data is merely an abstraction. It indicates only what a particular study discovered about a particular situation, and sometimes the "facts" do generate false conclusions. As a case in point, evidence suggests that athletes achieve higher grades while their sport is in season than when it is not (Eitzen and Sage, 1986). When this relationship was first observed, early conclusions were that athletic participation somehow stimulated intellectual congruence. But it is now recognized that other factors can account for this finding, not the least of which is the athletes' desire to remain eligible for the team.

In other instances, research results could be given too much credit as sources of ultimate truths. An example was the data that assigned intelligence to inborn, limited, and strictly measurable conditions. However, intelligence is now seen as multifaceted and highly variable (Margolis, 1987), with the potential for dramatic changes throughout a person's lifetime (Spitz, 1986).

Furthermore, data may sometimes be responsible for generalizations that are too widely applied. Suppose a researcher studied the fitness levels of five hundred male and five hundred female students at McCaskey High School in Lancaster, Pennsylvania. Is it possible to conclude that this study revealed something about the fitness levels of all American high school students? Or, does it represent only Pennsylvania students? Or even all the students at McCaskey High School? In reality, it shows only the scores made by one thousand students at a particular high school at a particular time.

The inferences within a study are sometimes harmless, as in the example of a physicist who once "proved" that a bumblebee cannot fly because its wings are too small to lift its body mass. But in some cases wrong deductions of the data can affect the directions taken by others who read the erroneously derived statements. It could lead to teachers making ineffective plans for the learning environment, or to coaches using inappropriate training programs, or to therapists organizing unsuitable rehabilitation schedules. The final application of research, then, comes in the rational interpretation of the meaning of the data.

THE VALUE OF SCIENTIFIC INQUIRY

Scientific inquiry rests upon the assumption that every natural event in the universe has a cause, and if the cause can be made to occur, then the natural event must follow. It is this cause-effect arrangement of "knowing this—then that" which has greatly influenced the way many of the affairs of physical education are appraised today.

To acknowledge a cause-effect relationship in matters subject to physical laws is sometimes easy. In this regard it is possible to describe, for example, the physical laws in effect when a golf club traveling at 130 feet per second crashes into a stationary ball. But there is a reluctance to accept the same cause-effect relationship in unpredictable events. The resulting flight of a struck golf ball is entirely ordered by physical laws, but the episode is much more difficult to comprehend when considering the unpredictable nature of the person actually swinging the club. Why is it that on hole number six a golfer can drop a 150-yard approach shot pin-high to the green, and then on the seventh tee slice a drive into the woods?

But even when the circumstances of human performance are highly variable, still a general belief exists that the component parts of any performance are available for scientific inquiry and explanation. It might therefore be concluded that *all* aspects of human physical performance are within reach of technological understanding. Such optimism has generated at least three major attitudes of science within the profession today:

1. The only way any aspect of human movement can be completely understood is to study it by scientific investigation.
2. The only way scientific inquiry can be conducted is to use the most sophisticated tools available to reduce the influence of speculation.

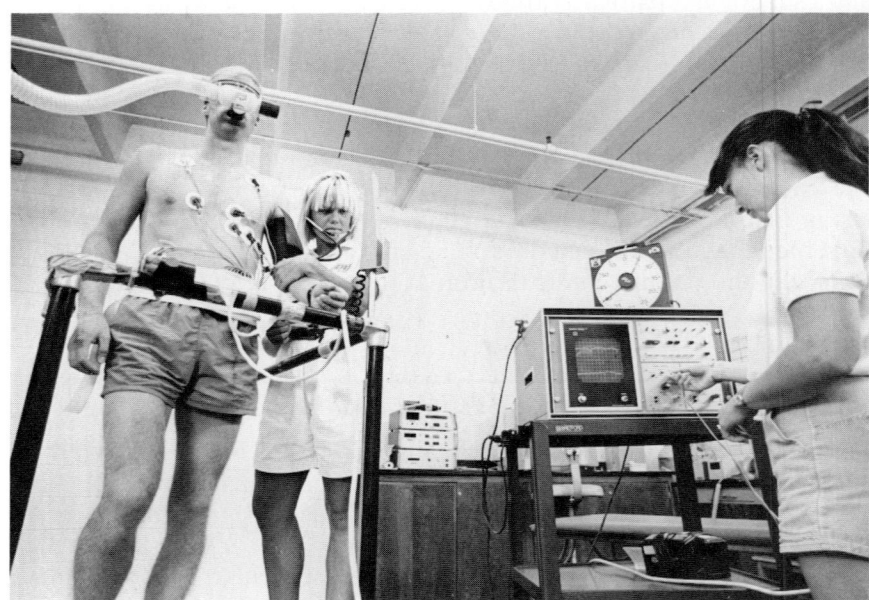

For scientific study to be accurate, sophisticated equipment is essential.
Photo by Tom Cherrey.

3. And then, when a particular aspect of human motion has been given scientific explanation, it becomes possible to create the conditions (cause) that will bring about the desired outcomes (effect). The final result is for a more efficient and influential profession.

IS ALL RESEARCH MEANINGFUL?

With the incredible proliferation of research-generated information becoming available on a daily basis, the problem of trying to sort the valuable studies from the not-so-valuable ones is inevitable. Scanning titles in any of the research publications can easily lead one to believe that much of the research has little application in the professional world. And yet, while the utilitarian value of a given piece of research may not be immediately apparent, every study does add to the total accumulation of knowledge.

A supposedly true story about Thomas Edison addresses the fact that he tried over one thousand different filaments for the light bulb without success. A friend inquired how he could be so persistent in the face of so many failures. "Failures?" Edison replied, "Think of it, I know one thousand things that don't work."

What may at first appear to be a "failure" in research because it seems to have no practical outcome actually does make a contribution. In some cases it shows, in effect, what not to do as well as what should be done in future studies. It reminds us which questions are important and which are not, not only adding bits of information to the total storehouse but also lending perspective to the profession.

DEVELOPING AN ANALYTICAL ATTITUDE

There is an enormous practical value to developing an attitude of being thoughtfully scientific. A willingness to question the nature of things—to seek the truth of any situation—gives dimension, intrigue, and discernment to every career venture.

For instance, what happens to learning if a teacher, accustomed to presenting a gymnastics unit in a particular sequence, decides to alter that sequence?

What is the outcome if a teacher abandons lectures and turns instead to open class discussions?

In baseball, does it really make sense to rely so faithfully on the sacrifice bunt?

Is it necessary for someone to learn certain footwork patterns to be able to hit successful backhands in tennis?

What occurs when a therapist introduces a new exercise regimen for a patient?

Should coaches have their athletes all eat the same, prescribed pregame meal?

How can health classes best be presented to motivate lasting habits of healthful living?

The important point is that not all research takes place in experimental laboratories or under sterile conditions with strictly controlled variables. One need not even be a researcher to do practical research. In the spirit of being inquisitive, one can perform what is called *action research*, which is literally any investigation of events in the real world. It could be mere observation of the results of a change in daily routine or simply charting the effects of existing behavioral patterns. The one criterion is that the observer be as scientific as possible, trying to see the truth of any situation rather than relying on guesswork or tradition. If this analytical attitude can prevail, then one can become more perceptive about everyday affairs and more capable of arriving at clear solutions to future circumstances.

THE IMPACT OF RESEARCH IN PHYSICAL EDUCATION

Research is often regarded as a force for change, and it clearly has had that effect in physical education. The scientific movement has accrued a fund of technological information that points to new directions and illuminates established values. The major effect has been to infuse the field with a spirit of inquiry. It is no longer acceptable to blindly believe that certain things are true. Consequently, thinking is not limited to the subjective realm, for research has provided the objective tools for discovery.

Traditional beliefs had long persisted. They became established, were repeated, and claimed a long line of believers. But now, in a massive switch of attitude, the profession has taken on a penchant for inquiring into every facet of human function. As a result, some older beliefs have been put aside, while others have taken on expanded dimensions, and new considerations have surfaced. Following are a few examples of how the results of research studies gave new insights into some traditionally held convictions.

1. *The natural athlete.* One of the earliest illustrations of objective study stemmed from the observation that some persons seemed to perform well at a wide variety of physical activities and were therefore con-

sidered to be "natural athletes." People concluded that skill was a general trait that was largely innate. Worst of all, some persons were cast as "motor morons," predestined for a life of incurable uncoordination. But a few investigators (McCloy, 1940; Brace, 1946; Henry, 1958) doggedly questioned this belief and set the profession to realizing, largely from their persistent research, that movement skills are many-dimensional, and that ability is not completely predetermined at birth, but can be markedly improved by proper instruction.

2. *Sports builds character.* One of the most frequently cited outcomes of sports participation is the idea that it somehow strengthens the positive "character" of individuals. While it appears true that a number of positive lessons can be learned through competition, the effects of sport can also be negated by too great an emphasis on winning, punishment for losing, and by negative role-modeling from cheating, substance abuse, and violence (Gilbert, 1988). As a result, low self-esteem may develop from receiving negative verbal and nonverbal messages of disapproval, aggressive behavior may develop from having leaders who fail to distinguish between assertive and aggressive behavior, excessive anxiety may occur from pressures to win, and depression and early dropout from sports may come from having continual negative appraisals of performance (Hellstedt, 1988).

3. *An athletic team must be "family."* An entrenched belief is that athletic teams will not perform well unless the players get along with each other. Surprisingly, some evidence shows that congeniality is not necessary for a team to win. In fact, winning teams tend to have more of a "businesslike" demeanor than one of close friendship. It's even possible that a certain degree of incompatibility may lead to increased effectiveness in performance (Coakley, 1986).

4. *Participation in sport teaches fair play.* Physical educators have always hoped that exposure to sporting activities, ranging from varsity competition to experiences in physical education classes, produces a sense of fair play among the participants. Although research on this concept is scarce, some indication is that, on the contrary, the outcomes could be the generation of unsportsmanlike conduct and antisocial aggressiveness, particularly in those sports that encourage violence (Stallman, 1977; Eitzen and Sage, 1986).

5. *Women should not engage in heavy exercise.* Of all the myths that surrounded physical activity, perhaps the most unfortunate are those that discouraged women from regular participation in exercise and competition. Most damaging of all may have been the beliefs that cautioned against vigorous exercise. But fortunately, research has demonstrated that sports participation has the same effects on the

vitality of women as men (Anderson et al., 1981) and that any differences in physiological function between men and women are more related to cultural and social restrictions than to limits in capacity (Wilmore, 1979). Furthermore, a trend has emerged whereby participation in sports is beginning to be seen as a positive trait by both males and females in their attitudes toward the opposite sex (Vickers, Lashuk, and Taerum, 1980). But a related myth that has tended to persist is that at high levels of competition, women display less confidence in their abilities than men and also show more common signs of "fear of success," which means that they are unable to handle the pressure of succeeding. Such beliefs are now being contradicted by findings that show no differences in confidence levels between the sexes, regardless of the intensity of competition (Lirgg and Feltz, 1989).

6. *Athletes need special diets.* At one time, the widespread misconception that high-protein diets were an absolute necessity for athletes prevailed. This led to disproportionate consumption of large amounts of red meat and milk, along with special protein supplements. Although some question still remains on this issue, a well-balanced diet may provide satisfactory nutrients for athletic performance (Hamilton, Whitney, and Sizer, 1988).

7. *Regular exercise results in mental health.* A relationship does exist between exercise and "mental health," however it may be defined. But there is an implicit assumption that exercise *produces* the qualities of a sound mind. Maybe it does. But as yet, we do not know whether the relationship is biochemical, neurological, social, or whatever (Sonstroem and Morgan, 1989). How one affects the other has not been determined, although the apparent relationship between mind and body remains unquestioned (Gauvin, 1989).

8. *Stretching reduces chances for injury.* Common recommendations are for persons engaging in a workout to stretch their muscles before and after the workout to reduce the potential for muscle pulls, cramps, or other injuries. Intuition alone seems to support this logic. Surprisingly, however, little evidence supports the belief that stretching either before, during, or after a workout reduces the incidence of injury (Cornelius, Hagemann, and Jackson, 1988). Furthermore, stretching does not appear to alleviate muscle soreness that often occurs after exercise (Buroker and Schwane, 1989).

9. *Running causes arthritis.* Osteoarthritis is the most common joint disease in the United States. Almost everyone has some pathologic signs by age forty, and the disease can be identified in the knees of 35 percent of the population by age thirty. Its cause is unknown, but

it has been thought to come about as a result of excessive impact-loading activity in the weight-bearing joints, such as from a longtime practice of regular jogging. So the original thought was that joggers were "spoiling their knees to save their hearts." But new evidence shows no reason to believe that jogging causes osteoarthritis (Pascale and Grana, 1989). In fact, running may actually slow the functional aspects of skeletal aging that are associated with the disease (Eichner, 1989).

10. *Performance is limited by oxygen supply.* One of the most fundamental beliefs in physical education is that performance of intense exercise is limited by the inability of the heart and lungs to supply oxygen for the energy demands of the active muscles. As a result, almost all explanations of the physiological adaptations to exercise cite increased oxygen diffusion into the bloodstream and better delivery to the muscles as the major factors that allow for training effects to take place. But evidence now accumulating shows that prolonged muscular contraction may be limited by other factors that have not characteristically been considered, particularly the way certain nutrients and chemicals (especially calcium) are utilized during contraction, and the structural limitations of the contractile elements in the muscles themselves (Noakes, 1988).

SUMMARY

Research is a process of discovery, the major goal of which is to determine cause-effect relationships, which in turn leads to the potential for regulating the events that are shown to be related to desired outcomes. It may seem that eventually, by this scientific process, all questions about human function will be answered. Certainly, many of the parameters appear to have been settled, yet much more remains to be accomplished.

The questions are especially problematical when one considers the complexities of the human mind. How is it that the minds of some people can get their attendant nervous and muscular systems together to become world-class athletes, while the great majority of the rest of us have trouble jumping rope?

It's the question-answer-question cycle of research that keeps it in momentum. So long as there are questions about human abilities, there will be work for research, and so long as there is research, there will be new questions about human abilities.

To the Reader

Perhaps the most important effect that research has had on physical education is the generation of an analytical framework. Much of what was earlier accepted within the profession was based on tradition, but tradition is no longer acceptable as the principle driving force today. Research does not discredit tradition, but it applies an inquiring attitude to it. All that is being asked is: What is the real truth?

Research, per se, is conducted within confined limits. It identifies a specific problem, then seeks answers through controlled investigation. But research originates from scholarly minds, and scholarship is a cultured form of inquiry. Thus, research is a product of, and also can foster, a naturally inquisitive mind. In this regard, research is central to the intellectual health of a discipline and serves to enliven those within it.

And so, at this early stage of your study, you are being presented with challenges that help you to acquire sophistication in your own sense of curiosity. You are surrounded by a community of individuals—professors and other students—with active inquiring minds. There is a collective natural fascination with conceiving and reconceiving ideas, and testing what seems to be fact. The process is one of gathering and verifying information, providing a liberal background toward conceptual scrutiny of all things.

Your formal study will equip you with the penchant for inquiry, which is the engine of discovery. Learning will become a kind of expressive imperative that will carry beyond your preparatory years. By giving an analytical approach to your study now, you will inherit the habit of examination and communication about the body of knowledge of the profession that will stand you in active readiness for your career. Inquisitiveness is, after all, something your mind cannot exhaust.

Suggested Projects

1. Find statements that you believe could not be supported by scientific analysis. Get these statements from the following sources: (1) comments made by your friends, (2) advertisements heard on radio or television, and (3) printed statements in the newspaper or magazines.
2. To carry this inquiry further, scan the library for journals that present research reports. Try to find some articles with conclusions that appear, by intuition alone, worthy of further research. Make suggestions about how that research might be conducted.
3. While scanning the research journals, make a list of commonly appearing terms that are used in the reports with which you are unfamiliar. Bring the terms to class for discussion of their meanings.

4. Select any aspect of human activity. Collect research articles on that topic. Note the conclusions. Is there agreement or disagreement among the results? Have a class discussion about how two similar studies can arrive at apparently different conclusions?

5. Think of a circumstance of human interaction that could be observed in your daily routine. Watch this interaction, taking notes about its characteristics for several days. Draw some hypotheses about the causes and effects of the informal data you have collected. Then devise some way to change the circumstances and their outcomes without being noticed by those involved in your ploy. Try for several days, and observe the effects.

References

Anderson, J. L., George, F., Krakauer, L. J., Shepard, R. J., and Torg, J. S. (Eds.). (1981). *The Year-Book of Sports Medicine, 1981*. Chicago: Year Book Medical Publications.

Brace, D. K. (1946). Studies in Motor Learning of Gross Bodily Motor Skills. *Research Quarterly, 17*, 242–253.

Buroker, K. C., and Schwane, J. A. (1989). Does Postexercise Stretching Alleviate Delayed Muscle Soreness? *The Physician and Sportsmedicine, 17*, 65–83.

Coakley, J. J. (1986). *Sport in Society: Issues and Controversies* (3rd ed.). St. Louis: Times Mirror/Mosby College Publishing.

Cornelius, W. L., Hagemann, R. W., and Jackson, A. W. (1988). A Study on Placement of Stretching within a Workout. *The Journal of Sports Medicine and Physical Fitness, 28*, 234–246.

Eichner, E. R. (1989). Does Running Cause Osteoarthritis? An Epidemiologic Perspective. *The Physician and Sportsmedicine, 17*, 147–154.

Eitzen, D. S., and Sage, G. H. (1986). *Sociology of American Sport* (3rd ed.). Dubuque, IA: Wm. C. Brown.

Gauvin, L. (1989). The Relationship between Regular Physical Activity and Subjective Well-Being. *Journal of Sport Behavior, 12*, 107–114.

Gilbert, B. (1988, May 16). Competition: Is It What Life's All About? *Sports Illustrated*, pp. 86–90ff.

Hamilton, E. M. N., Whitney, E. N., and Sizer, F. S. (1988). *Nutrition: Concepts and Controversies* (4th ed.). St. Paul, MN: West Publishing.

Hellstedt, J. C. (1988). Kids, Parents, and Sports: Some Questions and Answers. *The Physician and Sportsmedicine, 16*, 59–71.

Henry, F. M. (1958). Specificity vs. Generality in Learning Motor Skills. *Proceedings of the College Physical Education Association*, 126–128.

Lirgg, C. D., and Feltz, D. L. (1989). Female Self-Confidence in Sport: Myths, Realities, and Enhancement Strategies. *Journal of Physical Education, Recreation, and Dance, 60,* 49–54.

Margolis, H. (1987). *Patterns, Thinking, and Cognition: A Theory of Judgement.* Chicago: University of Chicago Press.

McCloy, C. H. (1940). A Preliminary Study of Factors in Motor Educability. *Research Quarterly, 11,* 28–39.

Noakes, T. D. (1988). Implications of Exercise Testing for Prediction of Athletic Performance: A Contemporary Perspective. *Medicine and Science in Sports and Exercise, 20,* 319–330.

Pascale, M., and Grana, W. A. (1989). Does Running Cause Osteoarthritis? An Orthopedic Perspective. *The Physician and Sportsmedicine, 17,* 157–166.

Sonstroem, R. J., and Morgan, W. P. (1989). Exercise and Self-esteem: Rationale and Model. *Medicine and Science in Sports and Exercise, 21,* 329–337.

Spitz, H. H. (1986). *The Raising of Intelligence: A Selected History of Attempts to Raise Retarded Intelligence.* Hillsdale, NJ: Lawrence Erlbaum Associates, Publishers.

Stallman, R. K. (1977). Professional Myths. *The Physical Educator, 34,* 139–144.

Vickers, J., Lashuk, M., and Taerum, T. (1980). Differences in Attitude toward the Concepts 'Male,' 'Female,' 'Male Athlete,' and 'Female Athlete.' *Research Quarterly for Exercise and Sport, 51,* 407–416.

Wilmore, J. H. (1979). The Application of Science to Sport: Physiological Profiles of Male and Female Athletes. *Canadian Journal of Applied Sport Sciences, 4,* 103–115.

Chapter 5

Exercise Physiology: Improving Physical Capacity

The Heart of the Matter

Muscle in Motion

Energy for Physical Activity

Science and Medicine Together

In the Subcellular World

Wellness: Good for Everyone

The Benefits of Regular Exercise

Cardiac Risk Factors

Exercise Prescription

Summary

To the Reader

Suggested Projects

References

The most long-standing interest in physical education has been the investigation of how the human body responds to various states of physical demands.

The profits of this investigation are found in knowing the factors that either positively or negatively affect human function.

With these determinations having been made, it becomes possible to offer individualized schedules for improving anyone's physiological state of being, ranging from competitive athletes to sedentary persons.

The end result is the general objective of potentially optimizing the physical and mental condition of all people.

A student, under the discerning eye of a professor, began a prescribed routine of exercise, persisted in that exercise, got tired, and quit. The professor wondered why.

Was it because not enough blood, with its baggage of energy supplies, was getting into the back street capillaries of the hungry muscles? Or was it because the blood could not effectively sweep away whatever biochemical refuse was being produced by the contracting muscles? Maybe the pump itself was too small for the job—after all, so much of us is vessels that laid end to end, they would make a small pipe reaching several times around the earth. Or maybe the student just said, "Enough of this."

The scene could have been at Harvard, in 1892, where George Fitz, M.D., began the first exercise physiology lab in the country (Rothshuh and Reisse, 1973). Or in a much more technological setting, it could have been yesterday, at a lab in Ohio or California or Wisconsin, where a treadmill-induced student sent electrical and mechanical messages from working muscles to electronic receivers that recorded, without error, every corporeal effort of that student.

It is a realm of exercise physiology, which is *the study of how the body, from a functional standpoint, responds, adjusts, and adapts to exercise* (Fox, Bowers, and Foss, 1988). It is the most venerable of the sciences in physical education.

THE HEART OF THE MATTER

Exercise physiologists are technologists. They use electrocardiograms and spirometers and pneumotachometers and other electronic paraphernalia to find answers to questions about human responses to exercise. For example, properly placed on the skin's surface, electrodes can pick up the electricity that is in a beating heart. It is there as a regular irregularity and can be measured by an electrocardiogram (ECG). Only a ten-thousandth of a volt is present during each heartbeat; still ten times more electricity than is produced in the brain by thought (Brustaert, 1989) and plenty of current to be recorded as an ECG. This electricity registers heart-cycle after heart-cycle, so long as there is graph paper and as long as the owner of the heart keeps it pumping.

The heart leaves a permanent record, there on the graph paper (figure 5.1). It shows the P wave, an electrical prime in the atria that depolarizes them and heralds their contraction. Then the QRS complex, the "spike" that correlates to the ventricles discharging their volume of blood into the aorta. Finally the T wave, a rounded upthrust that registers the electrical preparation of the ventricles for their next cycle. Seventy times a

Exercise Physiology: Improving Physical Capacity 71

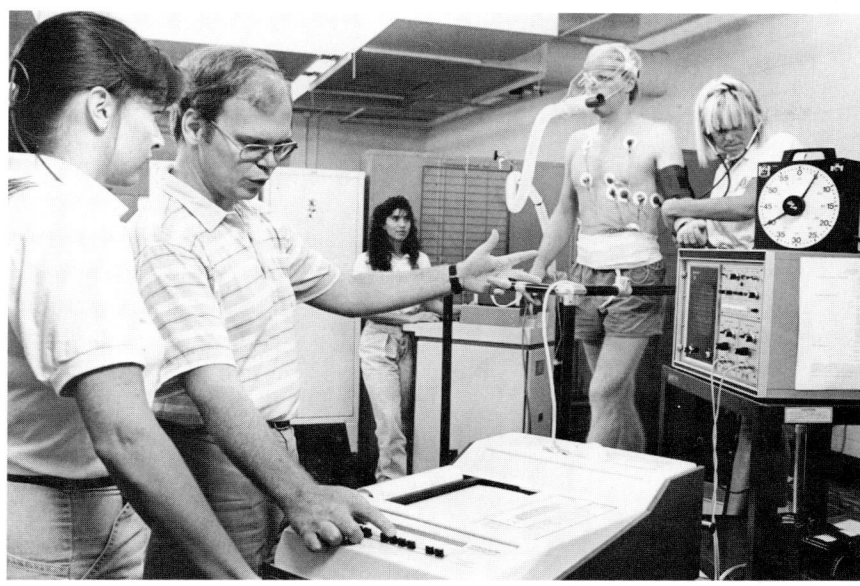

An electrocardiogram (ECG) is an extremely valuable measurement tool to the exercise physiologist.
Photo by Tom Cherrey.

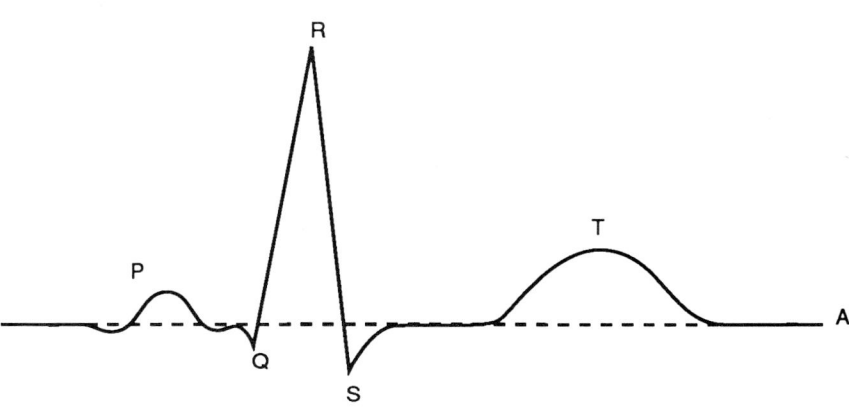

Figure 5.1 An ECG.

minute (much more often during exercise)—this cycle happens three thousand million beats in an average lifetime.

The exercise physiologist sees the ECG as a report of the electrical events that produce mechanical events. The document is there, permanent and clear. But the interpretation is not so clear. So the exercise physiologist, a technologist in collecting the record, now becomes a cryptoanalyst. The clinical usefulness of the ECG is manifest fact, a matter of physics. But the whole-heart affair that produced the record, and consequently the living meaning of it, needs the discerning eye of the physiologist turned cardiac detective.

The electrocardiogram probes the very core of life. In the hands of a physician, it helps with a diagnosis or may clinch it. For the exercise physiologist, it tells of how the heart is responding to the stress of physical exertion. It's important news, for what may show up in the graphic record are signs of tissue damage, or abnormalities in cardiac rhythm, electrical conduction, or oxygen supply.

The ECG is an autobiography of the heart, and it has inspired a wealth of useful—indeed life-giving—research in exercise physiology. Moreover, learning to administer and interpret an ECG has helped many a student to obtain a first job in a health clinic, hospital, or cardiac rehabilitation center.

MUSCLE IN MOTION

The wall of the right ventricle is so thin that if held up toward the sun, the light comes through. The left is heavier, but still seemingly too spindly to do its share in dispensing 300,000 tons of blood in a lifetime. Yet the heart meets its day-and-night appointments with clockwork regularity. And it does its work without bothering to ask the brain for a job description.

Not so of the skeletal muscles. They lie quiet until given work orders. There are 434 skeletal muscles. By weight they make up 40 to 45 percent of the body. On a good day, when all your backhands are going crosscourt to the far corner, your muscles feel like none of you. On a bad day, they can feel like all of you.

All muscles contract, whether voluntarily or involuntarily. It is their single genius. They can only pull, never push. By pulling, they do their daily chores of digestion, of respiration, of standing hair on end, of getting you to class on time. Exercise physiology studies the electrical, chemical, and mechanical events of contraction. The objective is to understand, and to maximize the functional efficiency, of every muscular contraction and therefore every system of the body.

The concerns are wide reaching. For a teacher, they tell about the fundamental neuromuscular processes that promote the acquisition and improvement of physical skills. For a coach, they center on how to arrange optimal training schedules for athletes. For an athletic trainer or a therapist, they define logical rehabilitation agendas. Other areas of study in exercise physiology tell the health club employee how to construct proper dietary programs for clients. Or they show an allied health professional how exercise can suppress asthma, diabetes, and other pathologies. For all of humankind, they demonstrate that degenerative disorders are amenable to positive change through physical activity and that regular exercise is a durable form of preventive medicine. And for everyone who studies exercise physiology, the learning will be housed in scientific justification for their future of optimizing, in whatever profession chosen, the internal combustion affairs of other people.

ENERGY FOR PHYSICAL ACTIVITY

Everywhere inside of us a fire is burning. It's a special kind of burning—that of life. We stoke the fire daily at mealtime, often between meals, sometimes at midnight when we are more asleep than awake—but wide awake on the scales the next morning.

We are what we eat, if one can trust a familiar adage. If that's true, should a bodybuilder eat lots of protein, and a basketball player plenty of carbohydrate? Or does it not matter?

The immediate source of energy for any muscular contraction is adenosine triphosphate (ATP), which is held in the muscle cells waiting to dispatch them into activity. But first the ATP must be sent into a complex chemical reaction that atom-smashes the ATP apart to liberate its potential. Any text in exercise physiology will note that ATP does its act by phosphorylation of adenosine diphosphate through the addition of an inorganic phosphate from the breakdown of PC to C plus P_i, and by glycolysis, which degrades glycogen to pyruvate and either lactic acid or acetyl-CoA. It's the memorization of chemical events like these that make you need that snack at midnight.

The energy liberated during this breakup of ATP activates specific sites on the contractile elements of muscles, causing the fibers to contract. But what is it that sets off the ATP cycle in the first place? Everything on the menu. And the chemical episodes in the digestive breakdown of food are just as confounding as the ATP sequence.

There are real-world applications for understanding this biochemistry. For example, the energy systems used for a sprint are descriptively different from those used for a marathon. A 100-meter dash happens in a hurry, so there isn't enough time for oxygen to be important in muscle contraction; therefore, ATP gets liberated *anaerobically* (without oxygen). But a marathon runner, by contrast, needs a more sustained supply of energy, and in this case ATP is broken down *aerobically* (with oxygen). Accordingly, appropriate and different dietary plans can be established to optimize the performance of athletes in either event. The marathon runner needs a plentiful supply of glycogen (a carbohydrate) stockpiled away in the muscles for this exhausting event. This cache of glycogen can be increased in volume by "carbohydrate loading," whereby the runner, in the days preceding the race, follows a regimen of three consecutive days on a diet low in carbohydrates, and then for the three days immediately before competition changes to a diet of spaghetti and pizza and chocolate cream cakes and all the other foods that weight watchers avoid.

Similar dietary management does not seem to affect the sprinter, however. In this and other athletic events of very short duration, the amount of carbohydrate in the diet is not a factor in the efficiency of muscular contraction and therefore does not markedly influence performance (Adams and Deitrick, 1983).

Actually, it's sometimes difficult to draw conclusions from nutritional research, for often considerable variability exists between different individuals on the same diet or within the same individual at different times (Cameron and Van Staveren, 1988). Notwithstanding this, the research has provoked appraisal of dietary customs that had been established only on the basis of years of tradition and belief. Following are a few examples:

1. Is an athlete's diet different from the best diet for anyone?

    Americans consume too much fat. Only 35 percent of the caloric intake should be fat, but it's closer to 45 percent in the average American diet (Baker, 1983). Reducing the fat intake makes good sense, and generally speaking, athletes need higher levels of carbohydrate in their diets.

2. How much extra carbohydrates do athletes need?

    It depends on the sport, but it should probably constitute 55 to 70 percent of the total caloric intake, the higher amounts being needed for athletes in demanding endurance events (Vander, Sherman, and Luciano, 1985).

3. Do athletes need extra protein?

    This is a confusing one. Some research evidence shows no increase in need (Asghar and Bhatti, 1987), modest need increases (Dohm, Tapscott, and Kasperek, 1987), or requirements of up to 100 percent over the needs of a sedentary individual (Lemon, 1987). Suffice to say that during exercise there is protein breakdown in the muscles (Wolfe, 1987), and while glycogen is acknowledged to be the main energy source, protein appears to play an important function in sustaining the whole metabolic apparatus (Brooks, 1987).

4. Should fluids be restricted during competition?

   This long-held belief has now been circumvented. Dehydration can disable an athlete more seriously than any other nutritional factor. A person can sweat away as much as 9 pounds of fluid and still perform well, provided there is sufficient water replacement during that performance (Sherman and Lamb, 1988).

5. Is extra salt advisable for athletes?

   Salt tablets at practice sessions were once common, but they were later found to be dangerous because of potentially serious disruptions in the electrolyte balance of the body (Fox, Bowers, and Foss, 1988). Replacement fluids during exercise need contain no sodium ions. During recovery some additional sodium may be needed, but normal salting of food is sufficient (Shephard, 1984).

6. Are there "high-energy" drinks that can help an athlete sustain performance?

   Gatorade and other "sweat replacers" claim that the mixtures (of water, glucose, sodium, chloride, potassium, magnesium, and calcium) enter the system faster than plain water. In fact they seem to be absorbed less rapidly than water because the glucose in them delays pickup by the bloodstream. The best drink is diluted juices (such as one part orange juice to four parts water) or just plain cool water (Whitney and Hamilton, 1987).

7. Is there a best pre-game meal for athletes?

   It should be high in carbohydrate and low in fat. Otherwise it should emphasize "digestibility," and perhaps more importantly, it should be finished three to four hours before competition (Hamilton, Whitney, and Sizer, 1988).

SCIENCE AND MEDICINE TOGETHER

If you see someone who appears drowsy, there's a chance that that person is in an exercise physiology class, sacrificing sleep to catch up on lab manuals. Exercise physiology is one of the more rigorous, technical areas of study in physical education. The topics are sometimes so heavy with chemistry and biophysics that completing a class seems like qualification for an M.D. certificate. Let's see now, was it alpha ketoglutatic acid or nicotinamide adenine dinucleotide that breaks down in the tricarboxylic acid cycle? Hans Krebs knew.

At first all is abstract. Then you realize that everything falls into a packet of scientific study without which one cannot give serious thought to human performance. Eventually, you begin to sense that it's impossible to know *enough* about the field.

But it does get medical, so much so that the term *sports medicine* is sometimes used as a synonym for exercise physiology. This is misleading, for sports medicine is an overall term that is liberally used to include the combined influences of physiological, mechanical, psychological, and cultural forces that pull and tug on human performance in sport (chapter 10 of this text is devoted to sports medicine). However, sports medicine has its essence of existence in exercise physiology, which supplies the hard science of understanding human dynamics. Furthermore, the body of knowledge that is exercise physiology finds its most salient application in the end objectives of promoting health and welfare, and in prolonging life, and therefore it can rightfully be aligned with the objectives at the core of medicine.

IN THE SUBCELLULAR WORLD

Exercise physiology has trespassed inward. In earlier days, research was largely confined to observing how people would respond to controlled exercise. Take the pulse. Measure the blood pressure. Collect expired air. Such observations are still done, but to understand what really causes adaptations to exercise, it was necessary to get to the inner sources of those changes.

So the cell was studied. It was sliced into thin sections and stained to look like a church window so its architecture could be seen under the microscope. Then came the electron microscope, and the human mind could reach inside to see the richness of the jewel box of life. The cell became a thing so large that it appeared like a big-screen television. And what was previously incomprehensible became comprehensible.

The interior of every cell is composed of organic and inorganic materials dissolved in water. Life is maintained there. The metabolic events that are in constant activity are now supplying answers to questions that prod at the mysteries of existence. How does the heart of a cardiac patient respond to specific types of exercise? How is metabolism affected by dietary manipulation? What happens when people age? What is quality of life? Every cell is in miniature what the organism is in whole. A muscle cell does in small what an entire muscle does in large. And so to study the heart is to study its cells. To know how the nervous system controls the heart and gives movement to the body is to study each neuron.

Histology and endocrinology and biochemistry and neuroscience and all the other disciplines look into the kernel of being. But only one of the sciences, exercise physiology, attends primarily to how exercise contributes to the overall well-being of body and soul.

WELLNESS: GOOD FOR EVERYONE

Then along came the concept of wellness. It started its locutional vogue as a hybrid term. Some dictionaries still do not even include it. But its meaning is extensive.

Wellness is not just a state of being, but a life-style—a mind-set that implies an active, positive approach to health. In the past, health was commonly defined as the absence of disease. By contrast, wellness is a process whereby an individual actively pursues an optimal development of the physical self through constructive use and management of all life choices that influence health. It includes self-responsibility for physical fitness, sound nutritional habits, alcohol and drug control, stress management, smoking cessation, weight management, and all other matters of comprehensive well-being (Rosato, 1986).

Wellness awareness emanated from the rapid growth of workplace fitness centers that multiplied in the 1960s. Corporations had realized that their best executives were too often becoming ex-executives. Companies were giving on-the-job preparation to management personnel only to find that many of them were becoming numbers on life insurance longevity charts. The executives-in-training were getting their leadership skills in readiness, but in the meantime their health was being ignored. So the corporations, not wanting to lose their qualified executives (to say nothing of the money invested in their training), began to channel resources into programs that would keep their employees physically able.

To think that the growth of such fitness programs was generated from a corporate sense of moral responsibility, or even more appealing, that it was a carryover from habits that were developed in school health and physical education programs would be convenient. But in truth, it was economical. Corporations simply did not want their executives having heart attacks after they had invested time and money in their apprenticeship.

The returns of the programs became realized in cost containment of medical care, and in decreased employee absenteeism, improved morale, increased productivity, job satisfaction, a feeling of well-being, an improved sense of community, and a feeling that the management cared about its personnel (Ellis, 1988).

Now the concept has spread to hospitals, community centers, medical clinics, agencies of government, private enterprises, and even schools and colleges (from where it should have originated in the first place). And although the startup of wellness may have been for economic reasons, the outcome is providing societal benefits that have long been the objectives of health and physical education. Such factors as alcohol and

Inquiry

A measure of lung function is one test of overall physiological fitness.
Photo by Tom Cherrey.

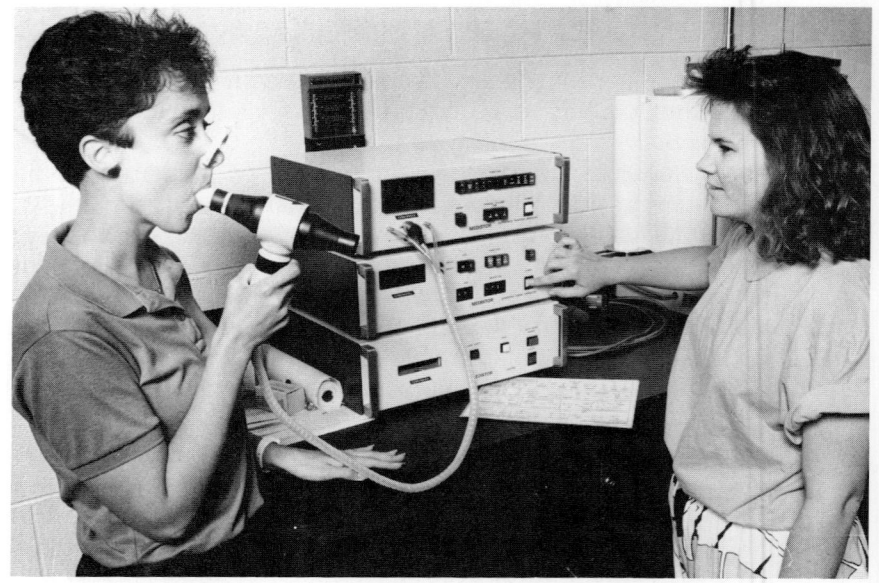

drug abuse, smoking, overweight, and chronic diseases that are linked to stressful life-styles are now being directly counteracted by wellness programs that seek to make positive behavioral changes. Wellness deals with the physical, nutritional, psychological, and metaphysical components of living. It's a total package.

Exercise is a central ingredient in this collective approach. When the first wellness programs began, the manifestations of a lack of exercise were not yet completely linked to well-being. Even in the early 1970s when aerobic programs emerged, the exercises were essentially limited to the improvement of cardiovascular endurance. But today, the whole person finds positive mental and physical benefits from the programs.

There is still work to be done. Attitudes about wellness are developed over a period of time, and waiting until someone enters the workplace could allow for chronic disease states to mature. Thus, the original and enduring objectives of school physical education to establish healthy life-styles remains today as important as ever. During the formative years, many life habits are established, so the target population for wellness should not be only in the corporate setting but also and especially with young people.

THE BENEFITS OF REGULAR EXERCISE

Public awareness about the benefits of achieving optimal states of physical and mental well-being is in fact growing. To an extent, this is a payoff of research coming from exercise physiology laboratories. In the past this research did not often reach beyond professional journals, but in recent years substantive writings about wellness concerns are appearing more frequently in newspapers, popular magazines, and in books for the general populace. Additional attention has come from regular programming and specials about wellness on television and radio.

An underlying stimulant to the current public interest is the recognition that exercise produces positive outcomes that have been clearly substantiated by well-controlled research. These known effects have paralleled to a great extent the evolution of research technology—the more sophisticated the techniques became, the more exacting and conclusive the results became. Yet some long-held convictions remain basically unchanged, albeit strengthened, by technological research. Three are most notable:

1. *Weight management.* Persons who are overweight are very likely to have directly correlated low levels of fitness (Haskell, 1989), indicating that weight problems occur from both overeating and "undermoving." The health risks of obesity are well documented; they include impairment of cardiac function, hypertension, diabetes, renal disease, gallbladder disease, pulmonary disease and/or impaired function, osteoarthritis, degenerative joint disease, several types of cancer, high cholesterol levels, and a psychological burden (McArdle, Katch, and Katch, 1986). Overweight, inactive individuals can achieve a more desired weight by caloric restriction and increased energy expenditure, with the best results occurring when both are modified (Zuti and Golding, 1976).

2. *Cardiovascular efficiency.* With regular exercise, blood pressure is lowered and the heart beats less frequently yet with increased myocardial power (Caspersen, 1987). This means less internal stress for the circulatory system and a more efficient operation of the entire apparatus. It results in a preservation of cardiovascular function at levels considerably above sedentary individuals. The improved cardiovascular state is in itself a significant mechanism that reduces the probability of coronary heart disease. It should be noted, however, that the only type of exercise that consistently and substantially is associated with lower coronary disease is habitual aerobic workouts for sustained periods (Morris, Everitt, and Semmence, 1987).

3. *Psychological benefits.* There is something therapeutic about exercise. Perhaps it is an emotional outlet—a way to reduce feelings of stress. Maybe it's the pleasurable sensation of having the body operate at a high level. Or perhaps it's the satisfaction of knowing one is doing something good for oneself. It might even be due to changes in blood or brain chemistry. Whatever the reason, exercise can refresh the mind. It is reported to generate a more positive self-image, a better ability to relax, and a heightened mental alertness (Noble, 1986).

CARDIAC RISK FACTORS

Galen, an ambitious Greek physician practicing in Rome, gave the blood vessels of the heart their name: coronary, meaning a circlet, or crown. Now the word coronary is crowned with mortality. It is a word for which the bell tolls. Near the last pages of any newspaper are notices with a short biography. Most are there because of a buildup of atherosclerotic plaque in their coronary arteries, leading to diminished blood flow. They may have been excited by some sudden blood-demand of physical effort or strong emotion (which tends vessels to spasm), but the blood could not be delivered. Then came a sudden severe pain, a feeling of suffocation, and the attack itself.

A person may survive a first heart attack, be felled by a second, or even a sixth. Survivability depends largely on the amount of tissue damaged. If blood flow is not completely blocked, the person may escape with angina (chest pains). But when the blood flow is totally cut off or reaches critically low levels, a portion of the heart muscle dies (clinically called a myocardial infarction). When it happens to someone we know, we may inventory our own life-style for a few contemplative days. We'll be more careful about our diet, stop smoking, think about getting more exercise, quit worrying about everything.

What are the chances that you will have a heart attack? Here's a gamelike test. It's called RISKO, originally devised by the Michigan Heart Association and further developed by the American Heart Association. RISKO is presented in table 5.1, which lists of some of the major conditions associated with an increased danger of coronary disease.

This test is an estimate. Some other factors are not included, such as glucose tolerance, or onset of diabetes, stress and tension in your life, personality type, and most important of the omissions, exercise habits. Nevertheless, this test is at least a general indication of your present potential for cardiovascular difficulty.

Table 5.1. RISKO. Cardiovascular Risk Appraisal.

MEN

Find the column for your age group. Everyone starts with a score of 10 points. Work down the page *adding* points to your score or *subtracting* points from your score.

		54 OR YOUNGER	55 OR OLDER
		STARTING SCORE: 10	STARTING SCORE: 10

1. WEIGHT

Locate your weight category in the table below. If you are in...

	54 OR YOUNGER	55 OR OLDER
weight category A	SUBTRACT 2	SUBTRACT 2
weight category B	SUBTRACT 1	ADD 0
weight category C	ADD 1	ADD 1
weight category D	ADD 2	ADD 3
	EQUALS	EQUALS

2. SYSTOLIC BLOOD PRESSURE

Use the "first" or "higher" number from your most recent blood pressure measurement. If you do not know your blood pressure, estimate it by using the letter for your weight category. If your blood pressure is...

		54 OR YOUNGER	55 OR OLDER
A	119 or less	SUBTRACT 1	SUBTRACT 5
B	between 120 and 139	ADD 0	SUBTRACT 2
C	between 140 and 159	ADD 0	ADD 1
D	160 or greater	ADD 1	ADD 4
		EQUALS	EQUALS

3. BLOOD CHOLESTEROL LEVEL

Use the number from your most recent blood cholesterol test. If you do not know your blood cholesterol, estimate it by using the letter for your weight category. If your blood cholesterol is...

		54 OR YOUNGER	55 OR OLDER
A	199 or less	SUBTRACT 2	SUBTRACT 1
B	between 200 and 224	SUBTRACT 1	SUBTRACT 1
C	between 225 and 249	ADD 0	ADD 0
D	250 or higher	ADD 1	ADD 0
		EQUALS	EQUALS

4. CIGARETTE SMOKING

If you...

(If you smoke a pipe, but not cigarettes, use the same score adjustment as those cigarette smokers who smoke less than a pack a day.)

	54 OR YOUNGER	55 OR OLDER
do not smoke	SUBTRACT 1	SUBTRACT 2
smoke less than a pack a day	ADD 0	SUBTRACT 1
smoke a pack a day	ADD 1	ADD 0
smoke more than a pack a day	ADD 2	ADD 3
FINAL SCORE EQUALS		

WEIGHT TABLE FOR MEN

Look for your height (without shoes) in the far left column and then read across to find the category into which your weight (in indoor clothing) would fall.

YOUR HEIGHT FT IN	WEIGHT CATEGORY (lbs.)			
	A	B	C	D
5 1	up to 123	124-148	149-173	174 plus
5 2	up to 126	127-152	153-178	179 plus
5 3	up to 129	130-156	157-182	183 plus
5 4	up to 132	133-160	161-186	187 plus
5 5	up to 135	136-163	164-190	191 plus
5 6	up to 139	140-168	169-196	197 plus
5 7	up to 144	145-174	175-203	204 plus
5 8	up to 148	149-179	180-209	210 plus
5 9	up to 152	153-184	185-214	215 plus
5 10	up to 157	158-190	191-221	222 plus
5 11	up to 161	162-194	195-227	228 plus
6 0	up to 165	166-199	200-232	233 plus
6 1	up to 170	171-205	206-239	240 plus
6 2	up to 175	176-211	212-246	247 plus
6 3	up to 180	181-217	218-253	254 plus
6 4	up to 185	186-223	224-260	261 plus
6 5	up to 190	191-229	230-267	268 plus
6 6	up to 195	196-235	236-274	275 plus
ESTIMATE OF SYSTOLIC BLOOD PRESSURE	or less	120 to 139	140 to 159	160 or more
ESTIMATE OF BLOOD CHOLESTEROL	199 or less	200 to 224	225 to 249	250 or more

Because both blood pressure and blood cholesterol are related to weight, an estimate of these risk factors for each weight category is printed at the bottom of the table.

Table 5.1. *Continued.*

WOMEN

Find the column for your age group. Everyone starts with a score of 10 points. Work down the page *adding* points to your score or *subtracting* points from your score.

		54 OR YOUNGER	55 OR OLDER
		STARTING SCORE 10	STARTING SCORE 10

1. WEIGHT

Locate your weight category in the table below. If you are in . . .

weight category A	SUBTRACT 2 / SUBTRACT 2
weight category B	SUBTRACT 1 / SUBTRACT 1
weight category C	ADD 1 / ADD 1
weight category D	ADD 2 / ADD 1

EQUALS / EQUALS

2. SYSTOLIC BLOOD PRESSURE

Use the "first" or "higher" number from your most recent blood pressure measurement. If you do not know your blood pressure, estimate it by using the letter for your weight category. If your blood pressure is . . .

A	119 or less	SUBTRACT 2 / SUBTRACT 3
B	between 120 and 139	SUBTRACT 1 / ADD 0
C	between 140 and 159	ADD 0 / ADD 3
D	160 or greater	ADD 1 / ADD 6

EQUALS / EQUALS

3. BLOOD CHOLESTEROL LEVEL

Use the number from your most recent blood cholesterol test. If you do not know your blood cholesterol, estimate it by using the letter for your weight category. If your blood cholesterol is . . .

A	199 or less	SUBTRACT 1 / SUBTRACT 3
B	between 200 and 224	ADD 0 / SUBTRACT 1
C	between 225 and 249	ADD 0 / ADD 1
D	250 or higher	ADD 1 / ADD 3

EQUALS / EQUALS

4. CIGARETTE SMOKING

If you . . .

do not smoke	SUBTRACT 1 / SUBTRACT 2
smoke less than a pack a day	ADD 0 / SUBTRACT 1
smoke a pack a day	ADD 1 / ADD 1
smoke more than a pack a day	ADD 2 / ADD 4

FINAL SCORE EQUALS / FINAL SCORE EQUALS

WEIGHT TABLE FOR WOMEN

Look for your height (without shoes) in the far left column and then read across to find the category into which your weight (in indoor clothing) would fall.

YOUR HEIGHT FT IN	WEIGHT CATEGORY (lbs.)			
	A	B	C	D
4 8	up to 101	102-122	123-143	144 plus
4 9	up to 103	104-125	126-146	147 plus
4 10	up to 106	107-128	129-150	151 plus
4 11	up to 109	110-132	133-154	155 plus
5 0	up to 112	113-136	137-158	159 plus
5 1	up to 115	116-139	140-162	163 plus
5 2	up to 119	120-144	145-168	169 plus
5 3	up to 122	123-148	149-172	173 plus
5 4	up to 127	128-154	155-179	180 plus
5 5	up to 131	132-158	159-185	186 plus
5 6	up to 135	136-163	164-190	191 plus
5 7	up to 139	140-168	169-196	197 plus
5 8	up to 143	144-173	174-202	203 plus
5 9	up to 147	148-178	179-207	208 plus
5 10	up to 151	152-182	183-213	214 plus
5 11	up to 155	156-187	188-218	219 plus
6 0	up to 159	160-191	192-224	225 plus
6 1	up to 163	164-196	197-229	230 plus
ESTIMATE OF SYSTOLIC BLOOD PRESSURE	119 or less	120 to 139		160 or more
ESTIMATE OF BLOOD CHOLESTEROL	199 or less	200 to 224		250 or more

Because both blood pressure and blood cholesterol are related to weight, an estimate of these risk factors for each weight category is printed at the bottom of the table.

Table 5.1. *Continued.*

WHAT YOUR SCORE MEANS

0-4 — You have one of the lowest risks of heart disease for your age and sex.

5-9 — You have a low to moderate risk of heart disease for your age and sex but there is some room for improvement.

10-14 — You have a moderate to high risk of heart disease for your age and sex, with considerable room for improvement on some factors.

15-19 — You have a high risk of developing heart disease for your age and sex with a great deal of room for improvement on all factors.

20 & over — You have a very high risk of developing heart disease for your age and sex and should take immediate action on all risk factors.

WARNING

* If you have diabetes, gout or a family history of heart disease, your actual risk will be greater than indicated by this appraisal.
* If you do not know your current blood pressure or blood cholesterol level, you should visit your physician or health center to have them measured. Then figure your score again for a more accurate determination of your risk.
* If you are overweight, have high blood pressure or high blood cholesterol, or smoke cigarettes, your long-term risk of heart disease is increased even if your risk in the next several years is low.

HOW TO REDUCE YOUR RISK

* Try to quit smoking permanently. There are many programs available.
* Have your blood pressure checked regularly, preferably every twelve months after age 40. If your blood pressure is high, see your physician. Remember blood pressure medicine is only effective if taken regularly.
* Consider your daily exercise (or lack of it). A half hour of brisk walking, swimming or other enjoyable activity should not be difficult to fit into your day.
* Give some serious thought to your diet. If you are overweight, or eat a lot of foods high in saturated fat or cholesterol (whole milk, cheese, eggs, butter, fatty foods, fried foods) then changes should be made in your diet. Look for the *American Heart Association Cookbook* at your local bookstore.
* Visit or write your local Heart Association for further information and copies of free pamphlets on many related subjects including:
  • Reducing your risk of heart attack.
  • Controlling high blood pressure.
  • Eating to keep your heart healthy.
  • How to stop smoking.
  • Exercising for good health.

SOME WORDS OF CAUTION

* If you have diabetes, gout, or a family history of heart disease, your real risk of developing heart disease will be greater than indicated by your RISKO score. If your score is high and you have one or more of these additional problems, you should give particular attention to reducing your risk.
* If you are a woman under 45 years or a man under 35 years of age, your RISKO score represents an upper limit on your real risk of developing heart disease. In this case, your real risk is probably lower than indicated by your score.
* Using your weight category to estimate your systolic blood pressure or your blood cholesterol level makes your RISKO score less accurate.
* Your score will tend to overestimate your risk if your actual values on these two important factors are average for someone of your height and weight.
* Your score will underestimate your risk if your actual blood pressure or cholesterol level is above average for someone of your height or weight.

Reproduced with permission. © RISKO, 1981. Copyright American Heart Association.

Being overweight and sedentary increases a person's risk of suffering a heart attack.
© John Foote/Photo Researchers, Inc.

EXERCISE PRESCRIPTION

In a perfect world, everyone would have a regular regimen of exercise. The physiological benefits qualify it as a therapeutic agent. And like any other therapy, the prescriptions for exercise levels must be thoughtfully administered. The dosage for one individual may not be appropriate for another.

Ideally, it would all start with medical clearance, which for persons over 35 should include a resting ECG and some blood-letting for cholesterol, glucose, and triglyceride levels. A thorough family history is also important to determine whether one is predisposed for cardiac distress.

Before prescribing an exercise program, to ascertain the level of intensity that can be safely tolerated is important. A review of present activity levels will be a help, but a more telling evaluation can be obtained from a test of *functional capacity,* which technically is the maximal ability to convert chemical energy into mechanical energy. The most common procedure for this determination is a *stress test,* or graded exercise test. The stress test usually consists of riding a bicycle ergometer or, more commonly, walking or running during a multistage treadmill test. In either case, the work load is gradually increased in a stepwise fashion until a predetermined target heart rate is attained, or the person indicates a desire to no longer continue, or until there are irregular blips on the ECG, which could signal a troubled heart. The primary purpose of the test is to detect for latent ischemic heart disease (local and temporary deficiency of blood in the heart), but the test is also useful in evaluating cardiovascular functional capacity and in evaluating the person's general response to a controlled dosage of exercise.

With all the necessary information accumulated, the objective becomes one of determining a program of activity that will provide the best outcomes for the person. Essential factors in achieving the goals are the type, frequency, duration, and intensity of the exercise. Although the schedule should be individually prescribed, the American College of Sports Medicine (1986) has recommended the following general guidelines as a basis for structuring any exercise program:

1. *Type.* The program should emphasize rhythmic, continuous endurance activities such as walking, running, cycling, swimming, and cross-country skiing. Stop-and-start activities like tennis and racquetball need to be vigorous rather than casual. One factor of caution, however, is that certain personality types (tense, stressful individuals) may actually have the positive effects of exercise negated by increasing their risk of coronary injury during prolonged, intense physical activity (Blair, 1988).

2. *Frequency.* For most people, three to five exercise days per week are recommended. However, in sedentary people or heart patients who are just beginning a program, more frequent and shorter exercise periods are more appropriate. Daily or twice-daily sessions of five minutes will lead to the most rapid adaptation for these persons.

3. *Duration.* There is no perfect exercise interval for everyone, but twenty minutes minimum and sixty minutes maximum will usually suffice. Low-intensity exercises should be continued for at least forty-five minutes, but sometimes one's body knows when to stop.

4. *Intensity.* Overall, the intensity of the exercise should require at least 60 percent of the maximal heart rate. A generally acceptable estimate of the maximal heart rate can be made by subtracting one's age from 220. Except in the case of athletes training for competition, exercising at intensities greater than 85 to 90 percent of the maximal heart rate does not produce additional returns of cardiovascular benefit. However, exercising at levels below the 60 percent minimum can still result in increased cardiovascular capacity, especially for persons of low fitness levels (Wilmore, 1989).

Often we are led to believe that an exercise schedule must be emphatically rigorous and prolonged to provide any desired benefits. Yet epidemiological research does not necessarily support this conclusion. Positive gains in one's overall state of health can be achieved by even modest increases in activity, particularly for sedentary persons (LaPorte et al., 1985). Therefore, what may be most important is that an exercise plan start off with attainable goals, however small, so that it offers the user encouragement rather than the discouragement of unreasonable short-term objectives.

SUMMARY

Systematized study finds great expression in exercise physiology. Research is probing for answers that are at the very center of human function and exist as the essence of life itself. The results have produced a comprehensive body of knowledge that has been at the forefront of advancements within the physical education profession and that often stands in collaboration with the interests of medicine. Today, this branch of study holds the attention of more professionals than any other.

Basic to exercise physiology is a continuing interest in how regular physical activity can contribute to one's well-being through improvements in functional capacity. The list of benefits is long. Following is a condensed index of those that are reliably documented by research (summarized in Astrand, 1987; Berger, 1982; and Seefeldt and Vogel, 1986).

Exercise leads to an increase in:

1. Coronary collateral vascularization.
2. General blood vessel size.
3. Efficiency of the heart muscle.
4. Efficiency of peripheral blood distribution and return.
5. Maximum oxygen uptake.
6. Cardiac output (stroke volume).
7. Capillary density in skeletal muscles.
8. Red blood cell mass and blood volume.
9. Fibrinolytic capability (dissolving of blood clots).
10. Electron transport capacity.
11. Activity of enzymes in skeletal muscles.
12. Structure and function of ligaments, tendons, and joints.
13. Growth hormone production.
14. Thyroid function.
15. Ability to use energy supplies during exercise.
16. Endurance during exercise.

17. Muscular strength.
18. Tolerance to stress.
19. Tolerance to environmental heat.
20. Prudent living habits.
21. Psychological feeling of well-being.

Exercise leads to a decrease in:

1. Blood cholesterol and triglyceride levels.
2. Glucose intolerance.
3. Difficulties with weight management.
4. Osteoporosis.
5. Production of lactic acid at given exercise levels.
6. Platelet stickiness and clotting.
7. Blood pressure.
8. Heart rate in both rest and exercise.
9. Vulnerability to dysrhythmias.
10. Probability of cardiac failure.
11. Neurohormonal overreaction.
12. Complications from surgery.
13. Perceived exertion at a given work rate.
14. Symptoms associated with psychic stress.

The profits of regular exercise are known, backed by a substantial volume of research. And yet, there are still unexplored areas. In the future, exercise physiology will add new evidence of even more benefits for an active life.

To the Reader

Understanding how the body functions during exercise is fundamental to all aspects of physical education. Maximizing physical capacity requires a knowledge of the physiological processes that mediate improvements in performance. This is obvious when considering athletes. But the information today has utilization for a more heterogeneous audience. New populations have become concerned with optimizing their own welfare. Business and industry have been caught up with exercise programs; heart attack patients are starting rehabilitation schedules earlier than ever; persons with asthma or diabetes are now using exercise to reduce the effects of their disabilities. Other degenerative diseases that once were prescribed rest are now responding to controlled exercise. And a general fitness awareness has penetrated the country.

The manifold ways that exercise affects this diverse population is important information. It is life-giving information. And it has broadened the realm of exercise physiology. Historically, the delivery system for many of the applications of physiological research has been the medical profession. But now, as exercise physiology takes up more and more of the concerns that were once considered only medical, the position of persons with such background becomes more favorable. There are, quite simply, new areas of jobs.

What is also becoming clear is that the medical profession is not as attractive as it once was. Recruitment into medicine has been negatively affected by legal matters in the profession itself and by the long years of preparation and inordinately rising costs of that preparation. As a consequence, entry into the helping professions via physical education has become more appealing. There are, and will continue to be, more qualified individuals in the health and wellness industry with solid preparation in exercise physiology. The trend toward healthy life-style management will continue, and the consequent job market in educational, community, corporate, and clinical areas should only expand.

To review the research topics that are common to exercise physiology, peruse the following journals: *The Research Quarterly for Exercise and Sport; Medicine and Science in Sports and Exercise; The Journal of Sports Medicine and Physical Fitness, The Physician and Sportsmedicine;* and *Physical Fitness/Sports Medicine.* In addition, attending a local health fair will provide discursive ideas about career avenues, and a visit to a hospital or rehabilitation clinic will offer the value of other vocational potentials.

Suggested Projects

1. Read about the interpretation of an ECG. Obtain a sample printout of an ECG record, and interpret the tracing. Describe the meaning of any irregularities that could appear. Compile a list of all settings in which an ECG is utilized, and discuss which of these may hold career promise.

2. Select a nutritional topic of your interest. Read the current literature and prepare remarks to be given to the class. Examples are: (1) how to maximize carbohydrate loading for a given event; (2) the protein and carbohydrate requirements of a given event; (3) comparisons of popular weight-loss diets; (4) relative influence of diet control and exercise on weight management.

3. Collect a variety of fluid replacement drinks. Compare the ingredients. Discuss their usefulness. Then consider the matter of water intake during prolonged exercise. Find out why unrestricted use of salt tablets could be dangerous.

4. Compile a class list of dietary habits and pre-event meals that were observed during participation in high school athletics. Hold an open discussion on their validity.
5. Discuss the interests that are common to exercise physiology and medicine. What joint research projects might be feasible? What career options could be available in areas of combined interest?
6. Visit several wellness centers, including both private and corporate locations. Inquire about the qualifications for employment and about what preparation could be made during the undergraduate years. Report the findings to the class.
7. Complete the RISKO scale. Then determine how you can alter your own life-style to improve your state of well-being. Draw up a contract stating your objectives for the remainder of the academic term, have it signed by your professor, and provide yourself with a pending reward for accomplishment of the objectives.
8. Write down your present exercise habits. Exchange your list with another class member, then compose a hypothetical exercise prescription for that individual.

References

Adams, G. M., and Deitrick, R. W. (1983). *Exercise Physiology Primer.* Costa Mesa, CA: Custom Publishing.

American College of Sports Medicine. (1986). *Guidelines for Exercise Testing and Prescription* (3rd ed.). Philadelphia: Lea & Febiger.

Asghar, A., and Bhatti, A. R. (1987). Endrogenous Proteolytic Enzymes in Skeletal Muscle: Their Significance in Muscle Physiology and During Postmortem Aging in Carcasses. In C. O. Chichester, E. M. Mark, and B. S. Schweigert (Eds.), *Advances in Food Research* (Vol. 31, pp. 344–451). San Diego, CA: Academic Press.

Astrand, P. O. (1987). Physiological Compared with Clinical Aspects of Physical Activities. In D. Macleod, R. Maughan, M. Nimmo, T. Reilly, and C. Williams (Eds.), *Exercise: Benefits, Limits, and Adaptations,* (pp. 385–394). London: E. & F. N. Spon Ltd.

Baker, R. D. (1983). Digestion and Absorption of Nutrients. In A. M. Brown and D. W. Stubbs (Eds.), *Medical Physiology* (pp. 191–208). New York: John Wiley & Sons.

Berger, R. A. (1982). *Applied Exercise Physiology.* Philadelphia: Lea & Febiger.

Blair, S. N. (1988). Exercise, Health, and Longevity. In D. R. Lamb and R. Murray (Eds.), *Perspectives in Exercise Science and Sports Medicine* (Vol. 1, pp. 443–488). Indianapolis: Benchmark Press.

Brooks, G. A. (1987). Amino Acid and Protein Metabolism during Exercise and Recovery. *Medicine and Science in Sports and Exercise, 19,* S150–S156.

Brustaert, D. L. (1989). The Endocardium. In J. F. Hoffman and P. DeWeer (Eds.), *Annual Review of Physiology* (Vol. 51, pp. 263–273). Palo Alto, CA: Annual Reviews.

Cameron, M. E., and Van Staveren, W. A. (1988). *Manual on Methodology for Food Consumption Studies.* New York: Oxford University Press.

Caspersen, C. J. (1987). Physical Activity and Coronary Heart Disease. *The Physician and Sportsmedicine, 15,* 43–44.

Dohm, G. L., Tapscott, E. B., and Kasperek, G J. (1987). Protein Degradation during Endurance Exercise and Recovery. *Medicine and Science in Sports and Exercise, 19,* S166–S171.

Ellis, M. J. (1988). *The Business of Physical Education: Future of the Profession.* Champaign, IL: Human Kinetics Books.

Fox, E. L., Bowers, R. W., and Foss, M. L. (1988). *The Physiological Basis of Physical Education and Athletics.* Philadelphia: Saunders College Publishing.

Hamilton, E. M. N., Whitney, E. N., and Sizer, F. S. (1988). *Nutrition: Concepts and Controversies* (4th ed.). St. Paul, MN: West Publishing.

Haskell, W. L. (1989). Exercise: Measurement, Dose-Response Relations, and Compliance. In J. S. Skinner, C. B. Corbin, D. M. Landers, P. E. Martin, and C. L. Wells (Eds.), *Future Directions in Exercise and Sport Science Research.* Champaign, IL: Human Kinetics Books.

LaPorte, R. E., Dearwater, S., Cauley, J. A., Slemenda, C., and Cook, T. (1985). Cardiovascular Fitness: Is It Really Necessary? *The Physician and Sportsmedicine, 13,* 145–150.

Lemon, P. W. R. (1987). Protein and Exercise: Update 1987. *Medicine and Science in Sports and Exercise, 19,* S179–S190.

McArdle, W. D., Katch, F. I., and Katch, V. L. (1986). *Exercise Physiology: Energy, Nutrition, and Human Performance.* Philadelphia: Lea & Febiger.

Morris, J. N., Everitt, M. G., and Semmence, A. M. (1987). Exercise and Coronary Heart Disease. In D. Macleod, R. Maughan, M. Nimmo, T. Reilly, and C. Williams (Eds.), *Exercise: Benefits, Limits, and Adaptations* (pp. 4–19). London: E. & F. N. Spon Ltd.

Noble, B. J. (1986). *Physiology of Exercise and Sport.* St. Louis: Times Mirror/Mosby College Publishing.

Rosato, F. D. (1986). *Fitness and Wellness: The Physical Connection.* St. Paul, MN: West Publishing.

Rothshuh, K. E., and Reisse, G. B. (1973). *History of Physiology.* Huntington, NY: Robert E. Krieger Publishing.

Seefeldt, V., and Vogel, P. (1986). *The Value of Physical Activity.* Reston, VA: American Alliance for Health, Physical Education, Recreation, and Dance.

Shephard, R. J. (1984). *Biochemistry of Physical Activity.* Springfield, IL: Charles C. Thomas Publisher.

Sherman. W. M., and Lamb, D. R. (1988). Nutrition and Prolonged Exercise. In D. R. Lamb and R. Murray (Eds.), *Perspectives in Exercise Science and Sports Medicine.* (Vol. 1, pp. 213–280). Indianapolis: Benchmark Press.

Vander, A. J., Sherman, J. H., and Luciano, D. S. (1985). *Human Physiology: The Mechanisms of Body Function* (4th ed.). New York: McGraw-Hill.

Whitney, E. N., and Hamilton, E. M. N. Revised by E. N. Whitney with M. A. Boyle. (1987). *Understanding Nutrition* (4th ed.). St. Paul, MN: West Publishing.

Wilmore, J. H. (1989). Exercise Prescription for Health and Fitness. In J. S. Skinner, C. B. Corbin, D. M. Landers, P. E. Martin, and C. L. Wells (Eds.), *Future Directions in Exercise and Sport Science Research* (pp. 13–22). Champaign, IL: Human Kinetics Books.

Wolfe, R. R. (1987). Does Exercise Stimulate Protein Breakdown in Humans? Isotopic Approaches to the Problem. *Medicine and Science in Sports and Exercise, 19,* S172–S178.

Zuti, W. B., and Golding, L. A. (1976). Comparing Diet and Exercise as Weight Reduction Tools. *The Physician and Sportsmedicine, 4,* 49–57.

Chapter 6

Biomechanics: The Science of Human Motion

The Relationship to Kinesiology

The Influence of Science

Descriptions of Movement

Qualitative Analysis: The Eyes Have It

Quantitative Analysis: Computers Tell the Truth

Kinematics, Kinetics, and Optimization

The Absolute Essentials of Performance

Implications for the Real World

Summary

To the Reader

Suggested Projects

References

Human physical movement may be viewed as a series of mechanical events that can be analyzed and described by using laws of motion.

Biomechanics is a science that utilizes the principles of physics and mechanics to describe the motion of the human body, most notably during the performance of sports skills, but including other dimensions of motion.

The general objectives of biomechanics are to determine the best techniques for the performance of any given movement skill and to analyze the performance characteristics of any person executing that skill.

Because biomechanics operates on the scientific principles of the laws that govern the motion of objects, it has application in any setting where humans are in interaction with their environment.

Inquiry

THERE was a time when all high jumpers would use the same technique: Approach the bar from an angle, thrust an arm and leg up and over, then follow with a whip kick, and the body would "roll" over the top of the bar. Then one day Dick Fosbury decided to go over the bar backwards in a twisting lay-back of the body. Soon everyone realized that in this style it was not necessary to get the body's center of gravity as high as with the old scissors-kick style, and widespread adoption of the "Fosbury flop" followed. Tennis players once hit mostly flat ground strokes, but now everyone hits topspin. Football field-goal kickers at one time approached the ball straight-on, but now they are soccer-style sidewheelers. Baseball pitchers used to throw big sweeping sidearm curve balls, but now the slider is common.

Virtually every performance aspect of every sport has been carefully watched and carefully analyzed. Some general questions were: Should the hip turn before the shoulders or at the same time? Should the foot land heel-first or toe-first? Should the arm swing straight forward or in an arc? In every instance where a skill (or a part of a skill) is analyzed, the overall question remains the same: What is the most efficient way to execute the movement?

Mechanics and physics join together for the study of human motion through biomechanics.
© R. M. Collins, III/The Image Works

Biomechanics is an area of study that *describes the motion of the human body by using the methods of mechanics and physics.* Mechanics is the science of *force* and *motion.* Physics deals with the properties of *matter* and *energy.* Together, these technologies combine to provide an objectively accurate means for discerning the qualities of human physical movement.

THE RELATIONSHIP TO KINESIOLOGY

Another term, *kinesiology,* is often used synonymously with biomechanics. Kinesiology technically means the science of motion, without particular reference to mechanics or physics. Presently, the term is broadly construed to mean "the study of movement." In this context, kinesiology can designate the sum total of all that is known about the physical properties of human movement, and thus it is sometimes taken to mean physical education itself.

Kinesiology is often given liberal interpretation, and its distinction from biomechanics is often cloudy. Courses and textbooks in kinesiology emphasize human anatomy and the musculoskeletal analysis of human movement. To study kinesiology is to study the elements of movement (bones, muscles, tissues, nerves) in the same way that an architect would study construction materials before designing a building.

Biomechanics evolved from kinesiology, sometimes acquiring the descriptor of "mechanical kinesiology." In application, it refers specifically to the laws and principles of human motion as set forth by mechanics and physics. It is an "active" science that explains the cause-and-effect of movement. Thus, kinesiology uses a broad focus to provide the informational background to study human motion, while biomechanics attends particularly to the force-motion relationships that are the exactitudes of movement. In a general sense, kinesiology might be thought of as telling *how* a movement happens, whereas biomechanics explains *why* it happens.

THE INFLUENCE OF SCIENCE

Some of the earliest and still lasting applications of science to human motion came from the adaptations of Isaac Newton's laws of motion. Newton had concluded that three main principles could account for motion: (1) the Law of Inertia, which states that an object in motion or at rest continues in that state until acted upon by some outside force; (2) the Law of Acceleration, which says that the acceleration of an object

Inquiry

Biomechanics describes the motion of the human body by using the methods of mechanics and physics.
University of Denver file photo.

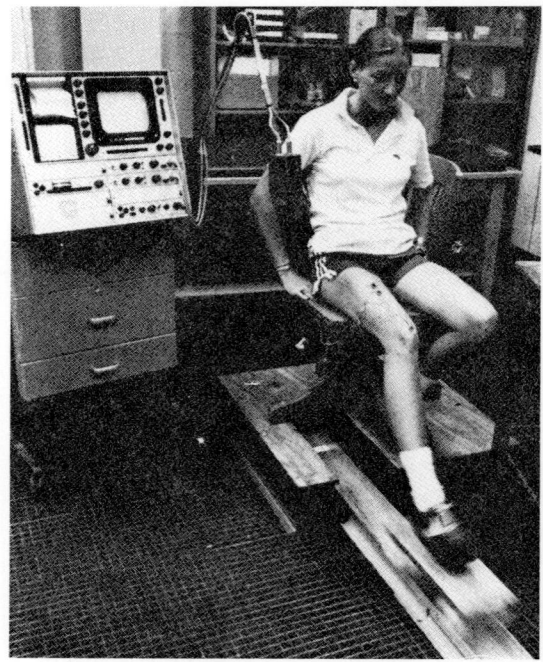

is directly proportional to the force causing it, and the acceleration is in the same direction as the force and is inversely proportional to the mass of the object; and (3) the Law of Reaction, which states that for every action there is an equal and opposite reaction.

When a tennis player hits a forehand drive, for example, the results of that drive are dependent on at least eight factors: (1) the speed of the oncoming ball, (2) the mass of the ball, (3) the speed of the racket at contact with the ball, (4) the mass of the racket, (5) the liveliness of the ball, (6) how tightly the racket is strung, (7) the direction the racket is traveling at contact, and (8) the angle of the racket face at contact. Newton's laws can explain all these factors and can provide a foundation for understanding all other sporting activities. These laws are not the only source of explanation, but they are prime examples of the application of science to human motion.

The most widely applied science is physics, which attends to the action of different forms of energy on matter in general. Mechanics is a specific system that uses the principles of physics to study the behavior of matter under the influence of forces. The conclusions of mechanics are purely scientific, and they apply to a wide range of research from galaxies to the most elementary particles of matter. When the study of mechanics is limited to living organisms, especially human beings, it is then called biomechanics, since the added prefix "bio" means "living."

Thus, the "living science" of biomechanics is every bit as exacting as physics, from which it evolved. Its analysis is unforgiving. It seeks the mechanical truth of every human movement by providing accurate answers about what is happening, why it happened, and to what extent it happened. All human motion can be explained by the laws and principles that govern force, and consequently all human motion is mechanically describable.

DESCRIPTIONS OF MOVEMENT

Biomechanics treats all motor functions, normal or abnormal, as mechanical events. The objective is to find the optimal nerve-muscle expenditure for any movement. Thus, for the top-level athlete there exists a perfect technique; for a beginner an acceptable technique; and for a handicapped person an adaptable technique. In this concept it might loosely be concluded that the body is a machine, with the skeletal system being a series of levers.

So construed, the movements of the body can be described in the same strict regard as any other mechanical device. Biomechanics has particulars to explain the qualities of human motion just as physics describes the action of inanimate objects. Movement could be, for example, "translatory," more commonly called *linear* motion, which is the movement of the whole body in one direction. Walking is linear movement; so is downhill skiing or swimming. But when the body moves in a circular path around a central point (the axis), the motion is called *rotary,* or *angular,* motion: a skater in a spin, a cartwheel, a somersault. However, most movements in sports are combinations of linear and angular motion and are called by the straightforward term *general motion.* A soccer player uses a constant interchange of angular and linear motion. So does a gymnast, or a hockey player, or a dancer. And a baseball or softball pitcher gives linear motion to an object, the ball, through the angular motion of the arm.

There are many other kinds of movement: displacement, velocity, acceleration, inertia, momentum, tangential velocity, radial acceleration, centripetal force, rebound angle, curvilinear, rectilinear. They all combine to provide an appropriate explanation of movement in all dimensions and to account for how 206 bones held in 43 major joints can combine with a couple of hundred muscles and several miles of transmitting nerves to get the body through daily routines or exceptional athletic accomplishment.

QUALITATIVE ANALYSIS: THE EYES HAVE IT

A tennis player, trying to improve a topspin serve, steadies, tosses, and hits. Assume you're the instructor. The player asks for suggestions. It happened so fast that you tell the player to hit another ball. Did the elbow lead the swing? Where was the weight at the moment of contact? Was the racket path forward and upward at impact? Did the wrist uncoil into the ball? Why are there so many variables?

Most of the time, in most situations, the only tools you will have for evaluating performance are your own senses. The most important one is your sight. A sense of biomechanical principles will help. In your memory, you will have a stockpile of physics and mechanics and more math than you ever cared to own. But in the field, when a tennis player says, "Fix my serve," you'll be reduced to a couple of eyes.

Trained eyes they must be. You'll be making a *qualitative analysis* of someone else's performance, which is to say, a subjective judgment. What did it *look* like? Assessment of human performance is often given with nothing more than the human eye and brain. Was there proper linear and angular motion? Were the body parts synchronized for a summation of force? Was the degree of flexion optimal? The determinations go on in microsecond intervals. It will seem like you always need to have with you a photocopy of all the charts in your biomechanics textbook.

Through experience, the observer of movement learns to recognize the components of skilled performance. Some of them can easily be seen. When the performance happens so fast that it's a mere blur to the eye, the components are sensed from the end product of the performance. Always there's a mental checklist, comparing what should have happened with what did happen. The checklist may be something like the following (adapted from Arend and Higgins, 1976):

Stage	Identify
Preobservation (before viewing performance)	1. Goal of the movement 2. Critical performance components of the movement
Observation	1. Aspects of the performance clearest in the observer's mind 2. Unnecessary movements and other signs of tension 3. Critical features executed and not executed
Postobservation	1. Degree of goal achievement 2. Efficiency evaluation 3. Instructional information for next performance trial

The preobservation stage of this scheme represents what an observer expects to find, this being the description of the optimal performance factors of the movement to be observed. The observation stage is what is actually occurring during each performance, and in most cases this means the observer must make ongoing judgments about what is being seen. In the postobservation stage, the observer critically evaluates the execution for the benefit of the performer, giving appropriate feedback (information about the performance) as instructional suggestions for the next practice trial.

QUANTITATIVE ANALYSIS: COMPUTERS TELL THE TRUTH

To the teacher with a trained eye, the tennis player may not be a difficult problem. After several viewings, the instructor might see that the serve difficulties originate from a locked front knee, a failure to bring the racket into the "back-scratching" position before the swing, or not enough upward thrust of the racket. "Such a thing is obvious," the teacher might say. Not so obvious are the solutions to the problems that biomechanics tackles in research laboratories.

In the lab, biomechanics becomes an exact science. It reshapes the fabric of the way human motion is interpreted. Special techniques have been created using computers, graphic images, and three-dimensional photomontages that capture the fantastic and delicate structure of the complexities of human movement. The camera has become the eye, and the computer the brain, as the two synchronize the elements of motion to show dimensions that defy accepted ways of thinking about movement. There is a respect for pattern, especially pattern that shows up repeatedly in different measures. For instance, should the sprinter take long strides or short, quick strides? The coach knows the answer. But the biomechanist turns this question (and all others) over to a science of reductionism. It doesn't really matter, the biomechanist says. What really matters is that the foot hits the ground while already into its backward driving thrust (Hay and Reid, 1988). The coach looks at a factor of secondary importance, according to biomechanics, and ignores (or doesn't think about) the most critical element.

What of the countless recreational joggers who have developed knee problems? Wear a shoe with more cushion, the shoe companies suggest. Build a shoe that will roll the foot into proper alignment with the knee, the biomechanist concludes.

Or consider the tennis players who are plagued by tendonitis. Give more flex to the racket so it will absorb the impact of the ball and relieve the trauma on the arm, say the racket companies. Wrong, says the right-again biomechanist, who proves that it's a stiff racket that provides the greater damping effect.

Computer-controlled measuring devices were providing the answers to these and a profusion of other problems. Time and force and

The use of computers in the biomechanics lab has opened a whole new world.
Photo by Tom Cherrey.

velocity and motion are now revealed through exacting measurement. The outcome is deterministic probability. Guesswork is gone. What may have appeared to the eye to be happening in a given movement may be revealed to be untrue by the computer. The science of biomechanics has drawn inexorably toward greater and greater order in every detail of human performance. In the process, long-held beliefs about the elements of any given motion may need to be discarded. Teaching and coaching strategies may need to change. It's a brave new world, today, in the computer-endowed laboratories of biomechanics.

KINEMATICS, KINETICS, AND OPTIMIZATION

Human motor behavior is a whole, but to understand the whole it is necessary to analyze the parts. In this regard, the science of biomechanics can be divided conveniently into two units, known respectively as *kinematics* and *kinetics*. Kinematics is a description of motion in terms of position, velocity, and acceleration. Kinetics is a description of motion that focuses on force as its cause. The end product of the two is *optimization,* which means determining the most (or a more) efficient way to perform a given task.

It is not difficult to appreciate the aesthetic qualities of a gymnast on the uneven parallel bars, every move blending into the next, every maneuver showing style and grace and fluidity. But it's another matter when trying to describe the action in precise mechanical terms. By using position and velocity and acceleration as the language of kinematics, it becomes possible to give a detailed account of the action.

Position refers to the *location* of a limb, or a ball, or a racket, or anything else, at some exact time in the continuum of a motion, beginning to end. It is the space and time dimension of motion.

Velocity is the *change* in position with respect to time. How did the limb, ball, racket, or other object change in position, and in what direction?

Confusing? On first hearing, it might be. No one ever said that biomechanics was easy.

Enter kinetics, which now describes the *causes* of any motion. It accounts for the agent that produces or tends to produce a change in the state of rest or motion of an object. A golf ball sitting on a tee is perfectly content to do nothing until acted upon by a force. Along comes an obliging clubhead. The ball then responds to absolute physical laws. It has no other choice. Its resultant flight gives away what happened at the moment of contact. A drive may have started out on-line but then may have arched into a foreboding slice that finished in a forest of trees alongside the fairway. Clearly, the clubhead was on a proper path at contact but the clubface was open. No doubt about it. Physical law tells the truth. So what is the remedy for this slice?

Not all problems are that direct. A golf ball and clubhead obey exact, perfectly describable laws. But the gymnast on the uneven parallel bars does not show the same obvious cause-effect relationships. The laws of physics are still in place, but so many parameters exist that learning the real truth may require video data fed into the polygraph computer. The eye and the brain, marvelous cybernetic devices that they are, will still miss some critical components in analyzing complex motor performance. But in the end, with eye and brain and camera and computer all working together, it is possible to identify all the base units of any performance, and then through optimization, to come up with appropriate estimates of the performance essentials for any given movement task.

THE ABSOLUTE ESSENTIALS OF PERFORMANCE

The final plan of optimization is to compose the absolute essentials of any performance—those skill components that are absolutely necessary for the most efficient execution of a task. They are the mechanics that all performers must utilize in order to execute the skill well. Furthermore, they could be interpreted as the only criteria necessary for efficient performance.

Every skill will have its own peculiar performance essentials. For some skills, the list may be quite extensive, and for others, it could be rather brief. For instance, to successfully shoot a free throw in basketball, the only prerequisite might seem to be to project the ball in a given critical arc toward the rim. If one observes professional basketball players, there appear enough stylistic differences to leave one with the conclusion that no common mechanical features exist among the players. However, on further analysis, similar features might be observed, such as the finger placement on the ball, a certain alignment between the ball and the elbow, or a certain sequential movement pattern for projecting the ball, and possibly others.

As another example, assume that a list of the absolute essentials were made for a tennis forehand. To arrive at this list, one might observe accomplished performers, assuming they would all demonstrate what must be achieved for skilled execution. The final list of essentials might include descriptions of the grip, body rotation, weight shifts, contact points, speed of racket head, direction of swing, and others. A curious finding, however, might be the absence of any definitive observations of footwork. Viewing accomplished players in action might lead one to believe that footwork changes with each forehand and is more related to the relative position of the ball rather than to any "storybook" performance. Consequently, the determination of a list of performance absolutes can also illustrate what should not be included because it does not appear to be an essential for skilled execution.

A classic early example of such a finding was the study by Breen (1967), who used film to analyze the swings of major league baseball players batting over .300, and compared them with the swings of hitters under .300. The analysis showed five factors, and only five, to be common in the swings of the .300 hitters. Thus, the distinguishing feature of these hitters was their ability to execute what appeared to be five performance essentials. In this case, footwork *was* important, but not in the regard that was commonly believed. It had been frequently stated that the foot placement in the stride of a hitter should be variable, depending on the location of the arriving ball. But the film analysis showed this belief to be false, for the .300 hitters were all planting their foot at the same place with each stride, while the under .300 hitters were not. So a variable foot placement worked against success in hitting, and yet every spring all over the country, baseball and softball coaches are still suggesting to hitters that they should "step into an outside pitch and away from an inside pitch."

What is important in these examples is that an understanding of biomechanical principles can create the proper frame of mind for observing performance. The observer will have science as a reference point, knowing full well what the laws of physics and mechanics have to offer.

The observer can then determine if what the eye sees agrees with the laws that apply to the given performance. Thus, a careful observer will be able to recognize those peculiar circumstances when physical laws do not necessarily agree with what makes sense in actual application. So a well-disciplined observer will use biomechanics as the foundation, knowing what to look for and what is important, but then must apply the art of critical evaluation.

IMPLICATIONS FOR THE REAL WORLD

In many cases, to know the *causes* of performance faults is difficult. A teacher or coach might attempt to correct a flawed performance on the basis of the observed results, without knowing the underlying causes of the results. The athlete's performance might then deteriorate further because attention might be directed to the wrong segment of the execution sequence.

Moreover, it's probable that in most cases the skill elements that should be emphasized for beginners are different from those for advanced players. Specific techniques may need to be subordinated to temporarily acceptable methods that have the advantage of offering some early success. The beginning golfer, for example, might be taught a stance and swing that will change with increasing experience. And a beginning tennis player would not logically be taught to topspin the forehand even though observations of accomplished players show this to be a universally common technique.

Biomechanical logic will clarify which performance factors need emphasis at the moment. Within each skill will be "subskills" that are the foundation for the final product. For a skilled performer these supporting elements will be precisioned mechanical factors, but for a beginner they will be approximations of the eventual objectives. Thus, every physical skill will have certain biomechanical "facts" that are the essential ingredients of successful performance for a given individual at a given experience level.

Furthermore, the application of biomechanical analysis, obvious as it is in sporting endeavors, also has value in other areas of human physical performance. For example, one recently developed area of application is in *ergonomics,* which is a science concerned with the interaction of humans and their technical environment. Often used as a synonym for human engineering, ergonomics attends to the design, use, and maintenance of machines and large-scale technical systems. The biomechanics of human motion is a principle component in determining the design of these systems, ranging from heavy construction equipment to interactive computers, and including the configuration of tools, instrument displays on cars and airplanes, and patient monitoring systems in hospitals. To optimize human-machine interaction, the machine or technical system must be compatible with the capabilities and limitations of the human user. This includes not only the configuration of the system but also the visual and acoustical displays, and the selection, arrangement, and combination of control elements. And as systems become more complex, it becomes increasingly vital to know as much as possible about the human biomechanical parameters that will be the basis of their design.

Relatedly, ergonomic investigations designed to ascertain the relation between the locomotor system and work injuries has been given high priority in occupational medicine. Biomechanical determinations are now being used to measure the degree of physical strain and potential danger to the human skeletal and physiological systems during work.

SUMMARY

The application of biomechanics has become widespread. Because the science deals with variables that are governed by the laws of physics, the principles can be injected into any circumstance where humans are interacting with the environment.

In sports the analyses that began with such direct observations as the Fosbury flop (Dapena, 1980) has now penetrated into every aspect of athletic endeavor. No turn of the hand or angle of the foot has been left unscrutinized. Biomechanics has even analyzed undramatic events such as sit-ups (Ricci, Marchetti, and Figura, 1981), walking (Kairento and Hellen, 1981), standing (Bajd, Kralj, and Turk, 1982), stumbling, (Suzuki et al., 1983), sitting (Wiktorin and Nordin, 1986), and even sleeping (Hoffman, 1989). In recreational activity, biomechanics has cast its discerning eye on rock climbing (Walker, 1989a), parachute jumping (Huston and Kamman, 1981), playground swinging (Walker, 1989b), and other activities of an incidental nature.

The essence of the science, however, has been to improve human performance in events of a sporting nature. To this extent, the effects of human movement analyses have been seen not only in changes in performance techniques but also in the design and manufacturing materials of sports equipment. The pole vault and tennis are examples where evolutions in performance technique led to drastic alterations of the equipment used. A particular contemporary example is cross-country skiing, where a new skating style has proved to be faster and is now used by virtually all competitors even though the equipment is not ideally suited to the technique (Nelson, 1989).

And in medical applications, the study of human movement dynamics has clear utilitarian value in orthopedic and other rehabilitative technology (Schmidt-Schönbein, Woo, and Zweifach, 1986). It has already found wide use in the design of programs for the rejuvenation of injuries sustained in sport (Winter, 1983). And it is finding new applications in such concerns as the mechanical dynamics of normal and abnormal cardiac function (Humphrey and Yin, 1989). Or in the quantification of responses to injury and the development and use of injury assessment devices and techniques for evaluating injury prevention systems (Viano et al., 1989). In short, wherever humans are interacting with the environment there is value for biomechanical assessment of that interaction.

To the Reader

The day may be just dawning for biomechanics. Advances in force transducers, photo and video techniques, and general microcomputer technology are making the potential instrumentation of human motion a state-of-the-art that seems to surpass imagination. Combined with the considerable amount of software now available, along with the low cost of computers, their convenience, and their portability, microcomputers will become more and more prominent outside the laboratory and academic environments. This will allow teachers, coaches, therapists, and other practitioners to monitor human movement on a continuous and scientific basis. Furthermore, the use of light-emitting diodes now permit the analysis of such otherwise illusive performance factors as the release characteristics of projected objects (from baseballs to javelins). Strain gauges are now being employed to analyze the forces generated on take-offs from a springboard or diving board, or the stress imparted to ski boots during downhill maneuvers. No aspect of human motion, no matter how incidental, is beyond the reach of technical sensing devices (Miller, 1989).

A danger in all this is to become overawed by the technology that has invaded the human movement sciences. So it is important not to lose sight of the original constructs of biomechanics. Microcomputers do not divorce biomechanics from the real world of subjective application. Rather, they encourage people to be purists in the analysis of human movement. And in fact, the use of complex technology is limited to national training centers and universities with a well-equipped lab.

Biomechanics has not lost the central ideal of attempting to improve human performance. Its major utilizations remain in educational and coaching settings. And the ability to critically analyze movement and recognize its causes are the absolute requisites for anyone who assists the performance of others. Thus, biomechanics has universal appeal and widespread value for any person who studies human action. No matter what the career goals may be, there is general merit in becoming a discerning analyst of the characteristics of human motion.

Suggested Projects

1. Select a specific aspect of any sport. Make up a list of what you believe are the absolute performance essentials for the skilled execution of that event. Read or distribute your list to classmates for their appraisal.
2. With the above list in hand, observe accomplished performers in the sport. Chart their execution characteristics by noting whether they are obeying the list of absolute essentials you have devised. Which do not seem apparent? Are there others you did not include?
3. Think of how performance techniques have changed in a selected sport (or sports) in recent years. Speculate on whether the changes may have come about from critical analysis of the mechanical principles that underlie the sport, and on what laws of physics may have prompted such change. Try to be as definite as possible in this appraisal.
4. Compose a similar list of changes that have occurred in the design and manufacture of sports equipment. Decide whether these changes are the result of an evolution in performance techniques or whether the equipment changes themselves have led to new performance styles.
5. Watch a beginning class in any physical education activity. What do you see as the common mechanical errors? Do certain subskill elements underlie the performance objectives of the class that should be learned by everyone before advanced techniques could be introduced?
6. Using a sport in which you actively participate, find a partner who also participates, and do a general mechanical analysis of each other's performance styles. Compare and discuss the evaluations.

References

Arend, S., and Higgins, J. R. (1976). A Strategy for the Classification, Subjective Analysis, and Observation of Human Movement. *Journal of Human Movement Studies, 2,* 36–52.

Bajd, T., Kralj, A., and Turk, R. (1982). Standing-up of a Healthy Subject and a Paraplegic Patient. *Journal of Biomechanics, 15,* 1–10.

Breen, J. L. (1967). What Makes a Good Hitter? *Journal of Health, Physical Education, and Recreation, 38,* 36–39.

Dapena, J. (1980). Mechanics of Translation in the Fosbury-Flop. *Medicine and Science in Sports and Exercise, 12,* 37–44.

Hay, J. G., and Reid, J. G. (1988). *Anatomy, Mechanics, and Human Motion* (2nd ed.). Englewood Cliffs, NJ: Prentice-Hall.

Hoffman, P. (1989). *Archimedes' Revenge.* New York: W. W. Norton & Co.

Humphrey, J. D., and Yin, F. C. P. (1989). Biomechanical Experiments on Exercised Myocardium: Theoretical Considerations. *Journal of Biomechanics, 22,* 377–383.

Huston, R. L., and Kamman, J. W. (1981). On Parachutist Dynamics. *Journal of Biomechanics, 14,* 645–652.

Kairento, A. L., and Hellen, G. (1981). Biomechanical Analysis of Walking. *Journal of Biomechanics, 10,* 671–678.

Miller, D. I. (1989). Microcomputers in Biomechanics Research and Applied Settings. In J. S. Skinner, C. B. Corbin, D. M. Landers, P. E. Martin, and C. L. Wells (Eds.), *Future Directions in Exercise and Sport Science Research* (pp. 209–221). Champaign, IL: Human Kinetics Books.

Nelson, R. C. (1989). Biomechanics for Better Performance and Protection from Injury. In J. S. Skinner, C. B. Corbin, D. M. Landers, P. E. Martin, and C. L. Wells (Eds.). *Future Directions in Exercise and Sport Science Research* (pp. 5–12). Champaign, IL: Human Kinetics Books.

Ricci, B., Marchetti, M., and Figura, F. (1981). Biomechanics of Sit-up Exercises. *Medicine and Science in Sports and Exercise, 13,* 54–59.

Schmidt-Schönbein, G. W., Woo, S. L. Y., and Zweifach, B W. (1986). *Frontiers in Biomechanics.* New York: Springer-Verlag.

Suzuki, S., Watanabe, S., Miyazaki, M., and Homma, S. (1983). EMG Activity and Kinematics of Human Stumbling Corrective Reaction during Running. In H. Matsui and K. Kobayashi (Eds.), *International Series on Biomechanics* (Vol. 4A, Biomechanics 8A, pp. 444–454). *Proceedings of the Eighth International Congress of Biomechanics.* Champaign, IL: Human Kinetics Publishers.

Viano, D. C., King, A. I., Melvin, J. W., and Weber, K. (1989). Injury Biomechanics Research: An Essential Element in the Prevention of Trauma. *Journal of Biomechanics, 22,* 403–417.

Walker, J. (1989a). How to Get the Playground Swing Going: A First Lesson in the Mechanics of Rotation. *Scientific American, 260,* 3.

Walker, J. (1989b). The Mechanics of Rock Climbing, or Surviving the Ultimate Physics Exam. *Scientific American, 260,* 118–121.

Wiktorin, C. V., and Nordin, M. (1986). *Introduction to Problem Solving in Biomechanics.* Philadelphia: Lea & Febiger.

Winter, D. A. (1983). Biomechanics in the Rehabilitation of Human Movement. In H. Matsui and K. Kobayashi (Eds.), *International Series on Biomechanics* (Vol. 4A, Biomechanics 8A, pp. 329–340). *Proceedings of the Eighth International Congress of Biomechanics.* Champaign, IL: Human Kinetics Publishers.

Chapter 7

Motor Learning and Control: The Mind in Action

Learning and Performance

Learning in Stages

Practice Makes Perfect and Other Myths

Brain in Thought: Information Processing

Motor Programs

Neuromotor Integration

Sensory Feedback

Thinking about the Brain

Summary

To the Reader

Suggested Projects

References

When learning a new skill, the brain relies on information arising from the senses to judge the effectiveness of each performance trial.

The brain in turn compares each trial with previous memory to modify the evolving movement into patterns that will achieve the desired results.

As a movement pattern becomes refined and mastered, it gets neurologically stored in the brain as organized "programs" that regulate future performances.

Consummate skill, then, is found in the optimal use of programmed movements and variations of those programs.

IMAGINE sitting in row 28, section H, at Wimbledon. You see a tennis player sprint in fluid motion to chase down a ball and arrive at the proper millisecond to thwack a cross-court winner. The player has said, subconsciously, "Feet do this; arm do that," and the appropriate muscles take the player from here to there, then send the ball to its appointed destination. A dozen times in that game, hundreds of times in that set, the player's brain tells the player's body what to do, and the muscle-machinery responds with finitely willed action. That is impeccable *control.*

But before that day, there were earlier times when even for this professional the contracting muscles got the body too close to the ball, or kept the elbow too crooked in the backhand, or sent the ball into the stratosphere. We've all been there, wondering if our cerebral self could ever get our sinuous self to do what we wanted. All of us—pro player and weekender alike—had to *learn.*

Not surprisingly, a discipline attends to this phenomenon. Its first name is *motor.* In context, it means human motion. Add *learning:* an enigmatic process of getting better at something. Together: *motor learning.* It designates an area of study that is concerned with *the conditions that can facilitate the acquisition and/or improvement of motor skills.*

If we add the word *control,* for *motor control,* we refer to another, related area of study that examines *the role of the central nervous system in regulating movement.* In combination, motor learning and control tell us how to acquire skill and become excellent in its performance.

LEARNING AND PERFORMANCE

But first, we must answer a major prefatory question: What is learning?

Is it a process of acquiring information? Or of knowing how to *use* information? Or being able to recite facts? Or is it an esoteric "knowing"?

Does it have different dimensions? In the past it was commonly divided into the three "domains" of cognitive (thinking), affective (feeling), and psychomotor (moving) learning. And it was believed that each type of learning had its own characteristics (Bloom et al., 1956; Gagné, 1970).

Most confounding of all, how can we tell when something is actually learned? After all, *that* is the final question in determining how successful instructional programs are.

In truth, learning must be *inferred* from some direct source of evidence. And the only real source available is performance, otherwise translated as *observable behavior,* otherwise translated as what someone

Motor Learning and Control: The Mind in Action

Motor learning and control tell us how to acquire a skill and become excellent in its performance.
University of Denver file photo.

does. It's a score on an exam. Or the number of volleyballs you serve into a marked area. Or whether you can recite your license plate number.

However, suppose one Saturday morning at the local golf course, you drill a three-iron off the tee at the 172-yard fourteenth hole and the resolute ball finishes in the cup. Could we conclude that you have learned a perfect golf swing as evidenced by your performance? Of course not, but somewhere you had learned a swing that increased the possibility of such a result happening. If you had golf lessons, they taught you to refine the mechanics of your swing and therefore led you to—in the classical definition of learning—a *change in behavior.*

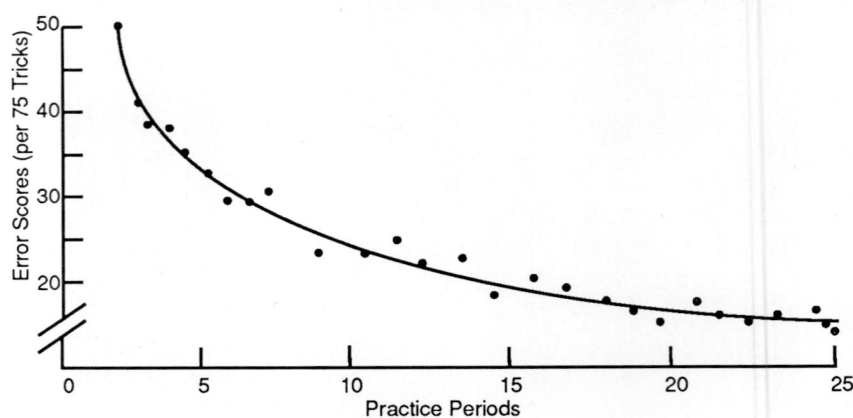

Figure 7.1 A sample learning curve.

Reprinted with permission from the *Research Quarterly for Exercise and Sport*, 1965, 39, 342–347. Research Quarterly is a publication of the American Alliance for Health, Physical Education, Recreation, and Dance, 1900 Association Drive, Reston, VA 22091.

Even so, not all learning automatically results in improvements in performance; therefore, learning might more accurately be considered as a *potential* for change in behavior. Or, as some definitions have it, learning is a "relatively permanent" change in behavior. So a complete description of learning might be *a relatively permanent change in the ability, tendency, or capacity to respond appropriately to a given situation.*

No matter how it's described, there are generally two assumptions about learning: (1) that it is improvement over time and (2) that performance becomes increasingly more consistent.

An example of such performance changes is illustrated in figure 7.1, which shows the achievements of forty college students learning to juggle (Trussell, 1965). The horizontal axis of the graph charts twenty-seven trials of seventy-five tosses in each trial. The vertical axis records the errors (uncaught balls) in each practice session.

As might be expected, the graph of this "learning curve" (the performance progress made over a series of trials) shows that errors decreased and performance tended to become more consistent with time. Even though the performance of any motor skill may be situational, fluctuating drastically from time to time and place to place, in the overall picture, improvements in the skill will show the trends illustrated in this example.

LEARNING IN STAGES

Learning apparently may progress in certain "stages" whereby the learner attends to different elements of a task as skill improves. There seem to be three such stages (Fitts and Posner, 1967), although they are no more distinct from each other as, say, being seven years old is from being six. In the first stage, learning is characterized by *thinking* about the performance and thereby attending to the mechanics of its execution. For example, when first learning to dribble a basketball, a youngster gives the attention of all senses to the ball. It must be watched; it must be consciously felt; often it may even be talked to. The learner thinks about how to keep this monstrous sphere under control, and accordingly this is usually called the *cognitive stage*. It involves a general process of "getting the idea of the movement" by sorting out what is *task relevant* as opposed to what is not important information (Gentile, 1972). The "feel" of the basketball each time it contacts the hand is a task relevant cue, while chatter from other students is not.

Then, with increasing practice, learners can become their own critics. Trial and error may show the learner that flexion in the wrist keeps the dribble more rhythmical, and a bend of the knees keeps the dribble closer to the floor. This is the *associative stage,* where success in the skill is consciously or unconsciously associated with doing certain acts of performance.

Finally the skill becomes virtually automatic. No longer does the brain need to give its attention to the mechanics of execution. This is the *autonomous stage* wherein the experienced basketball player dribbles the ball as though it were attached, ball-to-hand, by an invisible rubber band. Now the player responds instead to the environmental demands imposed by the moment-to-moment changes in a game.

In fact, when a player gets to the autonomous stage, thinking about the mechanics of the skill may actually interfere with its performance (Adams, 1971). In most skills, under game conditions, attention must be given to the dynamics of the game and not to the executional acts. As a blithe example, Yogi Berra, onetime New York Yankee great, had the annoying habit at bat of swinging at baseballs that were out of the strike zone. His perturbed manager, Casey Stengle, once implored Yogi to "think about hitting" in his next turn at the plate. So, determined, Yogi watched three called strikes go by, then strolled back to Casey and said, "Hey, I can't think and hit at the same time!"

PRACTICE MAKES PERFECT AND OTHER MYTHS

To improve skill, one must practice, and as everyone has heard, practice makes perfect. Or does it? While no practice certainly equals no perfection, *how* one practices is what determines progress in motor skill acquisition. This general curiosity has been of long-standing interest in motor learning and was in fact the original concern that coalesced motor learning into a discipline. Following are a few brief examples of the conclusions that have emerged from a massive accumulation of research:

1. The amount of total time one devotes to a skill is usually proportional to mastery of the skill, even to the point of practicing beyond a given level of achievement. Such "overlearning," as it is called, will strengthen the general motor memory of the skill and insure its reliability in the future (Schendel and Hagman, 1982).

2. It is usually more effective to have concentrated (massed) practice sessions without long rest periods between trials if the skill to be learned is *discrete,* meaning that it has a definite beginning and end (e.g., golf swing, baseball throw, or tennis serve). But if the skill is *continuous* (e.g., swimming, running, or gymnastic routines), there is a bit of an advantage to having more rest between practice trials (Adams, 1987).

3. Skills can be rehearsed as a whole, where the skill in its complete form is practiced; or they can be broken into part practice, where supporting segments of the whole skill are sharpened. Usually, whole practice is best for not-so-difficult skills or for those skills that have sequentially interdependent units, while part practice can benefit skills that are highly complicated (Oxendine, 1984).

4. A teacher's judicious use of *knowledge of results* (information provided to the learner about their performance) can positively affect skill acquisition if given at a time when it can be assimilated by the learner before the next practice trial and if it has content that is specifically instructional and appropriate for the skill level of the learner (Salmoni, Schmidt, and Walter, 1984).

5. The learner should be encouraged to "internalize" the skill. In fact, the ultimate test of achievement may be how well a learner can correlate the naturally occurring internal bodily sensations of a motion with the visual reports of the results of the performance (Magill, 1989).

6. In the spirit of a picture being worth a thousand words, the demonstration of a motor skill can convey important conceptual information about performance to observers. Verbal descriptions of motor

skills have the inherent risk of providing different meanings to different receivers, but a demonstration offers information in unadulterated form for the equitable interpretation of all viewers (Gould and Roberts, 1982).

7. For all skills, the practice should resemble as closely as practical the actual final performance demands (Shapiro and Schmidt, 1982).
8. Cognitive rehearsal (sometimes called *mental practice*) of skills can produce enhanced performance, particularly when used in conjunction with overt, physical practice (Suinn, 1986).

BRAIN IN THOUGHT: INFORMATION PROCESSING

The driving force behind every thought is a couple of handfuls of walnut-textured, cement-colored tissue. An average of three pounds. Much of it water. But the most intricately packed living matter known. There are at least a hundred billion cells crammed into every human brain (Steward, 1989).

The first function of the brain is to be a receiver. It hears news from all the senses. It gets microsecond accounts of what is going on inside and outside the body. They tell the brain how warm the day is, how difficult the statistics assignment is, the difference in weight between two baseball bats, whether the hips were locked during a golf swing, even the state of alertness of the brain itself.

Enormous numbers of nerve-news messages come railroading into the brain every fraction of a second. But the brain deciphers all the neuron reports, then decides what is important at the moment, and assembles plans for responding. It's an electronic microswitching called *information processing,* which is a term generously used to refer to *all the affairs of brain function that occur between a stimulus and a response.* In the most basic of diagrams it can be represented as in figure 7.2:

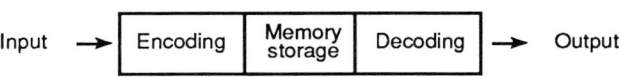

Figure 7.2 Information processing.

Operationally, input (sensory information) is encoded whereby the messages are put into some form of "code" that the brain can better understand and hold more effectively in its memory storage. And then, when an output is required, the messages are decoded, or translated back into useable responses.

Implicit in this operation is the viewpoint that memory storage is not an exact replica of any experience, but rather some kind of "representation" of that experience. The encoding process generates a schematic portrayal of the important features of the input and stores that sketch somewhere in its memory stockpile. It's a mathematical-neurological transformation of three-dimensional insights into a timeless and spaceless order that only the brain itself understands. The brain, it seems, deals in charades.

MOTOR PROGRAMS

After the metaphysical brain has scrutinized sensory information about any given situation, it prepares orders for potential responses. Decisions about how to act are based on the association of many factors, including past experience. When a motor response is needed, the brain scans its memory library for an appropriate set of ordered movement commands that can be plugged into the muscles for accountable action. These programs had previously been stored away as motor programs that exist as collections of "prescriptions" for movement dimensions. They are not exacting blueprints of precise motor patterns, but rather are held in retentive readiness in the brain's favorite form: as abstractions.

These programs get a real apprenticeship in new situations. For example, a first experience on a racquetball court can produce a bewildering encounter of doing little more than watching a ball obey physical laws of rebound. But in time the bounding angles of the ball become perceivable, and then the attention can be given to getting oneself into position to retrieve each ricochet. Eventually, the rebounding ball becomes a stimulus for the brain to pull from its memory a timely sequence of learned motor programs for a swing of appropriate strength and of proper direction—and all this in lighteninglike efficiency.

But first there had to be a general understanding of the design of the game. What is its objective? How does the ball rebound from each wall? Where is the best place on the court to be? The beginner has to develop a universal *schema* of racquetball. Generalized conceptions of how one responds, motorically, to the demands of this confined activity have to be learned. Compensatory reactions have to be established, and once in place, these general motor plans can then become refined into more specific responses (Schmidt, 1985). This evolving process of getting better has a productive yield of not only more effective execution of the skills of the game but also a more efficient microswitch operation of using the right programs at the right times.

Another example: Say you are an experienced center fielder. There's a runner on second. The batter drives a base hit in front of you. While approaching the ball, you never consciously think about the mechanics of fielding and throwing. Those schemas have been learned earlier and laid away in the mental remembrance of running and catching and throwing. So you simply pull from this storehouse the general programs for fielding and throwing. But nothing specific yet. You also draw from your memory the awareness that the runner on second is likely to try to score. As you field the ball, you have your throwing program at the ready. You take a quick glance to the runner. Going or holding up? Going! So your throwing program gets instant sanction. You tell your muscles, "Throw the runner out at the plate!" And as you coil your body into kinetic preparation for this mighty toss, your accommodating brain calls into play smaller component parts of the throwing program to narrow down the point of aim and inform the enlisted muscles of how much arc to give to the ball. And then, after the runner has been called out, your brain must practice humbleness as your teammates applaud your colossal heave.

NEUROMOTOR INTEGRATION

It's a marvel, to say the least. If one considers the enormous computational exchanges that must go on inside every human head for such an ordinary act as tying one's shoelaces, then the not-so-ordinary acts that occur in the athletic world are difficult to comprehend. There must be an incredibly scintillating spatiotemporal circuitry happening in the brain that allows the vast galaxy of electrical affairs to become refined motor performances.

This much is known: Motor plans are modulated as a whole, in preparation for their execution, by a special part of the brain called the basal ganglia, which is a mass of nerve cell bodies in the core of the brain between its hemispheres. As the plan is set into motion, it is refined by the cerebellum, which is that part of the base of the brain you cover when you fold your hands behind your neck to do sit-ups.

Atop this package is the motor cortex, a swath of brain that runs ear to ear in an arch underneath the headset you wear to listen to your stereo. The motor cortex has lines of nerves that run directly into the spinal cord and link up with motor neurons therein. All orders for movement are

Inquiry

Computerized recordings can show the neuromuscular integration of motor responses.
Photo by Tom Cherrey.

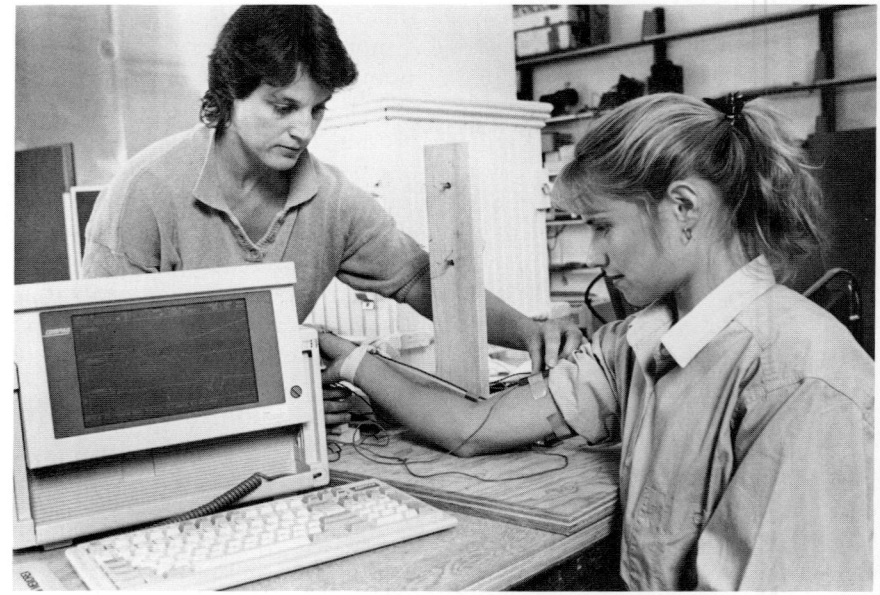

sent over these routes, but the orders are issued by the motor cortex only after it has consulted in continual microsecond meetings with its two advisors, the cerebellum and the basal ganglia. The connections that exist between these three allow for a constant flow of messages that interplay to control motor behaviors (Brooks, 1986).

There is some belief that the motor cortex is the library where all volumes of motor programs are held in a vast reference system, ready for checkout (Carew, 1985). When the motor cortex is in need of a particular action, it presumably scans its holdings and then decides on the appropriate command, whether it be a frequently used program such as the one for walking or a long-unused program such as the one that can be reanimated for riding a bicycle after years of not having done so (Purves, 1988).

Interestingly, the collections of motor cortex neurons that evoke a certain muscle group into activity are often located immediately adjacent to the neurons that control the muscle groups that produce the exact opposite action. This feature allows for a closer communication between the two, with the result being that when one muscle group is asked to contract (as, for example, to throw a baseball), the next-door neurons ask their muscle groups to refrain from joining the activity. This cooperative venture allows one set of muscles to contract while the opposing muscles relax (Kandel and Schwartz, 1985), a fortunate arrangement to say the least.

The basal ganglia appears to play the critical role of starting the micro-events that translate the brain's abstract thought into voluntary motor action. It may have the ability to create and initiate the generalized schemas that ultimately result in volitional motor activity. And it is possible that this mechanism is concerned with the pertinence of movement—the giving of intent, order, and efficiency to motor actions (Bridgeman, 1988).

But the ultimate polish of movement comes from the cerebellum. Its net effect is to smooth out or exert fine control over movements that are already in progress (Brooks, 1986). The cells of the cerebellum are tightly packed and highly organized, as if to show that by being orderly themselves they are more ready to perform their function of refining intentional movements. It adds composition to movement and makes adjustments in control when necessary. It is to movement what a conductor is to an orchestra.

SENSORY FEEDBACK

And then, during most performances, the brain listens to sensory news from the muscles about how the willed action is going. It's a *feedback* system where neural progress reports are continually being fed back into the brain.

Feedback is a natural product of any movement. When you shoot a basketball, you often know before the ball gets to the hoop whether it's on target or not. Your muscle sensors tell you so. Or, if you're coming down that beastly Thunder Alley run at Vail you must rely on fraction-of-a-second accounts from your muscles to tell you how to get through each mogul. Thus, motor performance can be a "closed-loop" system because the brain maintains a constant monitoring of the feedback information (a constant "loop" of information) to make compensatory adjustments while the movement is in progress.

However, if speed is the critical element, there isn't enough time to process the feedback information, so the mode of control becomes a *feedforward* system, also called "open-loop," in which feedback is either absent or ignored during the movement. Thus the sprinter, crouched in the blocks awaiting the signal, has only a motor program for an explosive start all primed to "feed forward" into the trained muscles. It's a one-way communication, brain-to-muscle, with no return loop. And it's also used if the movement is well learned, when in that case one can intentionally ignore the feedback generated during an action, as for example in a golf swing, where attending to feedback would detract from concentration on the swing itself.

Most movements are, in fact, feedback dependent, no matter how subtle the information may be. Especially when learning new skills or in performing movements of long duration, constant two-way communication between the senses and the brain is critical for adjusting the speed, direction, and intensity of the action to optimize the results.

THINKING ABOUT THE BRAIN

Possibly, no more than two or three million cells in the entire brain are specifically designed to be motor neurons (Rothwell, 1987), a surprisingly small number of the hundred billion that make up the total cell count of the brain. This is particularly unseemly in view of the fact that the only way the brain can expressively respond to any stimuli is through some manner of motor movement, and therefore logically the brain should have set more of its cells to specializing in neuromotor activities.

However, growing evidence suggests that no cells are exclusively motor in function. Rather, they may have both sensory and motor qualities (Purves, 1988) and might therefore be called "sensory-motor," a term that was freely used in the earlier days of motor learning. Furthermore, the search for a "motor area" in the brain has only led to an expansion of the locality rather than a localization of it (McMahon, 1984). Thus, we find that the brain, for all its presumed subdivisions and localized assignments of responsibilities, is nevertheless an integrated and computational network of cooperation. Whatever the precise relationship is among the areas of the brain that appear to have a role in controlling movement, the notion of teamwork remains clear.

Plato once said: "The mind exists for movement." In truth, the brain does spend much of its time on motor affairs and as such demonstrates that the motor really is also mental. And it further illustrates the basic principle of harmony—not only between brain and body but also among the various partitions of the brain itself. In the final view, we are reminded once again of what the ancient Greeks knew philosophically and we now know from research: that it is a thinking, feeling, emotional, responsive mind that sends the body into action. It's a *whole person* out there on the tennis courts.

SUMMARY

Motor learning, as an area of concentrated interest, has produced a considerable storehouse of information about how the learning of different motor skills takes place. It has investigated the variables that determine how rapidly one can learn and how long the learning can last. The real-world utilities of these reports are most obvious for teachers and coaches seeking the most effective ways to arrange practice of skills for their students and athletes.

The realm of motor learning has largely been to describe the environmental conditions that will facilitate learning and performance. Now motor learning has become supported by motor control, which inquires how the brain organizes the sensory signals it receives and plans for appropriate responses. So the investigations have, in effect, gone from appraising events outside of people to considerations of the internal affairs of the human mind.

Motor control looks at how motor actions are planned, how they are organized and executed, how they are controlled, and how feedback is used. In combination, both motor learning and motor control offer the rewards of explaining how individuals mentally represent and plan for movement and how the processes can be facilitated.

To the Reader

To examine the interest areas of contemporary motor learning and control, scan some recent volumes of the following periodicals: *Perceptual and Motor Skills,* the *Journal of Experimental Psychology,* and the *Journal of Motor Behavior.*

After you have viewed these journals, most of the primary considerations that are issues of motor learning may appear to be solved, and the present-day research, as represented in the pages of these publications, may appear to be exclusively oriented toward motor control. In fact, the earlier research in motor learning had lulled a sense of security into the field as principles of skill acquisition became generously accepted. But most of these guidelines had been established on the basis of controlled laboratory research, which was quite removed from the dynamic real world of the learner. And so there has been a determined call (e.g., Christina, 1989; Stelmach, 1989) and an actual trend to take the research of motor learning into the gymnasiums and onto the fields where the interactions of teacher/student and coach/athlete are occurring.

Thus, with motor learning about to burgeon again, and with motor control still fledgling in its emergence as a widespread discipline, the diversity and potential impact of these fields is uncompromising. They hold great promise, especially for someone interested in research.

You can supplement your preparation in these fields with courses offered by other departments. Psychology and biology departments may have courses in physiological psychology or other courses that deal with the internal control of physiological function. Studies in sensation and perception, as well as in the behavioral neurosciences, will provide useful background. They will be valuable for anyone with a career aspiration of assisting and improving people's goal-directed motor behavior.

Suggested Projects

1. Collect a number of definitions of learning. Are there common agreements among all of them? Think of some examples where performance is not necessarily indicative of learning.
2. Try to recount the experiences you had in learning a new motor skill. How did your teacher or coach help, either by method or communication, in your acquisition of that skill?
3. Consider how the "schema" theory of skill attainment may have affected your early stages of learning a skill. To what extent is it now utilized during your performance of that skill?
4. Have any of your athletic skills reached the autonomous stage? If so, how do you now use sensory feedback during their execution? To what do you attend during performance?
5. Read accounts of how the brain processes information and stores it as memory (particularly the holographic theory first suggested by Karl Pribram). On the basis of what is known about information processing, what suggestions does this have regarding the value of demonstrating motor skills compared to verbalizing about them to learners?
6. Assuming the brain operates in abstractions, or "pictographic representations," it may be concluded that all information is transposed by the brain into visualizations. On this assumption, verbal descriptions of motor skills should have the potential to generate effective and accurate mental pictures for learners who hear those descriptions. To this objective, compile a list of written statements that describe specific motor skills with words that have high visual value, presumably creating an appropriate visualization of the skill in the mind of a listener.

References

Adams, J. A. (1971). A Closed-Loop Theory of Motor Learning. *Journal of Motor Behavior, 3,* 111–149.

Adams, J. A. (1987). Historical Review and Appraisal of Research on the Learning, Retention, and Transfer of Human Motor Conditions. *Psychological Bulletin, 101,* 41–74.

Bloom, B. S., Engelhart, M. D., Furst, E. J., Hill, W. H., and Krathwohl, D. R. (1956). *Taxonomy of Educational Objectives, Handbook I: Cognitive Domain.* New York: David McKay.

Bridgeman, B. (1988). *The Biology of Behavior and Mind.* New York: John Wiley & Sons.

Brooks, V. B. (1986). *The Neural Basis of Motor Control.* New York: Oxford University Press.

Carew, T. J. (1985). The Control of Reflex Action. In E. Kandel and J. H. Schwartz (Eds.), *Principles of Neuroscience* (2nd ed.) (pp. 457–468.) New York: Elsevier Science Publishers.

Christina, R. W. (1989). Whatever Happened to Applied Research in Motor Learning? In J. S. Skinner, C. B. Corbin, D. M. Landers, P. E. Martin, and C. L. Wells (Eds.), *Future Directions in Exercise and Sport Science Research* (pp. 411–422). Champaign, IL: Human Kinetics Books.

Fitts, P. M., and Posner, M. I. (1967). *Human Performance.* Belmont, CA: Brooks/Cole.

Gagné, R. M. (1970). *The Conditions of Learning.* New York: Holt, Rinehart, and Winston.

Gentile, A. M. (1972). A Working Model of Skill Acquisition with Application to Teaching. *Quest Monographs, 17,* 3–23.

Gould, D., and Roberts, G. C. (1982). Modeling and Motor Skill Acquisition. *Quest Monographs, 33,* 214–230.

Kandel, E., and Schwartz, J. H. (Eds.). (1985). *Principles of Neuroscience* (2nd ed.). New York: Elsevier Science Publishers.

Magill, R. A. (1989). *Motor Learning: Concepts and Applications* (3rd ed.). Dubuque, IA: Wm. C. Brown.

McMahon, T. A. (1984). *Muscles, Reflexes, and Locomotion.* Princeton, NJ: Princeton University Press.

Oxendine, J. B. (1984). *Psychology of Motor Learning* (2nd ed.). Englewood Cliffs, NJ: Prentice-Hall.

Purves, D. (1988). *Body and Brain: A Tropic Theory of Neural Connections.* Cambridge, MA: Harvard University Press.

Rothwell, J. C. (1987). *Control of Human Voluntary Movement.* Rockville, MD: Williams and Wilkins.

Salmoni, A. W., Schmidt, R. A., and Walter, C. B. (1984). Knowledge of Results and Motor Learning: A Review and Critical Reappraisal. *Psychological Bulletin, 95,* 355–386.

Schendel, J. D., and Hagman, J. D. (1982). On Sustaining Procedural Skills over a Prolonged Retention Interval. *Journal of Applied Psychology, 67,* 605–610.

Schmidt, R. A. (1985). The Search for Invariance in Skilled Motor Behavior. *Research Quarterly for Exercise and Sport, 56,* 188–200.

Shapiro, D. C., and Schmidt, R. A. (1982). The Schema Theory: Recent Evidence and Developmental Implications. In J. A. S. Kelso and J. E. Clark (Eds.), *The Development of Movement Control and Co-ordination* (pp. 113–150). New York: John Wiley & Sons.

Stelmach, G. E. (1989). The Importance of Process-Oriented Research: A Commentary. In J. S. Skinner, C. B. Corbin, D. M. Landers, P. E. Martin, and C. L. Wells (Eds.), *Future Directions in Exercise and Sport Science Research* (pp. 423–432). Champaign, IL: Human Kinetics Books.

Steward, O. (1989). *Principles of Cellular, Molecular, and Developmental Neuroscience.* New York: Springer-Verlag.

Suinn, R. M. (1986). Models from Behavioral Clinical Psychology for Sport. In J. S. Skinner, C. B. Corbin, D. M. Landers, P. E. Martin, and C. L. Wells (Eds.), *Future Directions in Exercise and Sport Science Research* (pp. 453–474). Champaign, IL: Human Kinetics Books.

Trussell, E. (1965). Prediction of Success in a Motor Skill on the Basis of Early Learning Achievement. *Research Quarterly, 39,* 342–347.

Chapter 8

Sociology of Sport: Society in a Capsule

Description without Prescription

Sport and Social Values

Sport as a Socializing Process

Socialization through Physical Education

Sports in Educational Settings

Equity and Discrimination in Sport

The Future of Sport

Sport Sociology in the Future

Summary

To the Reader

Suggested Projects

References

Sport, at whatever level and no matter how organized, occurs in a social context, with social parameters and processes at work in every event.

Sport is a reflection of the society in which it exists and is capable of influencing societal values.

Because sport is a prominent and highly visible force in society, its position and influence warrants study just as any other social factor does.

The objective is to describe the position that sport holds in society, to determine if any malpractices exist, and to examine the socializing effects that sport has on its participants.

SPORT is alluring. It holds the attention of more people on given Sundays than church does. Newspapers give it more ink than the business, economic, or political news. The *World Almanac* gives it more coverage than science. There are more television hours devoted to sport than to any other theme. Americans spend more money betting on sports than on the purchase of books. Universities are usually more known for their athletic teams than for their academic quality. Athletes are more widely known than politicians.

Sport is a passion. It is the basis for argument, for common bonds, for identity, for liberation, for elation, for frustration. It is simultaneously laudable and damnable, pure and corrupt. It is the opiate of the masses.

Sport is an element of American life so pervasive that it touches and influences status, race relations, business life, clothing design, family life, the economy, language, and ethical values. And so, if one seeks to understand the nature of human behavior, then sport cannot be ignored.

Consequently, an area of physical education focuses on the relationship between sport and society. It is *sociology of sport,* which attends to *the study of the structure and effects of organized sport.* The concerns are how sport influences, and is influenced by, economics, politics, religion, mass media, and all other social forces. It focuses on the social processes that occur in sport and how people (and society) are affected by the interactions that occur from sport in all types of settings.

DESCRIPTION WITHOUT PRESCRIPTION

Whenever people interact with one another on the basis of some sort of accepted ground rules of social conduct, they are said to have a social organization. As a defined field of study, sociology is interested in the structure and composition of social organizations rather than in the characteristics of the individuals who make up the group. It searches for the effects that social groups have on human behavior, and not so much on how individuals influence the group (Gilbert, 1989). In a practical sense, sociology examines the whole (the group) to find out how it affects the parts (persons within the group) instead of vice versa.

Sociological investigations have tended to be descriptive—that is, they attempt to find out *what is,* with less attention given to *what ought to be.* The research generally does not impose judgments on the findings and therefore is often called nonjudgmental, or value-free, research. It usually is also nonethical, implying that no moral codes or social laws are applied to the findings.

Accordingly, the characteristics of sociological research are that: (1) it *describes* existing conditions, (2) then attempts to *discover relationships* among the variables of each setting, and (3) attempts to *explain* why those relationships exist.

SPORT AND SOCIAL VALUES

Values are beliefs or ideals. They provide social criteria for assessing what is desirable or acceptable behavior in specific situations. In this regard, sport is a value receptable for society. It disseminates and transmits social values. It can influence the social status of participants, and in turn the participants (prominent sports figures) are often held as symbolic representations of social values. Therefore, sport can be considered as an avenue for transmitting values to its participants. We assume, for example, that youngsters who participate are learning not only about the sport itself but also "to play the larger game of life." Inherent in this belief is the further assumption that the values that are acquired are desirable and reflect the normative expectations of society. And so sport is considered to magnify and accentuate some value orientations of society.

Sport and society share many of the same values.
Photo by Tom Cherrey.

What might these society/sport values be? According to an earlier writing (Edwards, 1973), seven common value themes are shared by society and sport: character development from experience, discipline and social order, competition and the facilitation of success, physical fitness, mental fitness, a religious ethic, and patriotism and love of country. More recently (Fine, 1987), the themes have been stated as effort to achieve, sportsmanship, teamwork, and the need to cope with victory and defeat. And another writing (Snyder and Spreitzer, 1989) suggests that they are courage, gameness, integrity, gallantry, and composure.

Legendary football coach Vince Lombardi had a poignant view:

> The goal of middleclass values is success; that is, in increasing accumulation of goods leading to higher social status. The means of success is hard work and continual striving on the part of the individual—a means that necessarily fosters elitism and class consciousness. The manner is basically puritanical: disciplined repression of present needs for the sake of future gratification, commitment to law and order accompanied by reliance on authority and tradition, and an optimistic pragmatism whose methods are always open to change. (Beuter, 1972)

Whatever the values happen to be, a general opinion exists among the public that sports can serve a positive function through the transmission of acceptable societal values (Eitzen and Sage, 1986), and on this basis sports are viewed as a potentially strong socializing agent.

SPORT AS A SOCIALIZING PROCESS

Socialization is the process of developing and molding an individual to behave in a manner that is consistent with the social expectations of a group. Because it imposes constraints in the range of acceptable behavior, socialization to some extent induces conformity. Sport can be an agent of this process within its own structural boundaries, and consequently sport is often said to be a *microcosm* of society; that is, sport is society in miniature.

Learning to be an athlete involves not only the development of appropriate motor skills but also the internalization of attitudes, dispositions, self-perceptions, and competitive behavior. It mandates mental skills that are necessary to respond to the strategic and social necessities of participation, including emotions that are often sport specific. Playing tennis, for instance, requires a somewhat different behavioral code than playing rugby. And playing tennis for a regional championship incorporates different behavioral allowances than playing your cousin during a family reunion.

Sociology of Sport: Society in a Capsule

Youngsters who gain positive support from parents and coaches can benefit significantly from competitive experiences.
© Alan Carey/The Image Works

It has long been held that participation in competitive sport has socializing effects. For example, we assume that sport engenders a value of competition. In fact, competition is a learned trait (Gordon, 1988), and sport appears to be one of the more emphatic avenues for learning about it (Hargreaves, 1986). By itself, competition can generate high levels of motivation to perform well and higher overall accomplishments than if competition were absent (Atkinson, McCarthy, and Phillips, 1987).

But competition generally allows only a few elite individuals (sometimes only one) to emerge with the top prize. That equates, in sports, to winning. And so there may be negative consequences for those who do not win. Feelings of inferiority or helplessness may surface, and low self-esteem may develop (Hellstedt, 1988), leading in some cases to withdrawal from the competitive scene (Coakley, 1986).

The effects of competition appear to be most penetrating for young players. At best, competition can be a forum for the positive pursuit of personal excellence. At worst, competition results in destructive rivalry, high levels of anxiety, self-depreciation, insensitivity toward others, cheating, and destructive aggressing (Smoll, Magill, and Ash, 1988). But youngsters who gain positive support from parents and coaches can benefit significantly from competitive experiences through the development of self-confidence and improved relationships with other players

(Scanlan, 1988). Furthermore, if games are designed to emphasize cooperation, the players can show increases in cooperative behavior not only in games but also in free play and classroom activities (Orlick and Pitman-Davidson, 1988).

Strangely, it is the outstanding athlete who sometimes acquires the least socialization. Athletically gifted youngsters may experience inordinate pressures to succeed, creating a desire to drop out of competition but making it difficult for them to do so because the message has become ingrained that winning is what counts in life (Nash, 1987). So the player becomes pampered and protected, and as the player gets older, more and more decisions may be made by other persons so that the player's "character" development is confined to performance criteria. In this sense, sports could be viewed as having a suppressing effect on socialization because of the safeguarding that many outstanding athletes receive.

In truth, no solid accumulation of evidence supports the contention that sports are a critical element in the socialization process (Eitzen and Sage, 1986). Nor is there substantial research that supports the concept that sports build character or good citizenship, or promotes any other desirable and valued personality traits (Snyder and Spreitzer, 1989). But these are statements that may be too cautious and far too general to be easily accepted by anyone who has played in this microcosm of life.

SOCIALIZATION THROUGH PHYSICAL EDUCATION

At a less intensive level, and to the extent that it brings people together for a common purpose, a physical education class could be considered as a potential agent for socialization. And it has always been assumed that desirable social behaviors could be taught through properly structured in-class experiences. In fact, physical education classes were some of the earliest settings used by sport sociologists to study the effects of group interaction.

Results have been disappointing, however. The first studies found the classes to have little if any effect (Bailey, 1977; Snyder, 1970), and later observations derived only speculative conclusions about any socializing consequences of participation (Chappell, 1986; Weiss and Bressman, 1985). Perhaps this is because physical education classes meet only a few hours a week on the average, and the range of social interactions tends to be limited. Moreover, participation is often compulsory, and this alone may dampen any sense of group affiliation (Dzewaltowski, 1989). Additionally, there is no reason to believe that physical education classes would influence behavior any more than other school experiences, for it's difficult to know (and studies have not been able to isolate) the specific reinforcers that are most important in people's lives (Foon, 1988).

Nonetheless, a shade of evidence holds that attitudes about play can be influenced by young people's experiences in structured play situations (Greer and Stewart, 1989) and that a quality loosely called "sportsmanship" can be promoted within specific activities. However, this behavior does not seem to generalize to other settings or activities (Giebink and McKenzie, 1985). Potentially, apparently the best strategies, at least for younger learners, are to offer activities with the intention of providing enjoyment and to give participants personal responsibility for their own behaviors within the activities (Valois, Desharnais, and Godin, 1988). This goal has been incorporated into the Physical Best program adopted by the American Association for Health, Physical Education, Recreation and Dance. Its objectives are to motivate children to participate in physical activity and improve their level of physical fitness. A central focus is to directly involve children in setting their own fitness goals, thus enabling them to perceive control over their own actions and to develop a stronger commitment to goal achievement (Pemberton and McSwegin, 1989).

SPORTS IN EDUCATIONAL SETTINGS

Not surprisingly, sociology of sport has given a great deal of attention to sport in educational settings, with mixed reviews. In general, the evidence questions the widely stated belief that sports are compatible with the overall goals of education. To a large extent, athletic programs are supported by schools for self-serving purposes. They are usually appraised internally by factors other than as educational experiences—in essence, did the teams win, and did the program make money? If any educational goals are achieved, they are more likely to occur at the elementary school level (Eitzen and Sage, 1986). At each successive level, sport becomes more serious, bureaucratic, and elitist, and therefore less "educational." Figure 8.1 illustrates the attributes of sports at different educational levels (Snyder and Spreitzer, 1981). In effect, sport moves from informal arrangements to corporate sport. Thus, in elementary and middle or junior high school, playing sports for their own sake, with the intrinsic rewards that can occur, is methodically replaced in time by selective participation and an increasing emphasis on winning as the atmosphere for the participants becomes more worklike.

Inquiry

Many of the inbred hypocrisies of sports are well known. At large colleges and universities, athletics are dominated by commercialism. Television contracts dictate when teams will play and even influence when time-outs are called during games. Teams have become dictatorships. Wins and losses become viewed as profit-loss statements. The athletic program is a business, to be inventoried like any other financial investment. This leads to flagrant recruiting violations and other outright immoral and illegal behavior on the part of coaches, alumni, and administrators. Athletes become interchangeable parts, as the manufacturing of champions is no longer a craft but an industry, calling for specialized laboratories, research projects, training camps, and even experimental sport centers (Eitzen, 1988).

The real surprise is not the existence of corruption in sport, but rather how widespread it is. Every year a list of major schools receives probation, and now in recent times smaller schools are joining the list. There is growing concern about the filtering down of unethical practices into the athletic programs of high schools (Eitzen and Sage, 1986).

Sport sociologists are making a comprehensive study of the structure of the megabusiness and are probing the long-established traditions of sports. In the process they are discovering the effects of abuse. The intent is not to discredit sports or to demean acclaimed benefits, but rather to reveal the inner workings and to document the shortcomings. The ultimate goal is to reinstate ethical sanity.

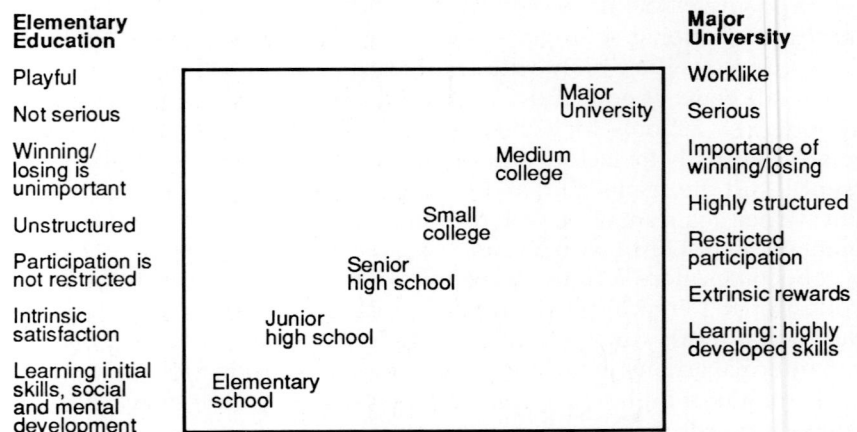

Figure 8.1 The attributes of sports at different educational levels.

From Snyder and Spreitzer, "Sport Education and Schools," in G.R.F. Luschen and G. H. Sage, *Handbook of Social Science of Sport,* Copyright © 1981 Stipes Publishing Company, Champaign, Illinois. Reprinted by permission.

EQUITY AND DISCRIMINATION IN SPORT

One particularly prominent area of interest for sport sociologists has been to investigate gender and racial discrimination in sports. Sometimes the findings have been appalling.

For too long, opportunities for athletic competition were virtually unavailable to women. Title IX made some changes. As part of the Educational Amendments Act of 1972, schools were required to provide equal sports opportunities to females. The effect of this, along with the women's movement, the general awareness of the benefits of health and fitness for all people, and the visibility of female athlete role models, was to increase female participation in sports. In high school athletics alone, during a six-year span from 1971 to 1977, the number of women participating on competitive teams increased over 600 percent (Westkott and Coakley, 1981). In the Olympics, female competitors have increased in number from less than eight hundred in 1968 to nearly two thousand in more recent games (Coakley, 1986). At the intercollegiate level, prior to Title IX only about 15 percent of college athletes were female, whereas today 40 percent are (Eitzen and Sage, 1986).

Furthermore, women are participating today in a wider variety of vigorous activities. Society has changed, and the enlivening experiences of athletic competition and recreational enjoyment are being pursued by both sexes, separately and together.

Today women are participating in a wide variety of vigorous activities.
Photo by Jim Bryant.

But despite these changes, sport continues in some regard to be associated with so-called "masculine" elements of culture, and the female in sport is still considered as somewhat of an anomaly. Sometimes girls and women experience a conflicting set of roles: They are expected to have "feminine" behaviors while also participating in vigorous activities (Csizma, Wittig, and Schurr, 1988). As such, females may receive signals of disapproval when participating in sports generally considered to be masculine. Yet studies of female athletes suggest that they do not themselves sense any role conflict (Jackson and Marsh, 1986) nor any differences in their competitive nature (Lirgg and Feltz, 1989). Moreover, these athletes are generally viewed to be more ethical in their sporting conduct than male athletes (Crown and Heatherington, 1989). And, female athletes are more well prepared academically for college than male athletes, besides doing better academically while in college and having higher graduation percentages (Birrell, 1987).

On another issue, some sport sociologists have held that sports have been not only racially oriented but also a magnet for racial discrimination. The National Football League did not have any black players until 1945, nor did major league baseball until 1949. The National Basketball Association was all-white until 1950. Some major universities did not have black athletes on any of their teams until the late 1970s. Today, more than half the players in professional football are black, and over 80 percent of professional basketball players are black (Eitzen and Sage, 1986).

Nonetheless, racial inequalities continue to be a recurring interest for sport sociologists. They examine such factors as the numbers of blacks in administrative and managerial roles. The National Football League, for example, did not have a black head coach until 1989. Always, the objective is to describe and to question, and then to aspire for true equality in athletics.

THE FUTURE OF SPORT

The basic construct of sports has not changed markedly over the decades. But the manner of presentation has. Technology has expanded spectator involvement, bringing the camera and microphone into every corner. Equipment made of space-age compounds has enabled athletes to hit a ball harder, to clear a higher bar, and to finish a race faster than would otherwise be possible. Biomechanists have computer-projected optimal performance styles. Exercise physiologists have found better ways to prepare for competition.

Maybe in the future athletes will have yet-unknown and legal chemical aids available to further enhance their performances. Maybe mechanical parts will replace joints and muscles to make the body ultra-efficient. Or electronic devices may be implanted in the muscles to generate perfect coordination. Maybe the real competition in the future will be between pharmacists and physicists.

Such visions are far-fetched, of course, but technology has become influential in sport today and will play an increasingly important role in the future. Thus, the term *technosport* is sometimes used to describe sport of tomorrow. It implies more than just the domination of technology in sport. It also suggests the use of cybernetic devices to eliminate errors, oversights, and mistakes. Coaching decisions will be made by computers. All of these projections are based on the idea that the only way to generate perfect performance is to give human behavioral control over to electronic circuitry. If so, emotion will have gone out of sport. Spontaneity will be unknown.

Or, the future might be in *ecosports,* where games will return to more natural, spontaneous, playlike behavior. The "new games" concept has already stimulated interest. In contrast to structured winner-loser athletics, the new games are designed to emphasize partnership between teams rather than competition.

Ecosports also suggests more involvement in recreational activities such as bicycling, hiking, rock climbing, scuba diving, the martial arts, orienteering, backpacking, and other pursuits that have no win-loss elements. The main objectives are to play and to enjoy playing. It is rejuvenation of the inner soul where participation is an end in itself, and it replaces the inactivity of spectatorship. It's back to nature through recreation.

What will *sports be like in the future?*
Photo by Tom Cherrey.

SPORT SOCIOLOGY IN THE FUTURE

Critics of sport sociology have suggested that too much emphasis has been placed on describing the negative aspects of sport. Much is now known about gender and racial inequities, violence, exploitation of athletes, cheating, use of drugs, excessive emphasis on winning, and violations of the "spirit" of sport. In the future, the discipline will take on new directions.

New concerns will be more related to how sport affects life-styles. For example, to what extent are values about sport changing, and how does this affect everyday life? Is the ecosports trend myth or reality? What role can sports play in reducing the alienation and depersonalization that technology has generated in life? What influence does sport have in marriage, child-rearing, or career formation? To what extent is nonparticipation in sport socially induced? What role can it have for retired persons? Why do people drop out of active participation? How can sports be more effectively arranged to deliver the positive social benefits that have always been the objectives?

The questions in the future will focus on human value orientations and how sport fits into the total picture of living in a technological society. The answers will not only describe new roles for sport but also will formulate actual strategies and effective action to make a more positive contribution to society. In the end, there may be few things more important to the health of society and its well-being than the manner in which it treats its sporting endeavors.

Summary

The various claims made about the social significance and assumed outcomes of sport presuppose an understanding of its nature. Much of what existed as standard belief came from speculation only. As a field of study, the sociology of sport has undertaken the work of uncovering the inner structure of sport and scrutinizing the social forces that affect its participants.

Part of the logic for studying organized sport originally grew from the conclusion that, since it was so prominent in society, sport simply could not be ignored. However, as a formal discipline, the sociology of sport is of recent vintage. Research began only in the 1960s, and a professional association of sport sociologists did not exist in North America until 1978 (the North American Society for the Sociology of Sport). Growth of the discipline has been admittedly slow, albeit steady. But the persuasive position that sport commands in society will lead more people to take a closer look at what sport is and what it might become. The outcomes can be to eliminate discrimination, exploitation, drug use, excessive emphasis on winning, and other inequities. And, as alternative sporting ventures become more defined, to clarify the meaning and value of sports on both individual and societal levels becomes increasingly possible.

To the Reader

Sports are said to serve many functions in society. They can be inspirational, satisfying, fun, enlivening, and health-giving. They have even been called the very foundation of democracy. But the "sacred" position of sport in American society has been shaken. Today the ramifications of autocratic and monopolistic organization within its structure has dethroned many of its inherent attributes.

Sociology of sport presents intriguing and revealing studies of sport and its roles in society. However, the product of such study can be downright depressing. The economic makeup of organized sport is overwhelming, and the political implications are disturbing, particularly when they are seen in the supposedly more immune areas like high school athletics and the Olympics. Some authors believe that sports have become such a nightmare that they will eventually undergo dramatic structural changes, or possibly even disappear.

But the final reason for studying sport is not to offer discouragement. Rather, by knowing about malpractices, one becomes sensitized to the events that cause them and the conditions that can be controlled to prevent them.

However, change will occur only if the people who want change will cause it to happen. Many of you will one day be directly involved with athletics, and the value of knowing the workings of sport will become even more obvious. To say that inequities and ill-disposed conditions exist in sports is not to say that you will automatically become part of the malignancy. The benefit of studying sport is seen in how the information is used to create a better atmosphere for the participants. In too many cases, play has become work and spontaneity has been replaced by bureaucratic control. But as a coach, a teacher, a future administrator, a parent, or in some other role, you can help to restore purity to an element of life that deserves it.

Suggested Projects

1. Construct a list of values that you believe are held as sporting ethic. Prepare another list of presumed values that are seen as desirable by society in general. Compare the lists, and discuss in class whether sport and society represent each other, and/or complement each other in the fostering of those values.

2. The research does not unequivocally support the concept that sports participation leads to the development of desirable personality characteristics. Yet most participants would probably believe that it does. Write a list of strengths that you, personally, believe you acquired from active involvement in sports, whether as a varsity player or in recreational pursuits. Share the list with the class for open discussion on the beneficial outcomes of participation.

3. Interview the athletic director at your school. Ask questions specifically relating to how money (including television and radio contracts, advertisements, and donations) may have been the bottom-line consideration in decisions about the athletic program.

4. What inequities exist in present-day sport? Have you personally observed any? What were, or are, the ramifications of these unjust practices?

5. In England, intercollegiate sports at many schools have traditionally been run entirely by the athletes. They draw up schedules, organize practice sessions, and determine team makeups. The only involvement of the college is to provide equipment and playing space, and the only involvement of other persons is to officiate games. How would this change the attitudes of players if such wholesale changes were made in American sport? Consider a range of circumstances from Little League baseball to big-time collegiate athletics.

6. What will sport be like in the future? How will increasing technology and presumed changes in social values affect sport as presently structured?

7. Assume you live in a society where sport is unknown. Further assume that you have been given the responsibility to create, for this society, a perfect sport. You must first determine what contribution you want this sport to make in your society, but thereafter the guidelines are without limitations.

References

Atkinson, G. B. J., McCarthy, B., and Phillips, K. M. (1987). *Studying Society: An Introduction to Social Science.* New York: Oxford University Press.

Bailey, C. I. (1977). Socialization in Play, Game, and Sports. *The Physical Educator, 34,* 183–187.

Beuter, R. J. (1972). Sports, Values, and Society. *Christian Century, 5,* 389.

Birrell, S. (1987). The Woman Athlete's College Experience: Knowns and Unknowns. *Journal of Sport and Social Issues, 11,* 82–96.

Chappell, R. H. (1986). Physical Education, Sport, and Recreation, and the Quality of Life. In J. A. Mangan and R. B. Small (Eds.), *Sport, Culture, Society: International, Historical, and Sociological Perspectives. Proceedings of the Eighth Commonwealth and International Conference on Sport, Physical Education, Dance, Recreation, and Health* (pp. 220–225). London: E. & F. N. Spon.

Coakley, J. J. (1986). *Sport in Society: Issues and Controversies* (3rd ed.). St. Louis: Times Mirror/Mosby.

Crown, J., and Heatherington, L. (1989). The Costs of Winning: The Role of Gender in Moral Reasoning and Judgements about Competitive Athletic Encounters. *Journal of Sport and Exercise Psychology, 11,* 281–289.

Csizma, K. A., Wittig, A. F., and Schurr, K. R. (1988). Sport Stereotypes and Gender. *Journal of Sport and Exercise Psychology, 10,* 62–74.

Dzewaltowski, D. A. (1989). Toward a Model of Exercise Motivation. *Journal of Sport and Exercise Psychology, 11,* 251–269.

Edwards, H. (1973). *Sociology of Sport.* Homewood, IL: Dorsey Press.

Eitzen, D. S. (1988). Ethical Problems in American Sport. *Journal of Sport and Social Issues, 12*(1), 17–20.

Eitzen, D. S., and Sage, G. H. (1986). *Sociology of North American Sport* (3rd ed.). Dubuque, IA: Wm. C. Brown.

Fine, G. A. (1987). *With the Boys.* Chicago: University of Chicago Press.

Foon, A. E. (1988). Reconstructing the Social Psychology of Sport: An Examination of Issues. *Journal of Sport Behavior, 11,* 223–230.

Giebink, M. P., and McKenzie, T. L. (1985). Teaching Sportsmanship in Physical Education and Recreation: An Analysis of Interventions and Generalization Effects. *Journal of Teaching in Physical Education, 4,* 167–177.

Gilbert, M. (1989). *On Social Facts.* New York: Routledge.

Gordon, M. M. (1988). *The Scope of Sociology.* New York: Oxford University Press.

Greer, D. L., and Stewart, M. J. (1989). Children's Attitudes toward Play: An Investigation of Their Context Specificity and Relationship to Organized Sport Experiences. *Journal of Sport and Exercise Psychology, 11,* 336–342.

Hargreaves, J. (1986). *Sport, Power, and Culture.* New York: St. Martin's Press.

Hellstedt, J. C. (1988). Kids, Parents, and Sports: Some Questions and Answers. *The Physician and Sportsmedicine, 16,* 59–71.

Jackson, S. A., and Marsh, H. W. (1986). Athletic or Antisocial? The Female Sport Experience. *Journal of Sport Psychology, 8,* 198–211.

Lirgg, C. D., and Feltz, D. L. (1989). Female Self-Confidence in Sport: Myths, Realities, and Enhancement Strategies. *Journal of Physical Education, Recreation, and Dance, 60,* 49–54.

Nash, H. L. (1987). Elite Child-Athletes: How Much Does it Cost? *The Physician and Sportsmedicine, 15*(8), 128–133.

Orlick, T. D., and Pitman-Davidson, A. (1988). Enhancing Cooperative Skills in Games and Life. In F. L. Smoll, R. A. Magill, and M. J. Ash (Eds.), *Children in Sport* (3rd ed.) (pp. 149–159). Champaign, IL: Human Kinetics Books.

Pemberton, C., and McSwegin, P. J. (1989). Goal Setting and Motivation. *Journal of Physical Education, Recreation, and Dance, 60*(1), 39–41.

Scanlan, T. K. (1988). Social Evaluation and the Competitive Process: A Developmental Perspective. In F. L. Smoll, R. S. Schmidt, and M. J. Ash (Eds.), *Children in Sport* (3rd ed.) (pp. 135–148). Champaign, IL: Human Kinetics Books.

Smoll, F. L., Magill, R. A., and Ash, M. J. (Eds.). (1988). *Children in Sport* (3rd ed.). Champaign, IL: Human Kinetics Books.

Snyder, E. E. (1970). Aspects of Socialization in Sports and Physical Education. *Quest, 14,* 1–7.

Snyder, E. E., and Spreitzer, E. A. (1981). Sport, Education, and Schools. In G. R. F. Luschen and G. H. Sage (Eds.), *Handbook of Social Science of Sport* (pp. 119–146). Champaign, IL: Stipes.

Snyder, E. E., and Spreitzer, E. A. (1989). *Social Aspects of Sports* (3rd ed.). Englewood Cliffs, NJ: Prentice-Hall.

Valois, P., Desharnais, R., and Godin, G. (1988). A Comparison of the Fishbein and Ajzen and the Triandis Attitudinal Models for the Prediction of Exercise Intention and Behavior. *Journal of Behavioral Medicine, 11,* 459–472.

Weiss, M. R., and Bressman, E. S. (1985). Relating Instructional Theory to Children's Psychosocial Development. *Journal of Physical Education, Recreation, and Dance, 56*(9), 34–36.

Westkott, M., and Coakley, J. J. (1981). Women in Sport: Modalities of Feminist Social Change. *Journal of Sport and Social Issues, 5*(1), 32–45.

Chapter 9

Sport Psychology: Inside the Mind of the Athlete

The Final Frontier

Brain in Emotion

The Activation of Arousal

Intervention Strategies

Who's in Control Here?

Go See the Movie in Your Head

The Transcendent Mind

Summary

To the Reader

Suggested Projects

References

Excellent athletic accomplishment demands not only preparation of the body but also appropriate psychological dispositions for performance.

The mental preparedness of an athlete can be improved, just as the physiological condition can, by strategically designed programs that bring about the desired results.

But for some athletes, the stress of competition induces uncontrollable anxiety levels or other psychological states that are inappropriate for skilled execution, with a consequent deterioration in performance.

To assist these athletes, intervention techniques have been devised to overcome the fear of competition or any other negative psychological influence on performance.

BOTTOM of the ninth. Losing by a run. Two outs. Runners on second and third.

The batter hesitates, feeling unequal to the moment. The game. The crowd. The cameras. The championship. Grind some soil into sweltering palms, force a few deep breaths, adjust the grip, arrange the stance. Brain, lungs, heart, muscles, all must be ready to act. Just a single. Just a single, and it's all over.

Strike one!

Step back from the plate. Why is the brain so alive with emotion? Why couldn't it be a humbler system, like the gnat that just flickered in front of the plate and got swatted. Why is time so distorted? Why is it so difficult to see? Realign the muscles. Prepare them to respond. Just a base hit. Just a crummy bleeder through the infield.

Strike two!

Step out again. Why is the mind so frenzied? Why does this small body have such a large head? Why are the fans so loud? Why is the bat so heavy? Why is the ball so small? Just a single. A lousy broken-bat, humpback, Texas-League blooper to right. Or maybe a walk. An error. An HBP. Anything.

Strike three!

On another, less intensive day, a student is in a beginning golf class. The novice tried, for the past three weeks, to send a ball into straight, parabolic flight. Cuffed at the ball for a hundred and eighty-seven swings, and got only an assortment of dribbles, slices, shanks, and hooks. How could anyone actually enjoy this impediment of a game? Grip the club more firmly, contort the face, blaspheme the ball, and repeat the trials. But there are still only dribbles, slices, shanks, and hooks.

A teacher had been providing a stream of verbal cues: "Keep your eye on the ball," "Shift your weight as you swing," "Keep your left arm straight," "Hit through the ball." And the more entangled the student became, the more the teacher offered additional proverbs. But the ball would not obey.

THE FINAL FRONTIER

We human beings are quite capable living organisms. But how easily disturbed and put out of order we can become. We are not always dependable, not always functional. Events that play on our brain can burden the muscles. Perhaps it's because the brain is a mind.

A skilled batter cannot respond to a moment of stress. A student cannot hit a golf ball. Both behaviors are related. Both are physical manifestations of states of mind.

This mind-body interchange has been happening ever since the first human tried to hit the first ball. But only recently has a field of study given attention specifically to the psychological factors that affect motor performance. Call it *sport psychology,* the latest and possibly the last of the sciences that focus on sporting endeavors. It deals with *the mental and emotional aspects of motor performance* by attempting to describe, explain, predict, and ultimately change mental behavior related to physical performance. Just as a coach endeavors to improve the motor skills of players, sport psychology helps athletes to work out personal problems, develop appropriate motivation and attitudes, and reduce anxiety. The end objective is to modify negative psychological influences and thus to facilitate skilled performance through positive mental approaches.

Exercise physiologists know how athletes can develop their best physical preparedness. Biomechanists can tell a performer about perfect executional styles. Sport psychologists probe into the athlete's mind, and thereupon they may have reached into the final hinterland of exploration to describe how humans function.

BRAIN IN EMOTION

The batter and the golfer: one skilled, one novice. The psyche that affects both is the same, in different settings, but with the same hindrance on performance.

It's a mental disarray, but it has a physical origin. It starts in an area of the brain stem that collects branches of all incoming sensory neurons in a great latticework of crossings and crisscrossings between the brain and the spinal cord. Called the *reticular formation,* it's a hoard of compact nerves located near the top of the spinal cord and penetrating into the core of the brain. The job of this island of neurons is to receive stimuli from every sensory source. From the optic nerves. From the acoustic nerves. From the extensor digitorium longus. From everywhere in the body, and all the time. It must be a noisy place.

Fortunately, the brain does not need to attend to all this profusion of stimuli. The grandeur of the reticular formation is that it appraises all incoming information and decides which of it is important enough to bother the brain's conscious attention. Thus, every human brain is saved the massive headache of having to acknowledge every bit of nerve-news that the senses feed into it.

We can be daily grateful for this service. Suppose you are attending a difficult lecture, and the light in the room is harsh, the chair is uncomfortable, there's commotion in the hall outside, your thumb hurts from being jammed in an intramural game, and you're hungry. Ignore all this, says the reticular formation, and attend to the lecture. Or, suppose you're standing over a final putt on the eighteenth green, and you know a miss will cost you a wager, and your new golf shoes are hurting your feet, and there's an airplane overhead, and a passing motorist shouts "Fore!" Your brain must tell you to focus on the putt, and that only.

Attention to important affairs is no problem. It's the unwanted attention to unimportant matters that gives us difficulty. It happens, for example, when we want to sleep and cannot because of worrisome thoughts racing through our heads. Or when we need a second serve to stay off a defeat in tennis, and our mind gets fixated on the fear of a double-fault. Our mind becomes charged with extra thought patterns that interfere with what it is we want to do. The reticular formation gets overloaded and confused.

All neural impulses and all thoughts are energy. Most of the time the reticular formation dissipates the unwanted energy by sending it to some unknown storage bin. But sometimes the coffers are full. And then the conscious brain gets bombarded with extra thought-energy that it does not want. In a fit of panic, the brain dumps the extra energy into the skeletal muscles. The result is a generalized increase in the level of tension that permeates the entire muscular system. No wonder the body feels "tight" when you lift a basketball for a crucial foul shot. It is. The normal cooperation of the muscles is hindered by an increased state of actual, physiological, tension. And so the muscles defy each other. The triceps and its companion muscles must try to project a basketball toward the hoop. Usually, under less stress, the biceps is calm, allowing the action of the triceps to occur unhindered. But in an emotionally tense situation, the biceps resists. It tightens up and fights against the normal motion of the triceps even though it does not want to. It can't help it.

THE ACTIVATION OF AROUSAL

There is a certain level of physiological tension which is neither too high nor too low for performing motor skills. It relates to a psychological energy level called *arousal,* which is a "readiness" to perform. Arousal comes in degrees. It is the state of emotional activation at any given moment on a continuum ranging from sleep on the low end to hysteria on the high end.

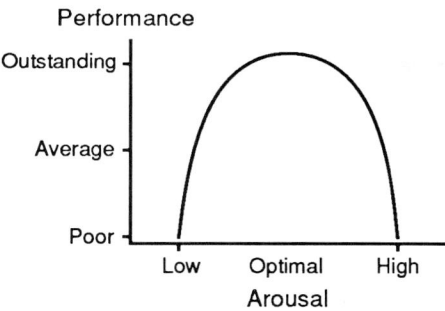

Figure 9.1 The inverted-U theory.

From A. V. Caroon, *Social Psychology of Sport.* Copyright © 1980 Mouvement Publications, Longmeadow, Massachusetts.

These variable states of arousal are controlled by the throttle of the reticular formation, whose function is to turn up or turn down the state of emotion so that the brain and body are prepared for whatever task is at hand. To explain this workings a so-called *inverted*-U theory was devised (Caroon, 1980) to describe a relationship between arousal and performance. The hypothesis predicts that there is a progressive enhancement in performance as someone's arousal level increases, but only up to some optimal point, beyond which further increases in arousal will lead to progressive decreases in performance efficiency (see figure 9.1).

A related concept (sometimes referred to as the Yerkes-Dodson Law) implies that the optimal state of arousal for any given task decreases as the difficulty or complexity of the task increases. The relationship is seen to be an inverse one in that the more complicated the task is, the lower the level of arousal should be for the best performance of that task. Conversely, when the skill is comparatively simple, the arousal level should be high. In figure 9.2, complexity is meant to be the degree of precision of movement required by a given motor skill; thus, optimal performance is a function of appropriately combining arousal levels with the relative degree of movement exactness that the skill requires.

In application, an "uncomplicated" task is one that does not require movements of great precision—weight lifting, for example. In contrast, golf is an example of a task that demands great precision of action. If the Yerkes-Dodson Law is correct, the level of arousal that would aid weight lifting would be too high and thus hinder the performance out-

Inquiry

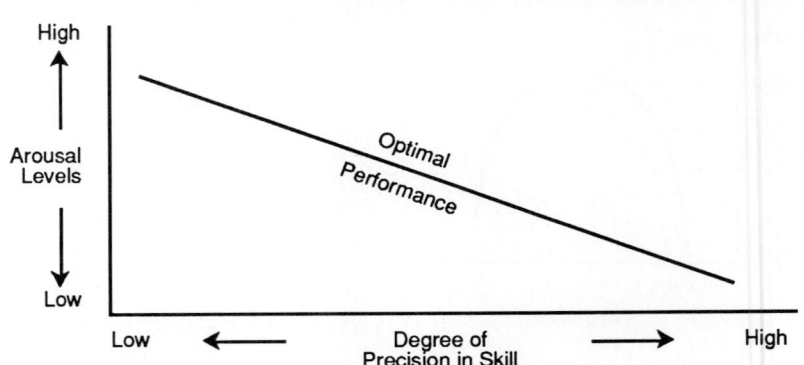

Figure 9.2 Hypothetical relationship of arousal levels to the degree of movement precision required by a given skill. In theory, higher arousal levels are more appropriate for skills of low precision, and vice versa.

comes in golf. Using this scheme, a hypothetical "match" can be made (see figure 9.3) whereby golf benefits from psychological states of calm, while weight lifting will be aided by higher arousal levels.

But the relationship is not so clinically absolute. Arousal is a performance factor that is variable from situation to situation and from individual to individual. Everyone has a certain threshold of emotion which, when it is breached, will hinder the performance of a given task. That threshold may be considerably higher for an experienced golfer compared to someone just learning the game. But when the experienced golfer's anxiety becomes too high for the normal free swing of a critical shot, and the beginner accumulates frustration because of repeated failures, both will have activated arousal levels that energize general muscle responses that are antagonistic to performance.

In another application, assume that an athlete is experienced as both a golfer and a football linebacker. To be successful in both sports, the athlete will have to learn to generate the appropriate emotional pitch for each contest. Or even further, a basketball player must adjust to the moment-by-moment changes of a game, since the arousal level that is proper when playing a pressing defense may be too high when the game pauses for that player to shoot free throws.

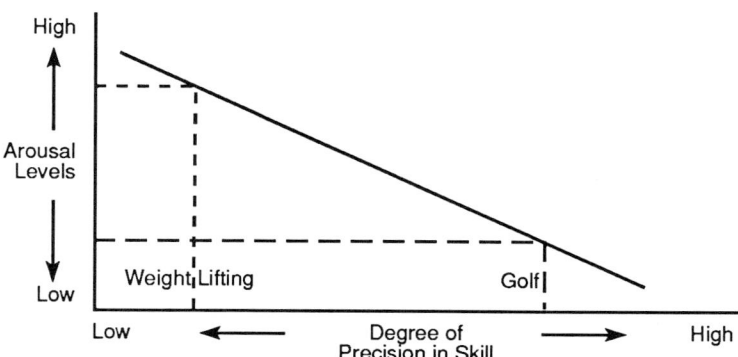

Figure 9.3 Assuming weight lifting to be a skill of low precision and golf to be one of high precision, appropriate arousal levels can be theoretically plotted.

INTERVENTION STRATEGIES

Coaches often deliver energizing talks to "psych up" their athletes in preparation for competition. Sport psychologists, in contrast, devote most of their attention to lowering arousal. They may be asked to intervene when an athlete has difficulty handling the anxiety of competition.

"Take a few deep breaths" is a quickly given suggestion as a remedy for arousal levels that are too high. And in fact, in a stressed state anyone is more likely to hold each breath longer or to take rapid and shallow breaths. So less oxygen is circulated and more waste product builds up in the muscles (Brooks and Fahey, 1987). The more appropriate response is to breathe as the fourth-grade music teacher tells everyone—with deep, slow, diaphragmatic inhalations.

But this is a situational "quick fix." Athletes who have difficulty handling anxiety need psychological intervention that has a more lasting effect. One technique of long-time use is *progressive relaxation,* first described by Edmond Jacobson (1938). This blanket term refers to alternately contracting and relaxing specific muscle groups, moving progressively from one muscle group to another. The objective is to gain an awareness and sensitivity to the actual sensation of tension as compared to relaxed states, and then to develop an ability to create appropriate relaxation as needed. In its simplest form, the technique involves tensing a single muscle group—for example, clenching the fist as tightly as possible for a few seconds and then letting go to allow all tension to run completely out of the hand. Over time, increased sensitivity is developed to smaller and smaller noticeable differences in states of tension, and ultimately the proper states can be self-generated according to the needs of the moment.

All other formats of relaxation training are variations of this central objective of being able to consciously reduce anxiety. When successful, these techniques allow one to willfully elicit a series of physiological reactions that include decreased muscle tension, lowered heart rate, slower respiration, and a change in brain wave patterns—from those that evoke negative thoughts to those that are associated with positive states of mind (Vander, Sherman, and Luciano, 1985).

Another technique is *systematic desensitization,* whereby in a quiet atmosphere, anxiety-arousing situations are consciously paired with low-anxiety events. For example, assume a basketball player has difficulty mediating stress during tense moments of games. The anxiety-prone athlete would meditate about events associated with games, such as going to the arena, and then assimilate thoughts that are stress reducing or nonthreatening, such as an amusing idea or memory of a camping trip. Once the imaginary trip to the arena no longer produces stress, the low-anxiety thoughts are paired to the next stage, such as suiting up for a game, and so on until the connection of stress-reducing thoughts is made to actual anxiety-producing events of a game.

Other coping strategies include self-talk techniques, where an athlete learns to carry on an internal dialogue that strengthens his or her conviction about having the competency to execute the required skills of an event. Sometimes meditative strategies such as Yoga and Zen are employed to generate proper frames of mind and self-monitoring of physiological responses. Occasionally hypnosis is used. All methods have the objective of altering the conscious mind of the performer and relieving anxiety.

Excellent athletes in all sports have developed ways of generating proper frames of mind for competition (LeUnes and Hayward, 1988). Many rely on past experiences to help them adjust to the unique requirements of each situation (Kerr, 1987). Even athletes who are successful in substitute roles appear to have learned how to adjust their arousal levels for entry into a game (Anshel and Wrisberg, 1988). So there is little doubt that top performance is related to the ability to handle stress (Poole, 1988). And likewise we know that properly chosen intervention strategies can have remarkable success in teaching troubled athletes how to control anxiety (Rainey and Cunningham, 1988). In sum, then, athletes must learn to handle stress, and for those who have difficulty, sport psychology has appropriate helping techniques.

Athletes must learn to handle stress.
Photo by Tom Cherrey.

WHO'S IN CONTROL HERE?

A concept called *achievement motivation* refers to an individual's "need" to perform according to a standard of excellence. This trait is stable, long lasting, and generally learned from others (usually parents) who were themselves high achievers (LeUnes and Nation, 1989). Athletic competition elicits this generalized "drivelike" desire to achieve excellence (Cratty, 1983).

A corollary reaction, called *motive to avoid failure,* is aroused not as a will to succeed, but rather as an expectancy that certain behaviors will lead to failure (Atkinson, 1978). In sport settings, often an athlete will perform in a fashion of trying to avoid making mistakes rather than with a spirited flair of giving one's all (Steigleder et al., 1978).

A strange human behavior is the *motive to avoid success.* It functions as an inhibitory tendency that acts against any motive toward success, even when success is possible. It could exist when an athlete perceives the consequences of success to be social isolation, a loss of close friends, guilt feelings, and even wondering about one's normality (Tresmer, 1976). Winning brings extra attention, recognition, and an expectation of repeat performances in future competition. Occasionally, a player does not want that responsibility and may intentionally perform below par. In

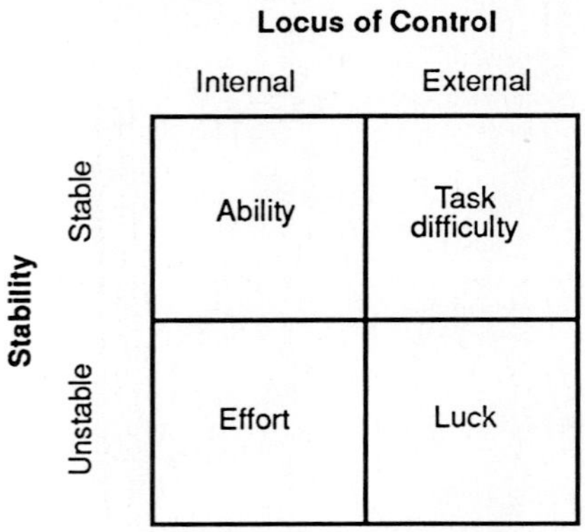

	Locus of Control	
	Internal	External
Stable	Ability	Task difficulty
Unstable	Effort	Luck

(Stability on vertical axis)

Figure 9.4 A classification of the factors that people use in explaining their successes and failures. By this classification, ability is seen as a stable (dependable over time) and internal factor, while luck is an unstable and external factor.

© 1974 General Learning Corporation. Used by permission of Silver Burdett & Ginn. All rights reserved.

one manifestation of this trait, a player may wish to avoid humiliating an opponent, and the athlete may be said to lack a "killer instinct."

In any case, in the end athletes seem to have reasons, whether consciously expressed or not, to explain their success or failure. Thus, their behavior is considered to have causes, which liberally interpreted means where they assign the credit or blame for their performance. In athletics, four elements have traditionally been cited: (1) ability, (2) effort, (3) luck, and (4) task difficulty. Ability and effort are considered as *internal* factors because they reside within the individual (they can be personally controlled), whereas task difficulty and luck are *external* factors (usually not controllable by the individual). Together they form the concept of *locus of causality,* or the degree to which people believe they are in control of their own sporting destinies (see figure 9.4).

As might be expected, athletes generally have a higher internal locus of causality than nonathletes (Robinson and Howe, 1987). Furthermore, they are more likely to attribute any situational failure to insufficient effort rather than to inability (Grove and Pargman, 1986). Sport psychologists have given considerable attention to these causality factors, and yet considerable question remains about how they affect the mind of the athlete during actual competition (Biddle and Jamieson, 1988). There is no question that athletes engage in spontaneous causal thinking, perhaps even considering the consequences of their performance, during the intensity of competition. But the fashion in which these thought processes become meaningful psychological properties during competition remains one of the great mysteries of sport psychology (McAuley and Duncan, 1989).

GO SEE THE MOVIE IN YOUR HEAD

In athletic endeavors, it's often mind over matter. The body can be tricked. It isn't always sure whether it did something or not. If something is vividly imagined, our body may think that it actually happened. So we can sit quietly and think about performing an athletic skill, and thereby actually put a bit of information programming into our nervous system.

It's called *mental practice,* or visual motor behavioral rehearsal, or imagery, all referring to the cognitive rehearsal of a motor performance without necessarily including any actual overt practice. And it works—for gymnasts (Meyers et al., 1979), for basketball players (Hamilton and Fremouw, 1985), for skiers (Suinn, 1972), for tennis players, (Cahill, 1987), for baseball batters (Gough, 1989), even for Frisbee players (Andre and Means, 1986), and seemingly for anyone who wants to improve athletic performance.

But mental practice is not a panacea or a lazy person's way to skill improvement. It appears to be most effective when used in conjunction with physical practice, and it tends to be more effective for experienced performers (Hecker and Kaczor, 1988).

The technique is not highly involved nor particularly difficult to learn. All that's involved is the creation of a strong mental image of successful performance. The more vivid the imagery, the better (Loehr, 1982). For example, mentally rehearsing a golf drive would include visualizing the fairway, focusing on the target, emphasizing the color of the ball resting against the green grass, even smelling the grass, hearing sounds around you, sensing the feel of the club in the hands, then your swing, and the sight of the ball disappearing into perfect flight.

Generally, visualization works best within the following guidelines (Loehr, 1982):

1. Mentally practice using all your senses. Try to develop and sharpen your ability to create vivid images of people, places, and events. The more detailed the imagery is, the more powerful are the effects.
2. Rehearse difficult physical routines or parts of performance that have given you difficulty in the past.

Inquiry

Mental practice can improve performance.
University of Denver file photo.

3. Practice creating and strengthening positive mental images throughout all aspects of your play. Replace failure images with successful ones.

4. Mentally rehearse positive emotional and psychological responses to difficult situations that may arise during competition. Imagine yourself staying calm, confident, and positive.

5. Establish a regular visualization routine to be followed every day. Many short sessions are better than long concentrated sessions.

Visualization does not take the place of physical practice. But physical practice that is accompanied by appropriate mental rehearsal is superior to physical practice alone. Some studies even show that visualization generates neuromuscular activity that matches that required for the overt performance of the skill being mentally practiced (Suinn, 1989).

Once the habit of visualization is acquired, it can be used anywhere and at any time. It is especially valuable just before a performance, when the generation of a strong positive image can greatly influence the execution of the skill. Moreover, visualization can be used to create positive attitudes about performance. Fear of failing, or anxiety about fans, or a feeling of being unequal to the task, or any other psychological barrier can be overcome by positive imagery. When the brain creates, the body listens.

THE TRANSCENDENT MIND

Several common factors are usually associated with the minds of accomplished athletes. They typically show high values of self-esteem (they feel good about themselves) and self-confidence (they believe they can do well) (Cratty, 1981). In competition, they can focus their attention on the demands of the event, often entering into states of mind that are different from the ordinary.

Sport has the potential for generating certain unusual states of mind for participants. In popular terms, they achieve *altered states of consciousness*. These states are different from "normal" states and are usually characterized by extraordinary awareness—a heightened sensitivity of the perceptual powers of the mind. They can be achieved through sport, or through various systems of meditation, biofeedback, stress management, or self-hypnosis.

Public interest in altered states grew dramatically in the 1960s. Such factors as overwhelming technology, fear of a nuclear holocaust, social isolation, and other alienating conditions may have contributed to an increased focus on ways to turn to one's inner self. Or, it could be that these achieved states are simply pleasurable in themselves. In Western societies, sport has been viewed as one of the more potent avenues for attaining such states of mind and may be the only way for the general population to gain heightened consciousness.

Altered states are often said to be transcendent experiences; that is, the person goes beyond, or transcends, normal states of being. In sport, such transcendence is frequently called a "peak experience." When athletes report such experiences, they usually describe them in terms of being at the peak of their power and functioning in an extraordinary state of coordination, as if being guided by a greater presence. They feel psychologically integrated and unified with their environment, and yet detached from the ordinary world (Murphy and White, 1978).

Sport provides opportunities for becoming absorbed. It encourages such dispositions as positive self-attitudes, focused attention, supreme awareness of the present, "letting go," and total involvement. By its very design, it entices states of mind that differ from everyday existence. Not much is known, yet, about these transcendent affairs of the brain. It's still a black box. It's still esoteric. In the meantime, it makes for an absorbing area of study for sport psychology.

SUMMARY

Sport psychologists have made a study of the athletic brain. They have discovered ways to prepare the mind for more effective performance. And they have developed intervention remedies for head cases. In total, they help athletes become better. Overall, their functions are the following (LeUnes and Nation, 1989):

1. Develop performance improvement programs through progressive relaxation, visualization, autogenic training, meditation, and other appropriate means that are designed to gain greater control over the psychological determinants of performance.
2. Use psychological assessment techniques including psychological inventories and measurements to aid in the counseling of athletes.
3. Improve communication between athletes and coaches through the use of tests, group techniques, and individual consultation, and always in an ethical manner.
4. Provide crisis intervention when athletes or coaches may be temporarily unable to function, and refer them to outside sources of help when necessary.
5. Provide consultative and program development for coaches, trainers, and others who work directly with athletes.
6. Function as a therapist or clinical psychologist, but only to the degree that their training permits, beyond which a sport psychologist must recognize when an athlete is in need of a professional clinician or a psychiatrist.

To the Reader

Today the person whose profession is involved with the dynamics of human movement must be both a scientist and a psychologist. The scientist must know how the body moves. The psychologist must know how the brain gives the body its orders.

It's not easy talking to the 1,350 grams that are a brain. It's not easy to deal with minds that are nonconstant, nonhomeostatic, better today or worse tomorrow, and never totally predictable. It's also not easy to be a sport psychologist.

At present all who call themselves sport psychologists have varied backgrounds. Most are physical educators. Few have had any internship or related field experiences. Few have backgrounds in assessment, intervention, and therapy techniques. Most are self-educated.

Responding to this varied preparational background, the United States Olympic Committee has made a series of recommendations for appropriate training in sport psychology. They relate to three broad areas—clinical, educational, and research—which are assumed to be the three most common workplaces. The guidelines are stringent and idealistic, but they may be of some influence in course selection if becoming a sport psychologist is an interest of yours.

To qualify for work in a clinical setting, the USOC has recommended having a degree in clinical psychology or psychiatry; and to work in an educational or research setting, the recommendation is for a degree in psychiatry or a doctorate in psychology. In all cases, the USOC is suggesting that the sport psychologist qualify for acceptance into the American Psychological Association (which has a division of sport psychology). In essence, this means holding a doctoral degree in psychology or a related field, although exception can be granted to "people of distinction in fields other than psychology."

Should these recommendations ever become adopted as a standard for certification as a sport psychologist (there is as yet no "certification"), it will mean persons in the human movement sciences will need to acquire the undergraduate course work in psychology to qualify for an advanced degree in that or a related field.

Suggested Projects

1. Think of a time when your emotional level was perfect for the athletic contest you were in. What created that appropriate state? Were you able to consciously bring yourself to that same harmony again in other competition? Speculate on the origins of such perfect states.
2. Interview a number of coaches at your school. Select a variety of sports ranging from those that require high arousal levels to those that seem to require states of calm for best performance. Ask the coaches what they do to generate the appropriate emotional states for their athletes.

3. Choose a simple task, such as tossing beanbags at a target. Have some volunteers take a given number of trials. On the basis of the results, split the volunteers into two equal performance groups. Have one group practice the task and the other group practice an equal number of trials but also include mental practice sessions. See if this leads to differences in the accuracy of the two groups.

4. Describe situations you have seen wherein the performance of an athlete was not that which might have been expected on the basis of the athlete's skill. Explain what may have caused that athlete to perform either better or worse than expected.

5. Discuss locus of causality. In what sports is it especially important to have an internal locus? Is an external locus ever beneficial? If possible, obtain copies of a test that determines whether someone has an internal or external locus. Administer the test to athletes, especially in a sport where there are offensive and defensive assignments, such as soccer. Discuss the results.

6. Eastern philosophy underlies many of the meditative techniques that are designed to generate altered states of consciousness, and as a result, meditation is widely practiced by the masses in eastern societies. Western societies are not generally experienced in such meditative techniques, and consequently sport has been called "Western Zen," meaning that it may be the only way for the American population to attain altered consciousness. Debate this point.

References

Andre, J. C. and Means, J. R. (1986). Rate of Imagery in Mental Practice: An Experimental Investigation. *Journal of Sport Psychology, 8,* 124–128.

Anshel, M. H., and Wrisberg, C. A. (1988). The Effect of Arousal and Focused Attention on Warm-up Decrement. *Journal of Sport Behavior, 11,* 18–31.

Atkinson, J. W. (1978). The Mainsprings of Achievement-Oriented Activity. In J. W. Atkinson and J. O. Raynor (Eds.), *Personality, Motivation, and Achievement.* Washington: Hemisphere Publishing.

Biddle, S. J. H., and Jamieson, K. I. (1988). Attribution Dimensions: Conceptual Clarification and Moderator Variables. *International Journal of Sport Psychology, 19,* 47–59.

Brooks, G. A., and Fahey, T. D. (1987). *Fundamentals of Human Performance.* New York: Macmillan.

Cahill, P. J. (1987). Mental Training for Tennis. *Athletic Journal, 9,* 16–19.

Caroon, A. V. (1980). *Social Psychology of Sport.* Ithaca, NY: Mouvement Publications.

Cratty, B. J. (1981). *Social Psychology in Athletics.* Englewood Cliffs, NJ: Prentice-Hall.

Cratty, B. J. (1983). *Psychology in Contemporary Sport* (2nd ed.). Englewood Cliffs, NJ: Prentice-Hall.

Gough, D. (1989). Improving Batting Skills with Small-College Baseball Players through Guided Visual Imagery. *The Coaching Clinic, 26,* 1–6.

Grove, J. R., and Pargman, D. (1986). Attributions and Performance during Competition. *Journal of Sport Psychology, 8,* 129–134.

Hamilton, S. A., and Fremouw, W. J. (1985). Cognitive-Behavioral Training for College Basketball Free-Throw Performance. *Cognitive Therapy and Research, 9,* 479–483.

Hecker, J. E., and Kaczor, L. M. (1988). Application of Imagery Theory to Sport Psychology: Some Preliminary Findings. *Journal of Sport and Exercise Psychology, 10,* 363–373.

Jacobson, E. (1938). *Progressive Relaxation.* Chicago: University of Chicago Press.

Kerr, J. (1987). Structural Phenomenology, Arousal, and Performance. *Journal of Human Movement Studies, 13,* 211–229.

LeUnes, A. D., and Hayward, S. A. (1988). Annotated Bibliography on the Profile of Mood States in Sport, 1975–1988. *Journal of Sport Behavior, 11,* 213–239.

LeUnes, A. D., and Nation, J. R. (1989). *Sport Psychology: An Introduction.* Chicago: Nelson-Hall.

Loehr, J. E. (1982). *Athletic Excellence: Mental Toughness for Sports.* Denver: Forum Publishing.

McAuley, E., and Duncan, T. E. (1989). Causal Attributions and Affective Reactions to Disconfirming Outcomes in Motor Performance. *Journal of Sport and Exercise Psychology, 11,* 187–200.

Meyers, A. W., Schleser, R., Cook, C., and Cuvillier, C. (1979). Cognitive Contributions to the Development of Gymnastic Skills. *Cognitive Therapy and Research, 3,* 75–85.

Murphy, M., and White, R. A. (1978). *The Psychic Side of Sports.* Reading, MA: Addison-Wesley.

Poole, R. C. (1988). Peak Performance Is Synonymous with Stress Management. *The Coaching Clinic, 25,* 1–6.

Rainey, D. W., and Cunningham, H. (1988). Competitive Trait Anxiety in Male and Female College Athletes. *Research Quarterly for Exercise and Sport, 59*(3), 244–247.

Robinson, D. W., and Howe, B. L. (1987). Causal Attribution and Mood State Relationships of Soccer Players in a Sport Achievement Setting. *Journal of Sport Behavior, 10,* 137–146.

Steigleder, M. K., Weiss, R. F., Cramer, R. E., and Feinberg, R. A. (1978). The Motivating and Reinforcing Functions of Competitive Behavior. *Journal of Personality and Social Psychology, 36,* 1291–1301.

Suinn, R. M. (1972). Behavioral Research for Ski Racers. *Behavioral Therapy, 3,* 519–520.

Suinn, R. M. (1989). Models from Behavioral Clinical Psychology for Sport Psychology. In J. S. Skinner, C. B. Corbin, D. M. Landers, P. E. Martin, and C. L. Wells (Eds.), *Future Directions in Exercise and Sport Science Research*. Champaign, IL: Human Kinetics Books.

Tresmer, D. (1976). The Cumulative Record of Research on "Fear of Success." *Sex Roles, 2,* 217–236.

Vander, A. J., Sherman, J. H., and Luciano, D. S. (1985). *Human Physiology: The Mechanisms of Body Function* (4th ed.). New York: McGraw-Hill.

Chapter 10

Sports Medicine: Keeping Active People Active

A Synthesis of Many Fields

Preparation of the Human Machinery

What the Outside Can Do to the Inside

The Critical Role of the Athletic Trainer

Duties of the Trainer

The Realm of Physical Therapy

Other Therapeutic Modalities

Summary

To the Reader

Suggested Projects

References

In any athletic, sporting, or recreational pursuit, there is an inherent potential for injury from the activity.

The rehabilitation of persons injured in sport has become a scientific enterprise of treating a wide variety of neuromuscular and musculoskeletal dysfunctions.

Relatedly, proper conditioning programs and knowledgeable supervision can reduce the potential for initial injury or for further aggravation of an incurred injury.

An encompassing collection of disciplines has combined to arrive at better techniques of preparing people for competition and of attending to injuries sustained in sport events.

THE American Indians, who knew and know of life, have always granted an honored position to individuals who are considered to have exceptional abilities for dealing with spirits. These individuals have served long apprenticeships and memorized the details of ritual that allow them to summon spiritual aid for the benefit of others. They are always prestigious individuals, usually exceptionally intelligent, and have strong, persuasive personalities. They hold a dignified place in the tribe, and their sacred office carries with it the value and reliability of their powers. They are the medicine men.

Among all tribes, the medicine man (or woman) serves as a physician, and some even have specialties such as curing specific diseases, broken bones, or wounds. Always their powers are used to restore, promote, and preserve the health and welfare of their tribe. They practice medicine—not in the technical sense of the word, but in respect to what their knowledge and energies are used for and what the results are.

In athletic settings, a collection of individuals holds a similar position. Their objective is likewise to use their energies, experience, and knowledge to benefit the physical and psychic welfare of their community. A broad term, *sports medicine,* describes this encompassing enterprise. It, too, has some definitional liberty. It does not really mean "medicine" in the dictionary sense. But the work of this endeavor has the same positive effect of human betterment.

A SYNTHESIS OF MANY FIELDS

In truth, sports medicine originated as an interest area among licensed doctors. Their attention was given to the medical aspects of sports participation, particularly the diagnosis and remediation of injuries. But today the term *sports medicine* has slipped those bounds and now includes at least the following: (1) athletic medicine, (2) biomechanics, (3) clinical medicine, (4) growth and development, (5) psychology and sociology, (6) nutrition, (7) motor control, and (8) physiology (Fox, Bowers, and Foss, 1988).

The scientific roots exist in physiology, which branches into exercise physiology and medical physiology, which then combines with other allied sciences to provide the arena of sports medicine. It could be viewed as in figure 10.1 (Morris, 1985).

Medicine, regardless of the qualifying objectives that are used to describe its domain, always infers a science that is concerned with the restoration and preservation of health. Thus, sports medicine defines its area of interest to be humans in sporting activities. Like any physician, the

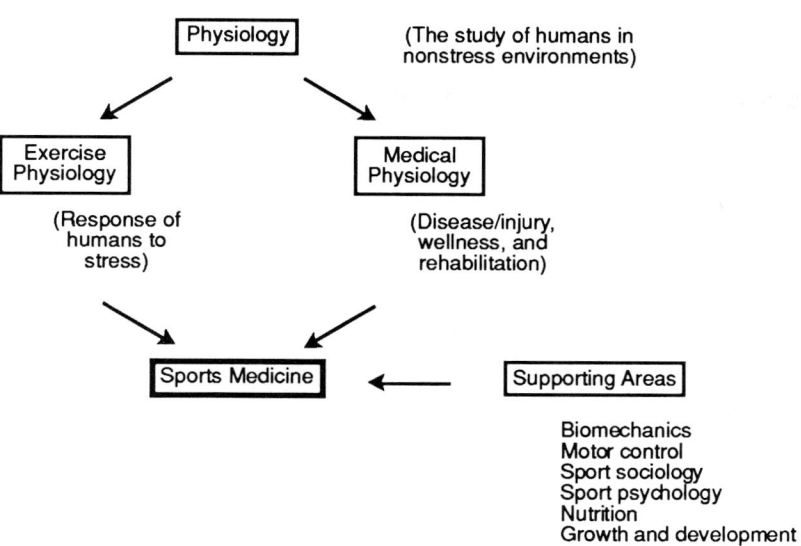

Figure 10.1 The arena of sports medicine.

individuals in sports medicine treat the "patients" with highly refined diagnostic and prescriptive skills that focus on exercise science. It draws a professional reservoir from physicians, educators, athletic trainers, therapists, biological scientists, and behavioral scientists (Morris, 1985). All combine for a broad understanding of how human beings work in their complex ways when participating in activities of a sportlike nature, whether it be for leisure or in preparation for an Olympic team.

PREPARATION OF THE HUMAN MACHINERY

The umbrella of sports medicine is large. But in its short history it has attended basically to two fundamental interests: (1) how to best prepare athletes for high-level competition and (2) how to rehabilitate those who are injured. A scenario emerges: Prepare them better, and they will be injured less.

The physical preparation of the athlete has been a long interest of exercise physiology. The contribution of the research from this field to the literature of sports medicine has been substantial. It is especially

Inquiry

The goal of sports medicine is to prepare athletes better so that injuries are fewer.
Photo by Tom Cherrey.

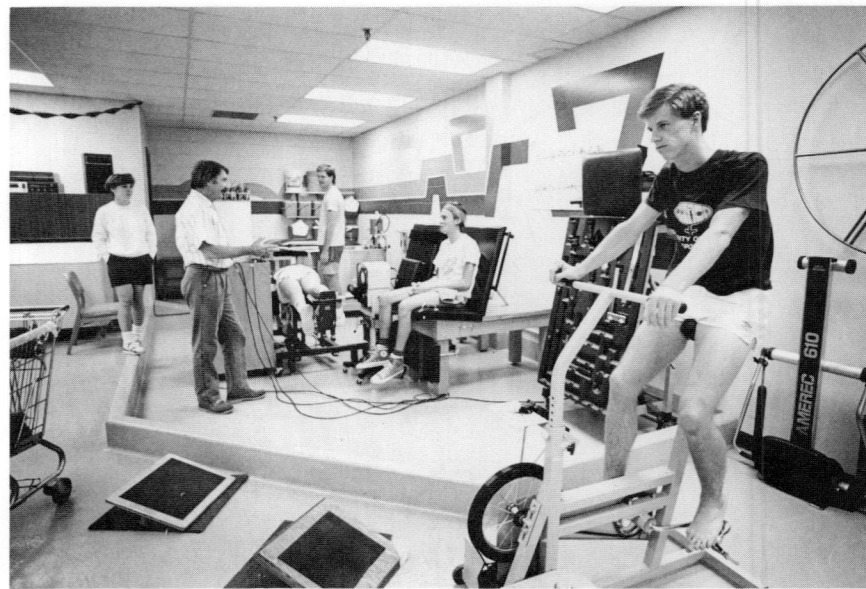

plentiful regarding the training of athletes. But several basic principles have continued to surface, briefly summarized below.

1. First is the *overload principle,* which states that strength and endurance will increase only when muscles are asked to do more than their normal daily routines. The greater the resistance that is offered (through heavier weights or exercises of longer duration), the more adaptations will take place. More precisely, a given threshold point must be exceeded before an adaptive response will occur. For example, the threshold for strength gains has been shown to be 40 percent of the maximum exertion a given muscle is capable of (McArdle, Katch, and Katch, 1986). And, since the maximum will increase as a result of training, so too will the threshold level. Thus, the application of the overload principle is now often called *progressive resistance exercise,* meaning that to sustain improvements in the size or functional capacity of muscles, they must be given increasingly more difficult loads of training intensity, duration, or weight resistance.

2. Exercise programs must also match the mode of training to the desired end effect. This is the principle of *specificity,* which declares that all training programs must be specific to developing the energy

systems used during the actual performance of the event for which the athlete is training. Exercise is selective in the kind of change it induces. If an athlete is undergoing a training regime intended to promote the endurance capacity of muscles, then in general only this capacity and not others will show improvement (Sale and MacDougall, 1981). In fact, for endurance events, training the systems of oxygen delivery and utilization is so important that it can allow athletes to be successful even if they neglect the training of all other energy systems (Noble, 1986).

3. The *reversibility principle* pronounces that the effects of training are transient. Any gains in the functional and structural status of muscles are dependent on continued use of the overload and specificity principles. If the training does not continue to increase in intensity, no gains will be observed. There are diminishing returns with time, and eventually the threshold levels for overload will be the same as maximum capabilities, and no further adaptations can occur. Then, training will have the effect of only maintaining the acquired high levels of performance capacity.

Surprisingly, in spite of the wealth of information that has accumulated, some common questions remain in limbo. A prominent one is how to develop power. Whereas raw muscular strength is highly susceptible to training, power does not seem to be (Berger, 1982). Strength training emphasizes the force component of movement, and not the acceleration component. Apparently, power has a high genetic base. It does appear that repeated maximal contractions of a muscle can magnify its capacity for power and decrease the chemical effects of fatigue, but the gains are minimal compared to those that can be attained in raw strength and endurance. The most important factor seems to be one's heredity (Noble, 1986).

WHAT THE OUTSIDE CAN DO TO THE INSIDE

Between 1959 and 1962 twelve football players in the United States died from heatstroke. In all cases, temperature, or the humidity, or both were high. Most of the deaths occurred in the first two days of practice, and all could have been prevented (Fox et al., 1966). By 1983 another fifty-eight football players had died as a direct result of excessive heat stress during practice or competition (McArdle, Katch, and Katch, 1986). This alarming trend catalyzed a concentration of investigations about how environmental stress can be a life-threatening consideration. It became a focused study area for sports medicine. Three of the more emphatic considerations are discussed below.

1. *Heat stress.* During exercise, the heat production of the body is considerable. Increased temperature can be self-perpetuating and dangerous.

   The best way to lose heat is from the evaporation of perspiration. But excessive sweating can deplete the muscles of electrolyte sodium chloride, causing *heat cramps,* especially in the abdomen and legs. Normal salting of food, however, appears to be a preventative (Hamilton, Whitney, and Sizer, 1988).

   Sometimes the body has shunted so much of its blood to the surface of the skin in an effort to get rid of internal heat that the flow to the brain begins to decrease. In response the brain sends itself into a form of shock called *heat exhaustion.* Still, the body's heat-loss mechanism of perspiration remains functional. It's when this stops that the situation becomes critical.

   When the core temperature of the body gets to 105° F the regulatory mechanism of perspiration may stop. Without this source for losing heat, the body temperature will continue to rise rapidly, in minutes, to exceed 115° F and result in death. It's called heatstroke, formerly sunstroke, and now more accurately *hyperthermia.* When it happens, the victim must have a substitute for the lost heat-dissipating mechanism. Douse the victim with the coolest water available. Fan the victim so the water evaporates. Or dump the person in a cool bath. Anything to resupply the external coolant mechanism. And right away. Hyperthermia is a true medical emergency.

2. *Cold stress.* Dampness and wind are the most devastating factors to be considered in cold stress—even more so than temperature. It is possible to die of *hypothermia* in temperatures far above freezing. In fact, most hypothermia deaths occur in the 30° to 50° range (Wilkerson, 1985).

   Until recently, hypothermia was a factor in sports and recreation only when survival was at stake following mishaps in activities such as skiing, climbing, or camping. However, with the increase in joggers, bicyclers, and other endurance weekenders, the potential for hypothermia has magnified. Most at risk are the unconditioned. The body tries to preserve its core temperature by vasoconstriction of the peripheral vessels, thus decreasing the flow of blood to the surface. But the core temperature can drop in spite of this response. It usually happens when an individual has concluded a workout, or even a walk, and rests in a damp, windy environment. If the heat loss continues, the core temperature can fall below 98°, and when it gets to

95°, the victim may not be able to respond to any common sense thought of self-treatment. When it happens on the athletic field, or otherwise near a warm bath, the treatment is to immerse the victim. If it happens in the backwoods during a camping outing, everyone with a sleeping bag knows what to do.

3. *Altitude.* An understanding of altitude physiology became important because of the many athletic contests held at moderate altitude, particularly starting with the 1968 Olympics at six-thousand-foot Mexico City, along with the tremendous increase in the popularity of mountain sports.

Exercise at high altitude is stressful because there is less oxygen pressure. Diffusion from the alveoli to the pulmonary capillary blood is decreased, with a consequent drop in the oxygen saturation of the blood. The most common and least severe manifestation is *acute mountain sickness,* where someone not accustomed to exercise or even living at high altitude will experience headache, nausea, vomiting, shortness of breath, and sleep disturbance. Extra fluids and a high carbohydrate diet seem to help (Auerbach, 1986).

More serious is *high altitude pulmonary edema.* It usually occurs above eight thousand feet, and mostly at night. The most sudden symptom is an absolute inability to breathe for about fifteen seconds, with repeated attacks of this inability. It's a sign that fluid is filling the alveoli and will eventually render them unable to diffuse oxygen at a normal rate. It can be fatal, and the only remedy is to descend at least one thousand feet.

THE CRITICAL ROLE OF THE ATHLETIC TRAINER

Approximately six million students compete in high school athletics today (Culpepper, 1986). Every year, at least one of every eight will sustain an injury that results in a loss of participation time (Weidner, 1989). And there are an average of thirty-four paralyzing injuries or fatalities annually that are directly related to interscholastic sports (Powell, 1987).

In football alone, 37 percent of all players are sidelined at least once every season. Football players comprise 18 percent of the interscholastic sports participants but have more than half of the injuries. And yet fewer than 10 percent of the nation's 15,500 schools that have football programs have a certified athletic trainer (Powell, 1987).

Overall, less than 20 percent of the high schools in America employ an athletic trainer (Weidner, 1989). Some high schools will have a physician in attendance during games, but more than 65 percent of all injuries occur in practice (Kulund, 1982). Furthermore, the frequency of injuries is nearly twice as high in schools that do not have an athletic trainer (Rankin, 1989). And most revealing of all, the average reinjury rate at high schools that have an athletic trainer is only 3 percent, whereas at schools that do not have a trainer, the average reinjury rate is an alarming 71 percent (Legwold, 1983).

Because of this dramatic injury and reinjury rate at schools that do not have an athletic trainer, the role of the coach as a provider of health care is to be seriously questioned. The majority of coaches (possibly as high as 70 percent) have not even completed a basic course in first aid (Weidner, 1989). So the coach often lacks the background knowledge of emergency first aid, cardiopulmonary resuscitation, or transport procedures. Moreover, the coach is placed in a conflict of interest situation in deciding when an injured athlete should return to competition. Thus, negligence can become an issue. Recent court decisions have increased the vulnerability of school districts to liability lawsuits from sports injuries and are holding coaches at a higher level of accountability. Multimillion-dollar lawsuits are now common (Weidner, 1989). School districts are keenly aware of this assailable position and know that employing an athletic trainer reduces the risk from legal liability. Yet they continue to base their decision mostly on whether the district can afford the salary (Ray, 1987).

DUTIES OF THE TRAINER

It's a busy place, the training room. Athletes taping for practice, pulled muscles getting heat treatment, a postoperative knee is getting rehabilitation, someone from a physical education class is getting attention for a poke in the eye, or an overweight English teacher is asking what to do for tennis elbow. The athletic trainer seems to be charged with the prevention and treatment of injuries for the whole school community.

The trainer is the link between the team physician and the coach, or the athlete and the coach. But like the quizzical interloper who wants free advice from a lawyer friend, the open door of the training room invites anyone else in the school to seek the aid within. Administratively, the trainer is responsible to the athletic director, but medically, to the team physician. The trainer carries out the team physician's instructions. However, most of the time the trainer operates independently, setting up and directing conditioning or rehabilitation programs for flexibility, strength, and endurance. The trainer also makes determinations about when an athlete should be held out of or returned to competition. The trainer also fits and checks protective equipment, advises coaches regarding the safety of their practice procedures, and may even be a health counselor for athletes. The day is long.

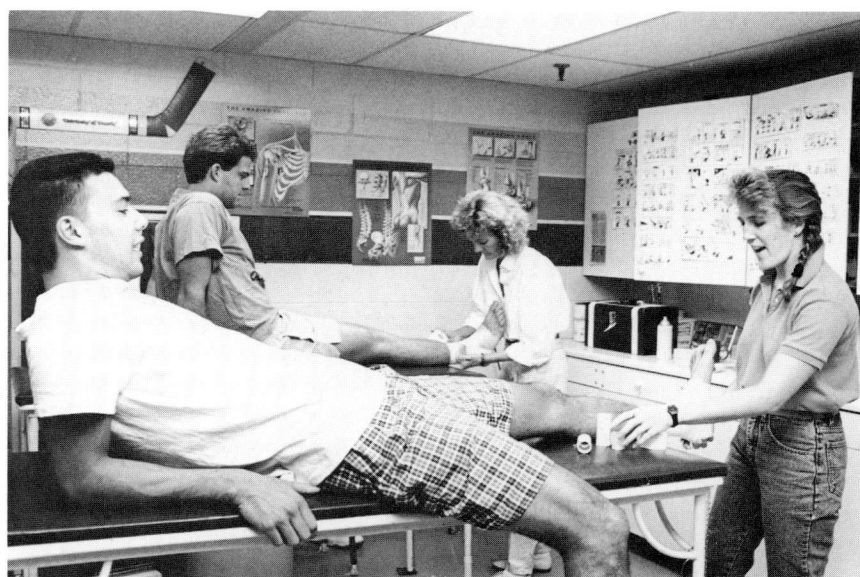

The training room is a busy place.
Photo by Tom Cherrey.

In spite of the hassled time that is asked of the trainer, well over 90 percent of those in the profession say they find it a highly rewarding and fulfilling job (Gieck, Lephart, and Saliba, 1986). And the "burnout" rate (a time in life when one's job is no longer interesting) is very low in athletic training compared to other professions (Capel, 1986). Apparently, trainers enjoy the busy world of their profession.

THE REALM OF PHYSICAL THERAPY

One gets a new respect for such a simple after-dinner performance as taking one's body out for a walk when one can't. Maybe a crunching tackle tore a medial meniscus. Or a landing after a rebound ripped the anterior talofibular ligament. Or a curve ball pulled the humeral head out of the glenoid. A physical therapist may be able to help relieve pain, restore function, prevent further injury, and return one to action as soon as possible.

As a profession, physical therapy was born in 1918 with the establishment of reconstruction aids in the United States Army who helped rehabilitate soldiers injured in the First World War. Since then there has been an incredible growth in the body of knowledge, the scope of the practice, the techniques of treatment, and most recently, the availability of jobs.

Opportunities for physical therapists have expanded dramatically in recent years.
Photo by Tom Cherrey.

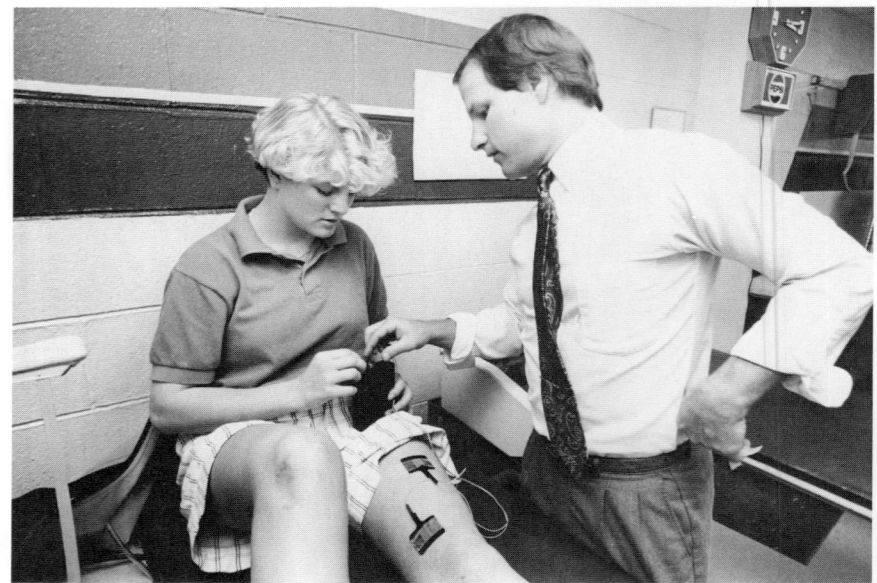

In the general picture, physical therapists are involved in the treatment of abnormalities of the muscular, skeletal, and nervous systems. Persons who are disabled as a result of pain, disease, injury, or developmental deferments are evaluated by the therapist, who then plans and administers an appropriate therapeutic program. Individualized programs may include (1) the use of physical agents such as heat, cold, massage, ultrasound, or electrical stimulation; (2) therapeutic exercises, especially to reinstate or improve strength, endurance, and range of motion; (3) patient and family education; (4) ambulation training; and (5) activities for daily living.

The physical therapist is legally and ethically responsible for planning, implementing, and evaluating programs of care for patients of all ages who are disabled from illness or injury, or were born with a handicap. Physical therapists perform tests and evaluation on the functional abilities of patients and work closely with physicians or other health practitioners to establish treatment objectives that are realistic and consistent with the patient's needs. This may include the need and use of braces or artificial limbs.

Sometimes a therapist will not be able to restore full functionality, either because no known technique will do so or because the condition occasioned by the malfunction is permanently debilitating (as is especially true with injuries to the central nervous system). In other cases, such as postoperatives or athletic injuries, the therapist concludes a total restitution of full muscular capacity.

The area of professional employment for therapists has expanded remarkably. In 1950, about 80 percent of all physical therapists worked in hospital settings. But today, they also work in doctors' offices, the patients' homes, health clubs, child development centers, nursing homes, research centers, clinics, athletic team training rooms, or in special facilities staffed entirely by therapists to whom patients are referred by doctors. The biggest increase has been in private practice, with projections that this setting will become even more prevalent in the future (Magistro, 1989).

OTHER THERAPEUTIC MODALITIES

Physical therapists are generally concerned with improving or restoring normal function of all the movement patterns of everyday living. Focus is usually placed on the actions of the larger muscle groups, the trunk, and the limbs. Another branch of the health professions, occupational therapy, concentrates on improving or restoring motor functions that are integral parts of basic vocational skills. The occupational therapist is more "task oriented" than the physical therapist, who is more "movement oriented." The occupational therapist sees movement as a means toward an end, with the final objective being to make the patient a more productive citizen and fully functioning self-reliant worker in their chosen trade. Thus, the occupational therapist does not usually employ the various mechanical devices familiar to the physical therapist, but may instead survey the needed motor skills of the patient's profession and then design tasks that match those required on the job.

One of the newer helping professions is recreational therapy. In general, the recreational therapist is likely to work with a wider range of individuals and in a wider range of settings, varying from a school for the mentally retarded where the attempt is to improve the students' self-concepts to a home for the aged where the objective is to slow the onset of senility. As the name suggests, recreational therapists use "recreation" as the tool, with movement programs planned to improve the personal and social attributes of individuals.

The recreational therapist may also work with a dance therapist, whose role is to use rhythm and total body movement to improve the same personal qualities. The results are often dramatic, especially in the case of individuals who have been hospitalized for mental dysfunction.

SUMMARY

America's infatuation with sports, which has produced a nation of spectators, is now taking the direction of producing active participants. An outcome of this has been an inordinate increase in the number of sport- and fitness-related injuries. The drastic rise in these disablements can usually be attributed to improper training techniques, poor levels of physical conditioning, or ignorance of the physical complexities of the activity (Scully and Barnes, 1989).

Often, the injuries are out of the realm of the everyday practices of the family physician. Moreover, many require extensive rehabilitation, which the general practitioner may not be equipped to handle. And so there has emerged a need for specially trained persons to attend to the injuries that are common to sporting pursuits.

In the most specific sense of sports medicine, three groups of physician specialists are involved: doctors of medicine, doctors of osteopathy, and doctors of chiropractic. Team physicians usually have a general practice, but there is a trend toward involving physicians with specialized training as orthopedists. They use a wide range of techniques to treat injuries and abnormalities of the skeletal and muscular systems. Doctors of osteopathy, like orthopedists, attend to the muscular-skeletal system and in addition offer manipulative treatment of the injury. Chiropractors do not use drugs or surgery, but use manipulation techniques, massage, ultrasound, and various temperature-controlled therapy modalities.

The generalist of sports medicine practitioners remains the athletic trainer, whose duties are more varied than any other. The more specialized individual is the physical therapist, who focuses on the rehabilitation of injuries.

Although sports medicine may seem to be an after-the-fact enterprise, being needed only after an injury, there is a preventative side to the field. One aspect of this prevention is in fact following an injury, where the intent is to restore function so that the potential for reinjury is minimized. Of equal importance, however, is the physiological investigation of new approaches to training techniques that not only reduce injury potentials but also optimize performance. Thus, the field encompasses an interrelated mix of disciplines, including exercise physiology as the principal contributor.

This preventative side of the field is becoming more apparent as society turns toward wellness applications of knowledge. As more and more Americans become aware of the health benefits of an active life-style, the need for public advice becomes more critical. And it further embodies sports medicine with the responsibility of seeking answers to such questions as how much exercise is optimal, how much is needed for minimum benefits, and which exercise habits are potentially harmful. The benefactors of this are everyone.

To the Reader

Plenty of jobs are connected with sports medicine. Every injury of any magnitude needs someone to attend to that injury. Obtain certification as a physical therapist, and you are a person in demand. Similar opportunities exist in athletic training.

But to become a person of sports medicine involves more than just having an interest in athletics. An athletic trainer, for instance, is not really in sport, but is a healer of others who are. The physical education teacher and the coach, having initiated their interest in sport as a participant, can still be a partial or at least a vicarious participant through their chosen roles. But the athletic trainer must effectively be removed from the melodrama, essentially waiting to be needed.

Furthermore, there's more to the craft than elastic tape and zinc oxide. The trainer must be somewhat of a psychologist, knowing who truly needs assistance and who is merely role-playing. The trainer must have the discretion to know when an athlete's desire to return to competition has superceded that athlete's readiness to do so. And a forthright relationship with coaches, who may want their athletes on the field even when hurt, is mandatory.

What does it take to become an athletic trainer? Sensitivity and a generally positive attitude toward other people are qualities that sustain professional athletic trainers as much as their technical skill (Deckard and Present, 1989). But it also takes time, and lots of it. The National Athletic Trainers Association, which is the national body that certifies trainers, has mandated curriculum requirements and an eight-hundred-hour clinical internship during which the student must intern in the athletic training room. Consequently, if you have interest in this profession, to seek early advice about the proper academic and internship paths to take is important.

If physical therapy is of intrigue, that can wait. You need the proper qualifying course work, but certification as a physical therapist is basically a postgraduate degree, generally encompassing two years of preparation after the bachelor's degree.

Suggested Projects

1. Find statistics on the incidence of injury in a given sport. Talk to a coach of that sport to compare his or her experience. Inquire what training schemes the coach uses to reduce the potential for such injuries.

2. Spend some time in the training room, especially in the late afternoon. Talk to the trainer and the student trainers, if there are any, about their day. Observe the routines that comprise the regular activities, and make note of the skills that are needed for this profession.
3. Locate a physical therapist. Try in particular to find someone working in private practice. Visit the site. Talk about the job, the marketplace, and the specialized education needed for certification.
4. Assume that you are the leader of a group of youths who are about to take a camping trip for a week in a cold or hot environment, or at high altitude. Make a list of the environmental injuries that could occur and the immediate treatment for each injury.
5. Recently, there has been considerable concern about injuries that are occurring in health clubs and fitness centers, particularly from aerobics classes. Often these injuries are sustained from exercise routines that were once accepted as standard but are now recognized as hazardous. Find out which routines have been discarded and what the more acceptable practices are today. Books on wellness are sources of information, as are professional journals and perhaps the health club itself.

References

Auerbach, P. S. (1986). *Medicine for the Outdoors: A Guide to Emergency Medical Procedures and First Aid.* Boston: Little, Brown.

Berger, R. A. (1982). *Applied Exercise Physiology.* Philadelphia: Lea & Febiger.

Capel, S. A. (1986). Psychological and Organizational Factors Related to Burnout in Athletic Trainers. *Research Quarterly for Exercise and Sports, 57,* 321–328.

Culpepper, M. (1986, May/June). More Health Care Needed for High School Athletes. *Athleticare,* pp. 1–3.

Deckard, G. J., and Present, R. M. (1989). Impact of Role Stress on Physical Therapists' Emotional and Physical Well-Being. *Physical Therapy, 69,* 713–718.

Fox, E. L., Bowers, R. W., and Foss, M. L. (1988). *The Physiological Basis of Physical Education and Athletics.* Philadelphia: Saunders College Publishing.

Fox, E. L., Mathews, D., Kaufman, W., and Bowers, R. (1966). Effects of Football Equipment on Thermal Balance and Energy Cost during Exercise. *Research Quarterly, 37,* 322–339.

Gieck, J., Lephart, S., and Saliba, E. (1986). NATA Certification: A 5 & 10 Year Follow-up. *Athletic Training, 21,* 120–121ff.

Hamilton, E. M. N., Whitney, E. N., and Sizer, F. S. (1988). *Nutrition: Concepts and Controversies* (4th ed.). St. Paul, MN: West Publishing.

Kuland, D. N. (1982). *The Injured Athlete.* Philadelphia: J. B. Lippincott.

Legwold, G. (1983). Injury Rates Lowered by High School Trainers. *The Physician and Sportsmedicine, 11*(11), 35–36.

Magistro, C. M. (1989). Clinical Decision Making in Physical Therapy: A Practitioner's Perspective. *Physical Therapy, 69,* 525–534.

McArdle, W. D., Katch, F. I., and Katch, V. L. (1986). *Exercise Physiology: Energy, Nutrition, and Human Performance* (2nd ed.). Philadelphia: Lea & Febiger.

Morris, A. F. (1985). *Sports Medicine Handbook: A Guide to the Prevention and Treatment of Athletic Injuries.* Dubuque, IA: Wm. C. Brown.

Noble, B. J. (1986). *Physiology of Exercise and Sport.* St. Louis: Times Mirror/Mosby College Publishing.

Powell, J. (1987). 636,000 Injuries Annually in High School Football. *Athletic Training, 22,* 19–22.

Rankin, J. (1989). Athletic Trainer Education: New Directions. *Journal of Physical Education, Recreation, and Dance, 60*(6), 68–72.

Ray, R. (1987). A Survey of Michigan School Superintendents' Knowledge of and Attitudes toward Athletic Injuries, Athletic Trainers, and Legal Liability. *Athletic Training, 22,* 311–315.

Sale, D. G., and MacDougall, J. D. (1981). Specificity in Strength Training: A Review for the Coach and Athlete. *Canadian Journal of Applied Sport Sciences, 22,* 87–92.

Scully, R. M., and Barnes, M. R. (1989). *Physical Therapy.* Hagerstown, MD: J. B. Lippincott.

Weidner, T. G. (1989). Injuries: Are Coaches Prepared? *Journal of Physical Education, Recreation, and Dance, 60*(2), 82–84.

Wilkerson, J. A. (1985). *Medicine for Mountaineering* (3rd ed.). Seattle, WA: The Mountaineers.

Part III

Applications

Chapter 11	**Teaching: Art and Science Together**
Chapter 12	**Coaching: Seasonal Challenges, Lifetime Rewards**
Chapter 13	**Special Populations: Considerations for the Handicapped**
Chapter 14	**Careers: Jobs Worth Doing**
Chapter 15	**Career Development: Getting Ready for the Real World**
Chapter 16	**The Future: Not Exactly Like the Present**

Applications

Chapter 11

Teaching: Art and Science Together

Components of the Job

A Managerial Manifesto

Profile of an Effective Teacher

A Matter of Method

Why Teach?

The Matter of Money

The State of the Market

Summary

To the Reader

Suggested Projects

References

Long recognized as an art, teaching has now become also a schematic approach to the method and management of the educational process.

It is now understood that certain performance characteristics will predispose one to success in the profession.

But when choosing a career, certain factors continue to be pressing issues in the decision-making process, in particular the salary structure and the availability of jobs.

Yet teaching remains in prominent position as a viable career choice and a contributor to the welfare of society.

Applications

TECHNOLOGY is everywhere. Microchips have changed the way we study data, communicate, travel, become entertained, balance our bank account, or select a running shoe. Everything has mathematical accessibility. It would seem that computers will eventually propel all things along a deterministic path, rule-bound like the planets, predictable like eclipses and tides. Science might reckon the future with absolute laws that will control its destiny.

But what will always remain are the lessons of giving direction to this burgeoning cybernation, and of keeping technology in some sort of moral order. Science does not automatically supply good sense and reason. Technology cannot, by itself, provide ethics.

There still exists, and always will, an important place for visionary people to give critical perspective to the technical world. Science will not run without human aid and will not advance without social scrutiny. Nor will science replace the profound meanings of life that are found in the world of living experience. So now more than ever before, teachers, not machines, will arrange for the experiences that will provide people with enlightenment in ways that technology cannot. Teachers will, perhaps better than anyone else, give people completeness of life. And physical education teachers will offer equilibrium to an otherwise data-processed existence.

COMPONENTS OF THE JOB

Physical education is a process that enriches the senses of people through learning experiences that forge the body, the mind, and the psyche. When properly administered, the provisions are lifelong aptitudes that sustain a sense of balance to the consciousness and a regard for one's own welfare. The consequences are life-giving.

But theory and practice are sometimes divided. The actual job of the physical education teacher includes an entangled array of divergent affairs that often have no relationship to the act of teaching. For example, if one were to observe a teacher for a few days, the teacher might be seen performing most or all of the following tasks:

1. Explaining a skill
2. Demonstrating a skill
3. Patrolling a hall
4. Handing out tickets
5. Taking attendance
6. Counseling or guiding
7. Collecting money
8. Disciplining

Teachers can enhance the lives of others.
Photograph courtesy of Camp Mishawaka, Grand Rapids, Minnesota.

9. Evaluating performance
10. Filling out reports
11. Talking with parents
12. Repairing equipment
13. Attending meetings
14. Arranging transportation
15. Making up tests
16. Planning lessons
17. Mediating an argument
18. Correcting tests
19. Distributing equipment
20. Collecting equipment
21. Unjamming a locker
22. Spotting for a performer
23. Explaining rules
24. Asking questions
25. Talking with teachers
26. Monitoring a study hall
27. Writing permission slips
28. Refereeing a scrimmage
29. Determining grades
30. Talking with students

A complete list might include a considerable number of other activities. Each of them might be necessary to perform the job of teaching, yet only a few are the actual acts of teaching. Consequently, the activities of teachers might be grouped into (1) instructional acts, which are those directly related to teaching, (2) managerial acts, or those related to administering a class, and (3) institutional acts, or those necessary for holding a position in an educational setting. And so, the preceding hypothetical list of teacher activities could be categorized as follows:

Instructional Acts

1. Explaining a skill
2. Demonstrating a skill
3. Evaluating a performance
4. Explaining rules
5. Asking questions

Managerial Acts

1. Taking attendance
2. Disciplining
3. Repairing equipment
4. Arranging transportation
5. Making up tests
6. Planning lessons
7. Mediating an argument
8. Correcting tests
9. Distributing equipment
10. Collecting equipment
11. Unjamming a locker
12. Spotting for a performer
13. Refereeing a scrimmage

Institutional Acts

1. Patrolling a hall
2. Handing out tickets
3. Counseling or guiding
4. Collecting money
5. Filling out reports
6. Talking with parents
7. Attending meetings
8. Talking with teachers
9. Monitoring a study hall
10. Writing permission slips
11. Determining grades
12. Talking with students

There is obviously more to the job of the teacher than the actual act of teaching. In fact, observations of teachers in all fields show that the average work day consists of a greater proportion of time given to managerial affairs than to events that can formally be defined as instructional (Altenbaugh, 1989). It is not surprising, therefore, to find that some research indicates managerial effectiveness more than instructional competence to be determinative of how long someone remains in the teaching profession (Cardinell, 1980).

A MANAGERIAL MANIFESTO

Class management is now regarded as not only central to the task of teaching but critically supportive of its effectiveness (Doyle, 1984). Physical education management covers a wide range of activities (roll call, enforcing safety rules, grouping students for an activity, gaining their attention, and so forth) that are not instructional acts but may affect the amount of time given to instruction. Because of the nature of the setting, physical education teachers spend a greater percentage of time on management affairs than teachers in other subject areas (Rink, 1985). It varies considerably, but in general at the elementary level about 25 percent of total class time is management, and in high school the proportion is about 22 percent (Luke, 1989).

Furthermore, research has used a wide variety of observational procedures and recording forms to reveal that the actual time students are actively engaged in learning experiences is often dismally small, perhaps averaging less than 10 percent in elementary classes and only 5 percent in high school (Metzler, 1985). There is considerable variation depending on the activity, but what is quite apparent is that overall the learning time in physical education is appallingly low compared to average learning time in classrooms (Lee and Poto, 1988).

It's a hazardous judgment, however, for most of the observations have noted only the time that a student is actively engaged in learning. That's rather like counting only the time the ball is alive in a football game.

A substantial amount of a physical educator's time is spent in class management.
© James L. Shaffer

Learning includes not only overt acts of rehearsing a skill but also cognitions. Acquiring a golf swing, for example, incorporates plenty of mental thought about the mechanics of the action. Such covert, cerebral engagements may average more than 12 percent of high school classes and over 20 percent of elementary classes (Paré et al., 1987).

Probably the most obtrusive of managerial acts is the need to respond to disruptive students. Evidence suggests that discipline problems are a major source of frustration among teachers (Charles, 1985), the one factor that detracts more than any other from instructional effectiveness (Sirotnik, 1982), a major reason why teachers leave the profession (Chapman and Lowther, 1982), a great concern among parents of students (Gallup, 1982) and the general public (Perry and Taylor, 1982), and that the whole matter of discipline is getting worse (Hutslar, 1986).

For students preparing to teach physical education, discipline is consistently ranked as the primary apprehension (Kirsch and McBride, 1987) and continues to be a repressive factor once on the job (Templin, 1989). Since every event is unique, it's a difficult aptitude to rehearse. No comprehensive theory of discipline management now exists. Ability to handle problems appears to accrue only from being in the workplace and discovering what does and does not achieve the desired results (Gallahue, 1985). However, one factor stands clear: Those teachers who have the lowest incidence of disruptive encounters are those who are effective behavioral managers (excellent review in Doyle, 1985). They have put their house in order. By judicious class management, they have reduced the probability of problems. They have suppressed discipline affairs with strategies of firm and fair codes of conduct that are consistently observed (Willie, 1987) and have focused on optimal learning environments (Myers et al, 1987). In sum, the most organized and well-prepared teachers have the least difficulties (Ban, 1982).

PROFILE OF AN EFFECTIVE TEACHER

Are the best physical education teachers, then, the best behavioral managers? It's a prime ingredient, but not the only one.

The search for the formula to effective teaching has been like the Holy Grail, often with the same illusive results. One earlier comprehensive volume (Dunkin and Biddle, 1974) concluded that teaching success was so complex an issue that it was difficult to know what comprised success in the first place. Another text on "master teachers" (Epstein, 1981) pronounced that great teachers are often "lucky enough to have had great students."

Most of the earlier studies of good teaching focused on personality factors and generally assumed that effective teaching and personal magnetism were related (Hamachek, 1975). Certain personal characteristics still appear to be supportive of effective teaching performance, mostly centering on the teacher being a skilled communicator and a compassionate person (Coppedge and Shreck, 1988). But the absence of specific criteria by which teachers can be evaluated has often led to judgments that are subjectively derived, not necessarily agreed upon, and frequently vague in meaning. So the research has filtered to using student achievement as a major tangible rating tool. Results have thereby shown that some teachers make more of a difference than others, and we now have some idea of the teaching behaviors that lead to effectiveness in instruction. In summary form, they appear to be the following:

1. *High expectations.* Students tend to achieve according to the teacher's expectations of them, especially in the earlier grades (Wayson, 1988). Accordingly, a teacher's expressed ideas about objectives can be a strong motivation for students, provided those expectations are reasonable and perceived by the students to be attainable. Furthermore, teachers must demonstrate confidence in their own ability to promote the learning and in the students' abilities to accomplish the stated objectives (Casanova, 1987).

   Unfortunately, there is indication that physical education teachers sometimes form expectations of their students based on such subsidiary factors as physical attractiveness, gender, and perceived effort (Martinek, 1989). These perceptions then tend to bias teachers toward their students and differentiate the teacher-student interaction. Better looking students get more attention (Martinek, 1981). Boys get more attention than girls (DeVoe and Gustafson, 1989). Skilled students get more positive feedback than the unskilled (Metcalf et al., 1986). Thus, the implications are that physical education teachers need to be conscious of providing fair and equitable treatment of all students, with reasonable expectations for each individual.

2. *Effective organization and management.* A stockpile of earlier research had shown that effective teachers have a great sense of what was called "orderliness" (Aitkin, Bennett, and Hesketh, 1981; Bennett, 1976; Dunwell and Wendel, 1976; Eble, 1980; Gage, 1978; Gensemer, 1980; Lovitt and Haring, 1979; Schlechty, 1976; Travers, 1973). It meant having responsible, goal-oriented behavior. Effective teaching was seen to be performed with intention and resolution, manifested through clear and definite objectives, with well-formulated plans for achieving those objectives. It more liberally implies good organization and management. As already indicated,

behavioral management is a great suppressant of discipline problems, while at the same time it is effective in stimulating student achievement (Emmer, 1987). Important factors within class management include the ability to minimize inactive time, presenting appropriate learning activities, a proper sequential ordering of activities, monitoring of student responses, and smooth transitions from one phase of a class to the next (Harrison, 1987).

3. *A supportive learning environment.* Praise that is spontaneous and genuine, and given in relation to specific accomplishments, is a reinforcement for further achievement (Labonty and Danielson, 1988). A willingness to help students through their learning by giving them necessary time and undivided attention will produce accelerated progress (Coppedge and Shreck, 1988). A positive learning atmosphere is, in fact, one of the elements of physical education that is highly valued by both teachers and students (Sherman, 1989). A sense of humor also seems to be a good benefit (Ziegler, Boardman, and Thomas, 1985).

Conversely, a negative climate produces negative results. Criticism can repress learning to a greater degree than praise will promote it (Harrison, 1987). Negative behavior is the exact antithesis of effective teaching (Cruickshank, 1986).

4. *Active teaching.* The best teachers are actively involved in the class via productive teaching. They are task oriented, focusing everyone's attention on the instructional content and objectives of the lesson, actively demonstrating, cuing performance, and providing ample feedback (McDaniel, 1986). They are rather like the referee who is in complete control of a game yet is accomplishing that dominion without attracting undue attention.

5. *Logical pacing of the learning.* Active teaching also tends to be related to instructional pacing that produces faster learning progressions than passive teaching. Organized teachers accomplish this with small steps that have a high probability for success and an overall plan of realistic stages toward the target objectives. Students are taken through the steps, each one a gradation of the previous step, at a pace that can be adapted to each individual's capability (Bruning, 1984).

6. *Maximal active learning time.* Active teaching produces active learning time. Generally speaking, the more time students have on-task, the greater their achievements will be (Cruickshank, 1986).

Unhappily, observations of physical education classes (Siedentop, Mand, and Taggart, 1986) have shown that students typically spend from 22 percent to 32 percent of their class time doing nothing.

More organized teachers have managed to minimize this "downtime" to provide for a greater percentage of involvement in learning. It relates, once again, to effective planning and class management. One research study (Phillips and Carlisle, 1983) concluded that active learning time is the single most important criterion of an effective teacher.

7. *Providing for mastery learning.* In the final analysis, active teaching coupled with proper pacing and optimal time-on-task will produce a mastery of all phases of a skill. Monitoring of progress in skill acquisition is vital and is accomplished by objective measures that show to both teacher and student how things are going. Careful and realistic evaluations, given at periodic intervals, should allow enough time for each step of a skill to be sufficiently learned to support the next stage. The product will be more confident students who acquire more lasting aptitudes (Doyle and Carter, 1987).

A MATTER OF METHOD

And what about the *method* of teaching? More preparatory attention is typically given to teaching methodology than to any other aspect of the job.

There's good news. The instructional techniques now available are the most effective in the history of education (Borko and Niles, 1987). They have been researched and time tested (Goldberger and Gerney, 1986; Rink et al., 1986). Best of all, they are supremely logical and direct.

Interestingly, in spite of the variety of teaching strategies available, virtually every format has its origins in one of two systems. One is a collection of philosophies generally referred to as *humanism,* and the other is a science-based technique called *behaviorism.* Together these two systems have influenced educational thought more than any other previous approach (Giroux, 1988). Their most positive feature is not only that they have made teaching more effective but that they have made learning more enjoyable and rewarding for the learners.

The basic difference between these two approaches lies in their assignment of the responsibility for learning. Humanists say students are quite capable of, and therefore responsible for, their own learning. In contrast, behaviorists state that teachers are more competent in stimulating learning and are consequently answerable for the process.

Humanism places confidence in self-discovered learnings. Humanistic teaching is never a matter of "telling" things to students; instead, it is made up of movements when a teacher and a student reach some insight into the nature of the learning. It establishes a permissive atmosphere in which students can make discoveries. The teacher encourages students to explore, giving cues when necessary and leading them to conclusions, but never imposing the answers. In physical education, this self-discovery method found a remarkable acceptance through a process called *movement education,* which relies on motoric experimentation and problem solving as its means (Gensemer, 1979). A student is never "told" exactly how to perform a motor skill but is encouraged to experiment with the possibilities to find the most efficient techniques.

The behaviorist model of teaching, on the other hand, is representative of a branch of psychology that attributes learning to the response to a stimulus. Given a set of circumstances (the stimulus), the reaction of people to those circumstances (the response) is predictable. Thus, all that is necessary is to organize the environment to provide the conditions known to produce the desired behaviors. Consequently, a behaviorist teaches according to a set of educational strategies whereby learnings are precisely presented in increasing levels of difficulty. Students are, literally, told how to perform motor skills rather than left to discover appropriate techniques for themselves.

The value in the two systems does not lie in the absolute use of only one method, but rather in the consolidation of the best elements of both. There are times when a teacher must allow for student experimentation and other times when the setting must be exactly organized. It varies in kind with the nature of the objectives of any given lesson. And appealingly, the judicious employment of appropriate methodology makes it more possible to be an effective teacher today than ever before.

WHY TEACH?

The major reason why people are attracted to physical education teaching is the opportunity it presents to be interactive with other people in a helping relationship (Beveridge, Gangstead, and McElroy, 1986). But there are an infinite number of other reasons why someone may want to teach. Following are a list of statements given by students in various preparation programs (collected by the author at three colleges):

- Teaching seems to be a fairly safe, low-risk occupation.
- There are many attractive side benefits.
- I really like the idea of having control over a class.
- Being an influence on the lives of students is appealing.

Every future physical educator has a personal (and probably, different) reason for going into teaching.
Photo by Tom Cherrey.

- I can't think of anything else to do with my major.
- The instruction I had in high school was so incredibly bad that I want to try to correct that situation.
- I really don't know what I want to do, so I'll teach until I find something else.
- I truly believe I can make a contribution to human betterment, especially through the positive outcomes that physical education offers students.
- I want to stay physically fit all my life, and in this profession I can do it.
- I like activity.
- I like the idea of being able to be outdoors much of the time.
- My parents were teachers, and they would really be pleased if I became one too.
- I love kids.
- It's a chance for me to stay young all my life.
- Teachers are my favorite people. I had good teachers all through high school, and it made me feel like I want to stay among them for a career.

- I want to coach, and I may have to teach along with it.
- It's something I've got to do until I can become an administrator.
- I like the respect that comes with the profession.
- I love sports, and I want to be around them as long as I can. At what other job can I be paid to be actively involved in sports?
- The vacations are great.
- It's a people occupation, where you can be with people all day—talking and relating—not like other jobs where your only contact is with machines or computers all day.
- It will allow me to express myself and to share knowledge with others.
- I like the challenge.
- It's a profession rather than just an occupation.
- You can still enjoy growth and improvement in your own thinking and feeling.
- It's a chance to be creative and to enjoy discovery.
- I really don't know why I want to teach; I just know that I do.

The reasons why someone can be attracted to the teaching profession can range from conscientious desires to influence society to such blithe logic as "June, July, and August." In any case, there is no more need to justify one's choice of teaching than any other career preference.

THE MATTER OF MONEY

It's no secret: Teaching is not the way to achieve financial independence. Low salaries are one of the major reasons why fewer persons are choosing to teach (Anthony, 1987) and may be the most important reason why one-half of those entering the teaching profession have left after seven years, two-thirds to three-fourths of them within the first three years of teaching (Templin, 1987). It is probably also the reason why nearly 30 percent of teachers moonlight with a second job (Sizer, 1984).

Since the Second World War, the real purchasing power (money earned compared to the cost of living) of teachers has declined compared to the national average (Wayson, 1988). In one ten-year period, from 1974 to 1984, the average teacher's salary rose 30 percent less than the average salary of other professional people (Sikes, Measor, and

Woods, 1985). All things considered, teachers continue to lose about one percent a year in their purchasing power (Altenbaugh, 1989).

Furthermore, teaching is not an occupation that rewards service and experience with salary increments. Raises are less for years of service rendered than the usual salary advances in other professions (Chapman and Hutcheson, 1982). In many cases, it takes a teacher a full career to double his or her salary (Templin, 1987). Worst of all, physical education teachers' salaries are below the midlevels of the salary scale for teachers in general (Evans and Williams, 1989).

An attempt at rewarding performance in teaching can be found in the establishment of merit pay as an incentive system. In this regard, the better teachers would qualify for the highest pay raises. Recommendations have included such supplements as bonus pay for teaching in disadvantaged areas and extra pay for all unused sick-leave days. But as yet the merit pay plans have received little support from the states (Jacobson, 1989).

However, teachers' salaries are normally quoted on the basis of a nine-month work year. If the average salary is projected to a twelve-month equivalent, teaching salaries rank quite favorably with other professions and rate considerably higher than the average industrial worker (Wayson, 1988). Thus, a teacher who elects to teach during summer sessions earns a far more equitable salary. And in fact, the average teacher's salary is above the national average for all wage earners, even when computed on only a nine-month basis (Alexander and Monk, 1987).

Furthermore, certain job benefits are often available to teachers that may not be common in other occupations, such as paid health insurance, tax shelter plans, pensions, or tuition-free college educations for faculty children or spouses of college professors.

In the final analysis, teaching does not offer the potential for untold wealth, nor for a quick accumulation of a sizable savings account. But the financial picture is more obliging than first believed. There is no fortune in teaching; nor is there financial famine. It just happens to be a median-level occupation in terms of monetary rewards.

THE STATE OF THE MARKET

Throughout the 1960s and early 1970s, teacher turnover rates produced critical teacher shortages. The burgeoning school-aged population, combined with an increased attrition from the profession and fewer new entrants, produced conditions in which the job market was wide open.

But in the late 1970s and early 1980s, when school populations dropped, the demand for teachers diminished. During this time, the supply of public school teachers exceeded the demand by 88 percent (National Education Association, 1982). In physical education, at one point as many as four qualified teachers may have been competing for every available job (Lambert, 1980). A general discouragement ensued as teaching became viewed as a difficult market to enter.

But now indications are that teacher shortages may again be resurfacing. Potentially, during the 1990s, there will be increasing shortages in science, mathematics, special education, computer science, English, and bilingual education (Dworkin, 1987). The total number of teaching positions available in 1995 is expected to be 1.88 million, an all-time high in this country (Griffey, 1987).

The situation for physical education appears less predictable, as projections do not always separate the field from education as a whole. It could therefore be speculated that vacancies might follow the trend of education in general, which would be favorable. However, one report (Templin, 1987) suggests that the supply and demand of physical education teachers will show no increase in demand through the mid-1990s.

The picture is somewhat clouded by the way figures of supply and demand are interpreted. Some announcements reflect the number of teachers who, at present, should be employed according to a specified standard of educational viability, which is usually set by the National Education Association. Since this "standard" indicates the optimal teacher-student ratio that would in theory provide for the best educational outcomes, such a reference base will invariably show a shortage of teachers. On the other hand, the statistics that show an oversupply of teachers are often based on the number of qualified teachers who are available in a given year but do not indicate the number who actually seek employment in teaching. In this regard, it is possible that fewer than three of every four students seeking certification in teaching are actually planning to become teachers (Rassekh and Vaideanu, 1987). So there is some room for interpretation of the supply/demand projections. Assuming that not everyone in physical education certification programs is actually planning to teach, further assuming that the total number in the certification programs is decreasing (Templin, 1987), and adding the projection for a small but definite increase in the public school student population through the 1990s (Rassekh and Vaideanu, 1987), one might arrive at a tentative conclusion that jobs in physical education should become easier to find. But the future is always disclaimed as a "probable," which is the only thing it can be.

SUMMARY

Many teachers start their first job with little idea of what it's really like to manage their own classes. Some find the experience frustrating. Initial difficulties in management may explain the high dropout rate among beginning teachers. But teachers who remain in the profession for seven years are likely to stay for many more, and consequently dropout rates are very low among experienced teachers (Murnane, Singer, and Willett, 1988).

Management skills are an essential ingredient for success in the teaching profession. Although a number of personality factors seem related to effective teaching, the ability to be an efficient manager of class activities appears as a constant. Unfortunately, the development of management abilities is a process that generally takes four to six years (Emmer, 1987), and this coincides with the fact that half of those who enter teaching leave the profession within the first seven years, perhaps before this ability matures. Conclusively, then, it seems that the better prepared one is with management capabilities, the more likely the transition into teaching will be a successful one.

Salaries continue to be a major issue in teaching and may in fact be the single most pressing reason for withdrawal from the profession. Yet curiously, money is not the most important factor for entry into teaching, and for those who remain in the profession beyond the initial transition period, money becomes even less of a concern as the rewards and satisfactions of the job itself become the more encompassing aspects of teaching (Blase, 1986).

To the Reader

A common difficulty in trying to decide on a career is not having enough information about the daily demands of a certain job. Consequently, this fragmentary information can lead to a romanticized view of a particular occupation whereby only the gratifying aspects of the job are noticed. Teaching may seem like a fairly independent vocation, with less constancy of demands on one's time than other jobs. But not readily obvious are the hours of preparing for classes, making up and grading exams, talking with parents, filling out reports, and attending meetings. And, virtually everything one does, or reads, or hears, or thinks can relate to the depth of one's instructional capacities. Therefore, teaching can literally consume the attention of every waking hour. It's easy to get compulsively preoccupied with it.

But teachers are, on the whole, rather content with their career choice (Chapman and Lowther, 1982). Compared to other occupations, stress levels are lower, the psychological benefits are higher, job security is higher, and there is a general feeling of contentment about one's contribution to society (Plevin, 1988).

Furthermore, some of the advantages of teaching are too subtle to be generally perceived. For example: the summer vacation. If you were employed in business and industry and decided to take an equal time off from your work (if indeed you could obtain such privilege), in your absence someone else would be doing your job, making sales to your clients, or otherwise climbing the corporate ladder. But free time in teaching has no strings attached: There is no need to maintain a business pipeline with the job while on vacation, and the psychological freedom this affords is refreshing, totally without vocational stress, and reinvigorating of one's energy for returning to the job.

And the job itself is far from mundane. No two days are exactly alike; thus, interest is easily sustained. The work atmosphere is such that it is seldom actually referred to as "work" in the sense of drudgery. The focus of teaching is people, not things, and therein lies an inherent continuing fascination.

Furthermore, teachers are largely in control of their own world, designing and directing learning experiences, with full liberty to experiment. It is a license for creativity—an art of implementing the science of knowledge, and thus the profession is often described as both an art and a science.

But all things considered, one heavy question can still hover: Will a job be waiting at the end of the degree? No guarantees, of course, but what is known is that the students who (1) are able to secure the greatest number of interviews for potential jobs, (2) are most likely to be offered a job, and (3) are ultimately perceived as the most successful teachers have several things in common. They are, first of all, high academic performers, typically ranking in the upper 20 percent of their high school classes and maintaining college GPAs of at least a "B" (Kowalski and Weaver, 1988). Also, they are involved in a variety of extracurricular activities as students (McLaughlin and Yee, 1988). Administrative officials who employ first-time teachers frequently cite a bias for hiring students who are active with extracurricular pursuits (including athletics), commonly even viewing this more favorably than high academic performance. And this may lead to another factor, which is the apparent ability of these students to teach and direct a wide range of activities (Travers, 1989). The final qualities that seem to generate the best chances for a job offer are those that emerge in an interview: effective communication skills, an obvious emotional and intellectual maturity, and a demonstration of genuine enthusiasm for the teaching profession (O'Hair, 1989).

Suggested Projects

1. Visit a teacher, and observe several classes. Make note of those activities that could be described as instructional, managerial, or institutional. Ask the teacher what the most difficult transitions were when first entering the profession.
2. Think of the best teachers you had in high school. Write down the characteristics that make you feel that way. Compare your thoughts with everyone else in class. Are there common themes? Discuss the comparisons.
3. Obtain a copy of *Teaching Physical Education* by Mosston and Ashworth. Read about the "spectrum of styles." Discuss the value of these different approaches to teaching.
4. Call the personnel offices of several local school districts. Inquire about the anticipated teaching needs over the next several years. If possible, talk directly with the Personnel Director to discover what general qualities are desired in the teachers hired.
5. Locate a school principal who is willing to discuss with you the background qualifications that are important for obtaining a teaching position in physical education. Meet the principal on-site for this interview, or have the principal come to your class to talk about qualifications.
6. Write down all the reasons you can think of for becoming a teacher. Write another list of negatives. Compare your balance sheet with others in the class.
7. The opportunity for role playing is found to be the most important process in the development of perspective about the events of teaching. On this basis, set up a mock situation whereby you will teach a skill of your choice to the rest of the class. React on your performance at its conclusion, and ask for commentary from the class.

References

Aitkin, M., Bennett, S. N., and Hesketh, J. (1981). Teaching Styles and Pupils' Progress: A Re-Analysis. *British Journal of Educational Psychology, 51,* 170–186.

Alexander, K., and Monk, D. H. (Eds.). (1987). *Attracting and Compensating America's Teachers.* Cambridge, MA: Ballinger Publishing.

Altenbaugh, R. J. (1989). Teachers, Their World, and Their Work: A Review of the Idea of "Professional Excellence" in School Reform Reports. In C. M. Shea, E. Kahane, and P. Sola (Eds.). *The New Servants of Power: A Critique of the 1980s School Reform Movement* (pp. 167–175). New York: Greenwood Press.

Anthony, P. (1987). Teachers in the Economic System. In K. Alexander and D. H. Monk (Eds.), *Attracting and Compensating America's Teachers.* Cambridge, MA: Ballinger Publishing.

Ban, J. R. (1982). A Lesson Plan Approach for Dealing with School Discipline. *The Clearing House, 55,* 345–348.

Bedwell, L. E., Hunt, G. H., Touzel, T. J., and Wiseman, D. G. (1984). *Effective Teaching: Preparation and Implementation.* Springfield, IL: Charles C. Thomas.

Bennett, N. (1976). *Teaching Styles and Pupil Progress.* Cambridge, MA: Harvard University Press.

Berliner, D. (1985). Laboratory Settings and the Study of Teacher Education. *Journal of Teacher Education, 36*(6), 2–8.

Beveridge, S. K., Gangstead, S. K., and McElroy, L. E. (1986). A Cross-Sectional Comparison of the Perceptions of the Role of a Physical Educator. *The Physical Educator, 43*(2), 75–81.

Billups, L. H., and Rauth, M. (1987). Teachers and Research. In V. Richardson-Koehler, D. C. Berliner, U. Casanova, C. M. Clark, R. H. Hersh, and L. S. Shulman (Eds.), *Educators' Handbook: A Research Perspective* (pp. 624–639). New York: Longman.

Blase, J. J. (1986). Socialization as Humanization: One Side of Becoming a Teacher. *Sociology of Education, 59*(2), 100–113.

Borko, H., and Niles, J. A. (1987). Descriptions of Teacher Planning: Ideas for Teachers and Researchers. In V. Richardson-Koehler, D. C. Berliner, U. Casanova, C. M. Clark, R. H. Hersh, and L. S. Shulman (Eds.), *Educators' Handbook: A Research Perspective* (pp. 167–187). New York: Longman.

Bruning, R. H. (1987). Key Elements of Effective Teaching in the Direct Teaching Model. In *Using Research to Improve Teacher Education* (pp. 75–88). Washington, DC: ERIC Clearinghouse on Teacher Education.

Cardinell, C. F. (1980). Teacher Burnout: An Analysis. *Action in Teacher Education, 2,* 9–15.

Casanova, U. (1987). What Should I Know about My Students? In V. Richardson-Koehler, D. C. Berliner, U. Casanova, C. M. Clark, R. H. Hersh, and L. S. Shulman (Eds.), *Educators Handbook: A Research Perspective* (pp. 295–456). New York: Longman.

Chapman, D. W., and Hutcheson, S. M. (1982). Attrition from Teaching Careers: A Discriminant Analysis. *American Educational Research Journal, 19,* 93–105.

Chapman, D. W., and Lowther, M. A. (1982). Teachers' Satisfaction with Teaching. *Journal of Educational Research, 75,* 241–247.

Charles, C. M. (1985). *Building Classroom Discipline: From Models to Practice.* New York: Longman.

Coppedge, F. L., and Shreck, P. (1988). Teachers as Helpers: The Qualities Students Prefer. *The Clearing House, 62*(3), 137–140.

Cruikshank, D. R. (1986). Profile of an Effective Teacher. *Educational Horizons, 64*(2), 80–86.

DeVoe, D. E., and Gustafson, J. A. (1989). A Descriptive Analysis of Individualized Teacher Behavior in Elementary Physical Education. *The Physical Educator, 46*(1), 13–17.

Doyle, W. (1984). How Order Is Achieved in Classrooms: An Interim Report. *Journal of Curriculum Studies, 16,* 259–277.

Doyle, W. (1985). Classroom Organization and Management. In M. Wittrock (Ed.), *Handbook of Research on Teaching* (3rd ed.) (pp. 392–431). New York: Macmillan.

Doyle, W., and Carter, K. (1987). Choosing the Means of Instruction. In V. Richardson-Koehler, D. C. Berliner, U. Casanova, C. H. Hersh, and L. S. Shulman (Eds.), *Educators' Handbook: A Research Perspective* (pp. 188–206). New York: Longman.

Duckworth, E. (1987). *"The Having of Wonderful Ideas" and Other Essays on Teaching and Learning.* New York: Teachers College Press.

Dunkin, R. R., and Biddle, B. J. (1974). *The Study of Teaching.* New York: Holt, Rinehart, and Winston.

Dunwell, R. R., and Wendel, R. L. (1976). *Foundations of Teaching and Learning.* New York: Praeger Publishers.

Dworkin, A. G. (1987). *Teacher Burnout in the Public Schools.* Albany, NY: State University of New York Press.

Eble, K. E. (Ed.). (1980). *New Directions for Teaching and Learning: Improving Teaching Styles.* San Francisco: Jossey-Bass.

Emmer, E. T. (1987). Classroom Management and Discipline. In V. Richardson-Koehler, D. C. Berliner, U. Casanova, C. M. Clark, R. H. Hersh, and L. S. Shulman (Eds.), *Educators' Handbook: A Research Perspective* (pp.233–258). New York: Longman.

Epstein, J. (1981). *Masters: Portraits of Great Teachers.* New York: Basic Books.

Evans, J., and Williams, T. (1989). Moving Up and Getting Out: The Classed and Gendered Career Opportunities of Physical Education Teachers. In T. J. Templin and P. G. Schempp (Eds.), *Socialization into Physical Education: Learning to Teach* (pp. 235–249). Indianapolis: Benchmark Press.

Gage, N. L. (1978). *Scientific Basis of the Art of Teaching.* New York: Teachers College Press.

Gallahue, D. L. (1985). Toward Positive Discipline in the Gymnasium. *The Physical Educator, 42*(1), 14–17.

Gallup, G. H. (1982). The 14th Annual Gallup Poll of the Public's Attitude toward the Public Schools. *Phi Delta Kappan, 64,* 37–50.

Gensemer, R. E. (1979). *Movement Education.* Washington, DC: National Education Association.

Gensemer, R. E. (1980). *Humanism and Behaviorism in Physical Education.* Washington, DC: National Education Association.

Applications

Giroux, H. A. (1988). *Teachers as Intellectuals: Toward a Critical Pedagogy of Learning.* Granby, MA: Bergin and Garvey Publishers.

Goldberger, M., and Gerney, P. (1986). The Effects of Direct Teaching Styles on Motor Skill Acquisition of Fifth Grade Children. *Research Quarterly for Exercise and Sport, 57*(3), 215–219.

Griffey, D. C. (1987). The Future of Graduate Study in Teacher Preparation in Physical Education. *Quest, 39*(2), 174–178.

Hamachek, D. (1975). Characteristics of Good Teachers and Implications for Teacher Education. In J. M. Palardy (Ed.), *Teaching Today: Tasks and Challenges.* New York: Macmillan.

Harrison, J. M. (1987). A Review of the Research on Teacher Effectiveness and Its Implications for Current Research. *Quest, 39*(1), 36–55.

Hutslar, J. (1986). Fizz Ed Problems and Solutions. *Journal of Physical Education, Recreation, and Dance, 57,* 70–75.

Jacobson, S. L. (1989). Merit Pay Incentives in Teaching. In L. Weis, P. G. Altbach, G. P. Kelley, H. G. Petrie, and S. Slaughter (Eds.), *Crisis in Teaching: Perspectives on Current Reforms* (pp. 111–128). Albany, NY: State University of New York Press.

Kirsch, R. A., and McBride, R. E. (1987). Physical Discipline Problems in the Gymnasium. *The Physical Educator, 44*(3), 355–359.

Kowalski, T. J., and Weaver, R. A. (1988). Characteristics of Outstanding Teachers: An Academic and Social Involvement Profile. *Action in Teacher Education, 10*(2), 93–99.

Labonty, J., and Danielson, K. E. (1988). Effective Teaching: What Do Kids Say? *The Clearing House, 61*(9), 394–398.

Lambert, C. L. (1980). What Can I Do Besides Teach? *Journal of Physical Education and Recreation, 51*(9), 74–76.

Lee, A. M., and Poto, C. (1988). Instructional Time Research in Physical Education: Contributions and Current Issues. *Quest, 40*(1), 63–73.

Lovitt, D., and Haring, N. (Eds.). (1979). *Classroom Applications of Precision Teaching.* Seattle, WA: Special Child Publications.

Luke, M. D. (1989). Research on Class Management and Organization: Review with Implications for Current Practice. *Quest, 41*(1), 55–67.

Martinek, T. J. (1981). Physical Attractiveness: Effects on Teacher Expectations and Dyadic Interactions in Elementary Age Children. *Journal of Sport Psychology, 3,* 196–205.

Martinek, T. J. (1989). The Psycho-Social Dynamics of the Pygmalion Phenomenon of Physical Education and Sport. In T. J. Templin and P. J. Schempp (Eds.), *Socialization into Physical Education: Learning to Teach* (pp. 199–217). Indianapolis: Benchmark Press.

McDaniel, T. R. (1986). A Primer on Classroom Discipline: Principles Old and New. *Phi Delta Kappan, 68,* 63–67.

McLaughlin, M. W., and Yee, S. M. (1988). School as a Place to Have a Career. In A. Lieberman (Ed.), *Building a Professional Culture in Schools*. New York: Teachers College Press.

MetCalf, T. M., Mancini, V., and Wuest, D. (1986). A Comparison of the Interactions of a Male and a Female Physical Educator and Their High- and Low-Skilled Students' Academic Learning Time-Physical Education (ALT-PE). *Abstracts of Research Papers 1986.* Reston, VA: AAHPERD.

Metzler, M. W. (1985). An Overview of Academic Learning Time Research in Physical Education. In C. L. Vendien and J. E. Nixon (Eds.), *Physical Education Teacher Education: Guidelines for Sport Pedagogy* (pp. 147–153). New York: Macmillan.

Murnane, R. J., Singer, J. D., and Willett, J. B. (1988). The Career Paths of Teachers: Implications for Teacher Supply and Methodological Lessons for Research. *Educational Researcher, 17*(6), 22–30.

Myers, D. E., Milne, A. M., Baker, K., and Ginsburg, A. (1987). Student Discipline and High School Performance. *Sociology of Education, 60*(1), 18–33.

National Education Association (1982). *Status of the American Public School Teacher 1980–81.* Washington, DC: Author.

O'Hair, M. (1989). Teacher Employment Interview: A Neglected Reality. *Action in Teacher Education, 11*(1), 53–57.

Parĕ, C., Mirette, M., Caron, F., and Black, P. (1987). The Study of Active Learning Time: Profile of Behavior. In G. T. Barette, R. S. Feingold, C. R. Rees, and M. Piĕron (Eds.), *Myths, Models, and Methods in Sport Pedagogy,* (pp. 255–261). Champaign, IL: Human Kinetics Publishers.

Perry, F., and Taylor, H. (1982). Needed: A Methods Course in Discipline for Pre-Service Teachers. *Education, 102,* 416–419.

Phillips, D. A., and Carlisle, C. (1983). A Comparison of Physical Education Teachers Categorized as Most and Least Effective. *Journal of Teaching in Physical Education, 2*(3), 55–66.

Plevin, A. (1988). *Education as a Career.* Washington, DC: National Education Association.

Rassekh, S., and Vaideanu, G. (1987). *The Contents of Education: A Worldwide View of Their Development from the Present to the Year 2000.* Bungay, England: United Nations Educational Scientific and Cultural Organization.

Reis, E. M. (1988). Effective Teaching Techniques: Implications for Better Discipline. *The Clearing House, 61*(8), 356–357.

Rink, J. (1985). *Teaching Physical Education for Learning.* St. Louis: C. V. Mosby.

Rink, J. E., Werner, P. H., Hahn, R. C., Ward, D. S., and Timmermans, H. M. (1986). Differential Effects of Three Teachers over a Unit of Instruction. *Research Quarterly for Exercise and Sport, 57*(2), 132–138.

Schlechty, P. C. (1976). *Teaching and Social Behavior: Toward an Organizational Theory of Instruction.* Boston: Allyn and Bacon.

Sherman, A. (1989). The Role of a Successful Physical Educator as Perceived by Physical Education Majors and Teachers. *The Physical Educator, 46*(1), 45–51.

Siedentop, D., Mand, C., and Taggart, A. (1986). *Physical Education: Teaching and Curriculum Strategies for Grades 5–12.* Palo Alto, CA: Mayfield.

Sikes, P. J., Measor, L., and Woods, P. (1985). *Teacher Careers: Crises and Continuities.* London: Falmer Press.

Sizer, T. R. (1984). *Horace's Compromise: The Dilemma of the American High School.* Boston: Houghton-Mifflin.

Stodolsky, S. S. (1988). *The Subject Matters: Classroom Activity in Math and Social Studies.* Chicago: University of Chicago Press.

Templin, T. J. (1987). Some Considerations for Teaching Physical Education in the Future. In J. D. Massengale (Ed.), *Trends toward the Future in Physical Education* (pp. 51–67). Champaign, IL: Human Kinetics Publishers.

Templin, T. J. (1989). Running on Ice: A Case Study of the Influence of Workplace Conditions on a Secondary School Physical Educator. In T. J. Templin and P. G. Schempp (Eds.), *Socialization into Physical Education: Learning to Teach* (pp. 165–198). Indianapolis: Benchmark Press.

Travers, P. D. (1989). Preparing for Teacher Employment: An Analysis of Job Applications. *The Clearing House, 62,* 263–265.

Travers, R. M. W. (Ed.) (1973). *Second Handbook of Research on Teaching.* Chicago: Rand McNally.

Wayson, W., with Mitchell, B., Pinnell, G. S., and Landis, D. (1988). *Up from Excellence: The Impact of the Excellence Movement on Schools.* Bloomington, IN: Phi Delta Kappa Educational Foundation.

Willie, C. V. (1987). *Effective Education: A Minority Policy Perspective.* New York: Greenwood Press.

Wittrock, R. C. (Ed.). (1986). *Handbook of Research on Teaching* (3rd ed.). New York: Macmillan.

Ziegler, V., Boardman, G., and Thomas, D. (1985). Humor, Leadership, and School Climate. *The Clearing House, 58,* 346–348.

Chapter 12

Coaching: Seasonal Challenges, Lifetime Rewards

A Typical Working Day

The Multiple Roles of a Coach

What Makes a Coach Successful?

Reasons for Coaching

Why Coaches Quit

The Teaching and Coaching Challenge

Evaluating Your Potential as a Coach

Summary

To the Reader

Suggested Projects

References

Coaching is a profession in which the hours are long, the pay is menial, the responsibilities are enormous, and the pressures are intense.

It is especially difficult for teachers who often do not have the energy or the time to give equal attention to their different roles of teaching and coaching, and often allow one of the roles to receive less commitment.

Yet coaching attracts more individuals than any other single vocational pursuit within academic settings.

Apparently, the satisfactions and intrinsic rewards to be derived from this profession outweigh the potential hazards and frustrations.

Applications

To see oneself as a coach is a euphoric vision. The drama of that position is readily imagined and captivating to the psyche. The sights, the sounds, the very feeling of being the leader of an athletic team is an image that comes easily to a wandering mind. Perhaps no other potential career holds the same kind of anticipated exhilaration as coaching.

A good coach is a tutor—one who educates, elicits what is latent, and helps players to be exact and exacting. The coach turns the awkward into the skilled, the unfocused into the determined. And having awakened the minds and bodies of others, the coach is vicariously enriched by the achievements of those who are actually performing.

A TYPICAL WORKING DAY

One of the first realizations that must be accepted about the coaching profession is how absolutely consuming it can be of one's time. For a coach, time is fluid. There is a given hour for the beginning and the end of practice, but the thoughts and emotions do not confine themselves to such a narrow time slot. The demands of coaching are relentless—a constant intrusion that filters into every aspect of the day.

Assuming a normal teaching schedule, a typical working day for a high school coach could look like the following (Sabock, 1985):

7:45–8:00	Hall duty or homeroom
8:00–11:00	Classes
11:00–11:30	Cafeteria duty
11:30–Noon	Lunch
Noon–3:00	Classes
3:00–3:45	Preparation period
4:00–6:00	Practice
6:00–7:00	Dress, shower, incidentals, go home
7:00–8:00	Dinner
8:00–9:00	Help children with homework, phone calls from parents or sportswriters, lesson plans, and so forth
9:00–11:00	Review game films or scouting reports

Time can become a blur. The typical coach will spend thirty to forty hours per week with duties directly associated with the team, including not only actual coaching acts but also planning for practices and games, studying films, arranging for transportation, and so forth (Sage, 1987). And this does not include meetings with the faculty athletic committee, or the community booster club, or league organizers, or equipment salespeople.

In part, a coach's commitment to the profession may be a product of a previous social environment. Coaches tend to come from blue-collar backgrounds where long hours of work and dedication to one's job are respected characteristics (Coakley, 1986). Structurally, sports and work can be viewed as similar. Both are identified by an "achievement principle" (McClelland, 1975), which is the tendency to strive competitively for socially recognized excellence. The work sessions themselves (practices) are frequently arduous, mechanical, and require high levels of endurance; thus, they resemble work more than play. Moreover, in contradiction to what coaching was originally meant to be, it is now frequently a very serious business. The spontaneous moments have decreased as the occupation has focused on productivity, involving discipline, authority, competition, organization, bureaucracy, a division of labor, mechanization, automation—in short, the production of a product, a winning team. To overcome the competition, a coach will often assume the work habits typical of business executives. Dedication and tenacity become the rule. The job can become all-consuming.

Coaching is not only glamorous. It's serious business. It's hard work. It's frustrating, soul-searching, gut-wrenching, and sometimes ruinous. There doesn't seem to be any middle ground, only total emotional involvement. No matter where they are or what they are doing, coaches seem always to have some part of their minds fixed on X's and O's. It can become an obsession. Yet people willingly commit to it, enjoy it, even thrive on it. It's a profession that is simultaneously intimidating and fascinating. It has potential for both frustration and elation. And so coaches operate in a sense of cognitive overdrive that forever hinges on optimism. Coaching is the focus of their energy: a mood, an attitude, a way of making their mark.

THE MULTIPLE ROLES OF A COACH

In addition to the duties of being a coach, other supporting roles must be assumed. They are often fulfilled continuously, sometimes with little or no awareness of their encounter. In fact, the actual act of coaching may turn out to be the easiest part of the job.

Many of the supporting roles are predetermined by the particular school and community where the coach works. The roles are expected behaviors, and they are obligatory in that the role-player must accept those behaviors in order to perform in the job.

Applications

A coach must often assume supporting roles both in the school and in the community.
Photo by Tom Cherrey.

Fundamentally, the supporting roles can be divided into those defined by (1) the school system and (2) the local community. They include at least the following:

Role Expectations in the Educational Setting

1. *Teacher.* The coach must be a teacher within the coaching position. Athletes do not come with perfect abilities intact; consequently the coach must have sound instructional capabilities for improving the quality of the athletes' performances.

2. *Organizer.* For conducting practice sessions, organization is absolutely essential. Purposeful behavior is a characteristic of successful coaches. There must be definite objectives for each practice session and an organized plan for attaining those objectives.

3. *Psychologist.* The days of the emotional, gimmicky locker-room pep talks may be gone. More importantly, the coach must be able to understand the athletes' personalities and be able to say and do the right things at the right times. This may be especially important for coaching individual sports, which tend to attract a more diverse group of personalities (Gill, 1986). Communication and motivational strategies must suit the different personalities of the team members.

4. *Counselor.* Athletes may develop a rapport with their coach and trust the coach's opinion in matters outside the athletic realm. Athletes may seek advice and guidance from the coach, particularly when support is not available from the home. Late-night telephone calls or visits from troubled athletes are not uncommon.

5. *Leader.* To the extent that an athletic team can be thought of as a business, the coach must be the chief executive officer. Athletic teams consist of individuals assembled for a common purpose, and for them to function well, a single person must hold final decision-making power. It is critical for the individuals in the group to know that their leader is entirely capable and ready to make those decisions.

6. *Disciplinarian.* Without discipline, team morale will suffer. Discipline does not mean punishment, but rather the expectation of punctuality, dependability, and commitment. Players need, indeed want, to have fair guidelines for their conduct. These guidelines provide the team with common values and a unity of purpose. And above all else, the coach must personify these expectations.

7. *School citizen.* It is easy and too often common for a coach to ignore school duties, miss faculty meetings, avoid committees, and so on. By shirking these duties, the coach will be viewed by the rest of the faculty as uncooperative and indifferent to the total operation of the educational system. A coach is held to the same responsibilities as any other faculty member. Moreover, a coach who demonstrates an interest in nonathletic school activities will probably gain extra respect of not only the faculty but the players as well.

Role Expectations in the Community

1. *Diplomat.* The public, like the educational community, will expect a coach to represent idealized behaviors. Often this requires diplomacy; discretion must be used in responding to the public's predictable questions about the team and the athletic program. The most difficult encounters may be with parents of players who disagree with the manner in which their son or daughter is being (or not being) used in games.

2. *Parental surrogate.* Many people believe that the characteristics displayed by players are somehow an outgrowth of the personality of the coach. While there may be some truth to this contention within the context of players' behavior during games, sometimes these associations carry over into the private lives of the players. A player who encounters trouble in the community may be viewed as a product of the coach; consequently the coach is partly blamed for

the troublesome behavior. A coach is often expected to be a guardian for the players, bestowing them with the same civil behavior that is expected from family influence.

3. *Politician.* This role is not so much a societal expectation as it is a necessary evil for the coach, regardless of its connotations. Knowing how to relate to influential community leaders will generate valuable social ties, both for the athletic program and for the coach. A well-timed golf game here and there, attendance at a church bazaar, a visit to the home of a troubled player—all add to the cohesion between the coach and the community, with potentially positive returns.

4. *Salesperson.* Coupled with the political sense just mentioned, a well-received coach may be a good salesperson, able to increase attendance at games and elicit additional revenue from the community. A coach may possibly be able to coerce community assistance for administering athletic contests (track meets require plenty of help), repairing equipment, or staging benefits. The coach might even recruit a volunteer assistant coach.

5. *Citizen of the community.* As a respected member of the community, a coach may be asked frequently to lend moral support at community affairs. Participating in civic groups, volunteering time for fund drives, making dedications, helping to organize social functions, delivering keynote speeches, being marshall of a parade, or merely attending community events are all expected of a coach—particularly of a winning coach and/or a coach of a so-called major sport. The number of these requests will likely be much greater in a small town because the community identifies with the coach and wants to use the image of the coach to promote its causes.

WHAT MAKES A COACH SUCCESSFUL?

In all these role dimensions, where one melds into another and where time is vague, who gets good at this profession? Everyone wants to be. Every coach wants to be effective at the central part of the job—to produce a team that performs well. What separates the best from the rest?

One of the earliest and still-cited investigations of coaches (Ogilvie and Tutko, 1966) concluded that they were generally inflexible, insensitive, and task minded. Later research was a bit kinder, indicating that coaches were organized and goal oriented (Caroon, 1980). One study even found coaches to be no different from the average college student (Mancini and Agnew, 1978). And one writing (Coakley, 1986) contends

What makes a coach successful?
Photo by Tom Cherrey.

that the better coaches are assertive without being insensitive, organized without being manipulative, and achievement oriented without being exploitive.

There is little doubt that coaching attracts persons with high energy levels for achievement. But in almost all cases, "success" within this profession is liberally interpreted to mean winning. With this as the criterion, identifiable factors do appear to consistently emerge as correlates of success.

1. *Knowledge of the sport.* A beginning prerequisite for success is to know the sport that one is coaching. Having a solid biomechanical understanding of the performance requirements of the sport is an absolute (Hennessy, 1989) and may be the one factor that, if absent, will prevent any other factors of game strategy or the personal characteristics of the coach from becoming effective (Claxton, 1988).

2. *Instructional competence.* Not only does the successful coach know the mechanics of skill execution, this knowledge is also communicated effectively to the players. Winning coaches have good instructional skills (Markland and Martinek, 1988) and spend more practice time in instruction than losing coaches (Sherman and Hassan, 1984). They also are effective in delivering their instruction in ways that are mechanically understood by the athletes (Griffey, Housner, and Williams, 1984).

3. *Positive feedback.* Good coaches show a liberal use of reward statements and high praise for the positive gains of their athletes (Lacy and Darst, 1985). They carry this habit into the actual games by maintaining an upbeat, supportive atmosphere (Wandzilak and Ansorge, 1988). In practice they encourage athletes to develop positive feelings about their abilities, and in fact the coaches openly display confident attitudes about the capabilities of both their athletes and themselves (Gould et. al., 1989).

4. *Organized practices.* Effective coaches use brief demonstrations and give short, precise verbal statements about what they want players to do. They waste little time. They are better at keeping their players involved and on-task during practice sessions (McKenzie, 1984).

5. *High expectations.* Successful coaches emphasize the exerting of effort and mastery of specific abilities. They focus on performance objectives and expect that their athletes will have high but realistic objectives of their own for achievement of performance goals (Chaumeton and Duda, 1988). In turn, the players who display the highest goals and exert the most effort are those who are more likely to have favorable interactions with their coaches (Sinclair and Vealey, 1989).

But what do the *players* want their coaches to be like? It's not much different from the descriptions of successful coaches. Players want their coaches to have a good knowledge of the sport (Schliesman, 1987), to conduct practice sessions that will effectively prepare them for competition (Garland and Barry, 1988), to provide good instructional feedback about their performances (Weiss and Friedrichs, 1986), to maintain a positive and supporting atmosphere (Dwyer and Fischer, 1988), and to be an effective decision maker (Gordon, 1988).

REASONS FOR COACHING

A common incentive for wanting to become a coach is to extend a positive experience with athletics. If playing is enjoyable, should coaching not be also? Such logic requires the same caution as concluding that being a filmmaker is every bit as pleasurable as going to the movies. There is much more to it than meets the eye.

According to one author (Keller, 1982), there are seven possible reasons why someone would want to coach:

1. *Liking for athletics.* Coaching is a way to continue an active affiliation with athletics and athletes.

Table 12.1 Reasons for Entering the Coaching Profession

	Response		
Reason	Male	Female	Total
1. I like to work with young people.	151	102	253
2. I have a keen interest in athletics.	148	101	249
3. It is a challenging profession.	128	78	206
4. I have had exposure to coaching at some level and enjoyed it very much.	100	63	163
5. I respected my former coaches and wish to follow in their steps.	67	43	110
6. To enhance my opportunity of securing a teaching position.	32	50	82
7. For financial reasons.	23	19	42
8. A member of my family is/was a coach.	20	10	30
9. Other	7	5	12

Reprinted with permission from the *Journal of Physical Education, Recreation, and Dance,* 1979, p. 40. The Journal is a publication of the American Alliance for Health, Physical Education, Recreation, and Dance, 1900 Association Drive, Reston, VA 22091.

  2. *Excitement of competition.* It is an opportunity to continue experiencing the excitement one had as a player.

  3. *Attention and recognition.* A normal human trait is to seek attention and recognition, and athletics provides an avenue.

  4. *Influence of a coach we admire.* The decision is influenced by a coach whose personality and coaching abilities were respected and admired.

  5. *Supplement to the livelihood.* It is rarely the only reason, but coaching is one way to add extra income.

  6. *Affection for students.* Helping each student-athlete to become a better person through athletic experiences is both a challenge and a responsibility.

  7. *Opportunity to teach.* Athletics is not only excitement but also a means for self-improvement, and the coaching position presents chances for significant teaching.

Responses to a questionnaire (Stillwell, 1979) that asked physical education majors at six Kansas universities why they wanted to coach showed that the most common reason was that they wanted to work with young people (see table 12.1). Sometimes researchers uncover a rather loosely defined "power motive" for wanting to coach (Coakley, 1986).

It's a trait that ranks high in business executives (Gilbert, 1989), but when discussed in connection with coaches, it often gets translated to "leadership." Thus, the power motive does not mean that coaches exert autocratic dominance over others, but rather that they enjoy the decision-making responsibilities that come with an influential position.

In fact, very little research has been done on why people enter the coaching profession. And in the final analysis, it does not really matter why other people want to coach. What is important is one's own personal reasons. When the will to do something is there, that in itself is adequate justification for doing it.

WHY COACHES QUIT

There are over 190,000 athletic teams in American high schools, involving approximately six million players. In a typical high school, one-third to one-half of the teachers are also involved in coaching (National Federation Handbook, 1989). Most persons who hold these dual roles as teacher and coach indicate they enjoy coaching more than teaching (Seagrave, 1981). Yet few coaches continue in this responsibility throughout their teaching careers. The standard length of service in the coaching profession is probably about fifteen years (Fouss and Troppmann, 1981).

Some earlier observations (Lackey, 1977) on why coaches leave the profession indicated that the major reason was a desire to enter another field of employment, and the major reason for being fired was not because of a failure to win, but rather because of difficult relationships with the players (see table 12.2). More recently, the same author (Lackey, 1986) indicated that the pressure to win in high school athletics had increased, and failure to win might now constitute the major reason for being fired. This pressure appears to come mostly from outside the school—from boosters, patrons, parents, and fans in general. In fact, a survey of 367 high school principals in Nebraska indicated that only 8 percent felt their coaches had any significant pressure from within the school to produce winning teams (Humphrey, 1987).

It has also been suggested that married coaches, especially those with children, are commonly plagued by the amount of time they must spend away from home, and this may be a major reason for their quitting (Sabock, 1985). Otherwise, a general explanation might be that unless the intrinsic values of satisfaction and enjoyment can be maintained, coaches will voluntarily leave the job. This implies that the rewards of coaching that were once present are either gone or no longer strong enough to overcome the job difficulties. Whatever the "fun" of coaching was, when it disappears, so do the coaches (Jones et. al., 1989).

Table 12.2 Reasons for Voluntarily Leaving and Being Fired from Coaching

Reason for Voluntarily Leaving	Percent of Total
1. Career changes	41.5%
2. Personal factors	26.6%
3. Pressures of the job	24.2%
4. Student-related factors	7.7%
(Total number was 164)	

Reasons for Being Fired	Percent of Total
1. Relationships with players and students	22.8%
2. Personal habits	20.9%
3. Failure to win	15.5%
4. Relationships with community	14.6%
5. Classroom performance	12.6%
6. Coaching ability	6.8%
7. Administrative relationships	4.4%
8. Peer relationships	2.4%
(Total number was 104)	

Reprinted with permission from the *Journal of Physical Education, Recreation, and Dance,* 1977, pp. 22–23. The Journal is a publication of the American Alliance for Health, Physical Education, Recreation, and Dance, 1900 Association Drive, Reston, VA 22091.

THE TEACHING AND COACHING CHALLENGE

The standard high school arrangement is one where coaches are first employed to teach classes in their area of certification and then are given extra pay for coaching responsibilities. There is a trend away from having the physical education teacher coach three different sports in season. The "one-sport" coach is now more common, thus coaches have by necessity been drawn from teaching disciplines other than physical education (Ellis, 1988), and this in part explains why it is not unusual to find high schools where half of the teaching faculty is also involved in coaching.

Those who play the dual roles of teacher and coach sometimes have difficulty in devoting equal energy to each role. While there may be complementary aspects to both, there are also unavoidable role conflicts. Teachers are expected to instruct competently and are evaluated on that basis. Yet a mediocre instructor is seldom fired. A coach could be an excellent mentor, with solid technical competencies, yet could be fired because of mediocre scoreboard results. Further, a coach who is fired might also be dismissed from teaching, irrespective of how competent the performance as a teacher may have been. An excellent teacher/losing coach is more likely to be terminated than a mediocre teacher/winning coach.

High school teachers who coach experience different demands and pressures than teachers with other extracurricular activities. Teams perform in public, and poor performance gets far more public criticism than mediocrity in the public presentation of other school events. In such a conditional system, teacher/coaches usually perceive their primary responsibility to be coaching, especially to be a winning coach (Massengale, 1981). Thus, role conflict is likely. Especially difficult is when the two roles impose conflicting messages of expected behaviors, particularly when the messages come from people both inside and outside the organization (Cherniss, 1980). Clearly, this can happen when the school evaluates someone internally as a teacher, but the public evaluates that same person as a coach.

Considering the different requirements and evaluations asked of teachers and coaches, role conflict is almost to be expected. And indeed, compared to other professions, role conflict appears to be especially prevalent among high school coaches (Sage, 1987), particularly among coaches who are physical education teachers rather than classroom teachers (Locke and Massengale, 1978). A predictable response in this conflict is for the individuals to reduce their involvement with the role perceived to be of lesser importance. In virtually every instance, it is the teaching that will become neglected (Sage, 1987). Coaching is more in-

Every teacher/coach faces a dual challenge—athletics and academics.
© Spencer Grant/Photo Researchers, Inc.

triguing, more pressure-inducing, and appears to have the greater rewards. So there may be an unpleasant grain of truth to the stories about the coach who "throws out the ball" for the physical education classes and then retreats to the office to plan for the next game.

Perhaps in recognition of this potential role conflict, some states allow a school to hire a coach without having to simultaneously offer that person a teaching position. And some states even allow a person to be hired as a coach who does not have any teaching certification at all. In Oregon, for example, in 1985 only 85.6 percent of the high school coaches had certification to teach (Sisley and Capel, 1985).

We should also recognize that role conflict does not automatically come with a teaching/coaching job. Indeed, some people actually thrive within these roles (Figone, 1989a). And even when there is conflict, it is still possible to perform the functions of both roles with a high degree of effectiveness.

EVALUATING YOUR POTENTIAL AS A COACH

Coaching is a volatile profession. A coach's tenure is often short. Pressures are intense, hours are long, the pay is generally menial, and the job can end on the whims of people who have nothing to do with education. Notwithstanding these hazards, the profession attracts people who see instead the potential for accomplishment and satisfaction, personal growth, community appreciation, or the intangible rewards of helping players to achieve performance excellence.

The questionnaire in table 12.3 may help you to evaluate whether coaching should be a part of your career aspirations (Jones et. al., 1989). Give yourself two points for each "yes" answer, and one point for each "maybe" response. Add up the total.

Table 12.3 Check your aptitude for coaching.

Can You:	Yes	Maybe	No
1. Handle long hours of physical work			
2. Handle long hours of mental work			
3. Talk with parents of players			
4. Organize a staff			
5. Listen to players' concerns			
6. Arrange for a game			
7. Lose with composure			
8. Win graciously			
9. Set training rules			

Applications

Table 12.3 *Continued.*

Can You:	Yes	Maybe	No
10. Discipline players			
11. Order uniforms			
12. Write a news story			
13. Make a speech			
14. Drive a bus			
15. Prepare an equipment bid list			
16. Keep playing statistics			
17. Be a good family person			
18. Mark off fields or line floors			
19. Be a role model for the team			
20. Be away from home			
21. Demonstrate skills and techniques			
22. Live with stress			
23. Use audio-visual equipment			
Have You:			
24. An even disposition			
25. Gained new sport knowledge this week			
26. Been an assistant			
27. Good physical health			
28. Good mental health			
29. At least ten books in your sports library			
30. Been to a sports clinic this year			
Are You:			
31. An athlete			
32. Sportsmanlike			
33. Cooperative			
34. Drug free			
35. A good teacher			
36. Safety conscious			
Do You:			
37. Like young people			
38. Know complex strategy of sport			
39. Know about liability			
40. Know conditioning fundamentals			
41. Like to teach			
42. Know how to pick a team			
43. Like to win			
44. Like to win fairly			
45. Know budgeting and purchasing			
46. Know how to raise money			
47. Know current rules			
48. Like attending to details			
49. Know ten other coaches			
50. Think coaching is fun			

Scoring
A score of 100 is impossible for most ordinary, truthful people.
A score of 75–99 = YES, you will probably be a good coach.
A score of 50–74 = YES, you can learn to be a coach.
A score of 49 or less = Are you sure that you are in the right field?

From Billie J. Jones, et al., *Guide to Effective Coaching*, 2d ed. Copyright © 1989 Wm. C. Brown Publishers, Dubuque, Iowa. All rights reserved.

SUMMARY

Preparing an athletic team for a game can be likened to preparing an orchestra for a concert. The players—the musicians—refine and expand their skills until they are ready for the public demonstration. The coach—the conductor—selects the most capable performers and cultivates their abilities to the highest possible degree. And during public performances, the most gifted of the group will play prominent roles.

The dates for the public presentations are known, so the leader must devise a practice plan to assure that the players are always ready on time. Playing techniques and performance patterns are prescribed by the leader and rehearsed by the performers. Strategy is devised and practiced. The leader concentrates on harmonizing the group into an integrated unit. Although some performers may become more celebrated than others, the contributions of all group members are important. And in the end, the public will make the final judgment of how well orchestrated the performances have been.

In another context, coaching is commonly assumed to be similar to teaching, yet there are distinctive differences. The atmosphere of teaching is often planned to reduce stress or tension, and to be particularly supportive of those having the most difficulty. Student self-discovery of information is frequently encouraged, and a cooperative endeavor among all students is not usually necessary for everyone to perform to the best of their abilities. In all cases, the students are expected to acquire new abilities from their experiences.

In contrast, athletic practice sessions are designed to hone abilities already learned. There is little time to allow players to self-discover new aptitudes. The sessions are often planned to induce stress for the very reason that the players must be prepared to perform under stress during competition. And cooperation among the members of the team is essential.

A teacher is obligated to provide equal learning opportunities for every student and to treat all students equitably. Sometimes this means that the best students are left more to themselves than the poor students. But the coach has selected an exclusive group and does not hesitate to give more time to those who will have major roles within the group. Less skilled performers are either eliminated from the group or are relegated to subordinate roles.

For the teacher, class sessions are spread over an academic year, giving students time to develop a wide range of abilities. For the coach, ten Saturdays can make a year.

But perhaps the most consequential difference is in the way teachers and coaches are evaluated. Teachers are appraised mostly by students, peers, and administrators, but the coach is often judged by the public.

No part of the school is more visible to the public than the athletic program. The performance of the athletes, the competency of the coach, even the adequacy of the facilities, are all constantly assessed by public observers, including the news media. At the center of this attention is the coach, who is often evaluated one way: How many victories?

To the Reader

If somebody described another job to you that had the same kinds of nuances, hazards, pressures, and foreshortened future as coaching, you probably would not be interested. Yet coaching may be the most universally attractive vocational application of the human movement sciences.

The main precaution to consider before choosing to coach is that the job is more than it may at first appear to be—more time-consuming, more stressful, more frustrating, more agonizing. It is not for the faint of heart or for those interested in financial reward (particularly when compared to time invested).

On the other hand, coaching offers more psychological and spiritual rewards than most other professions. The elation that can come from coaching is possibly unmatched elsewhere—there are moments of unabashed ecstasy that, unless experienced, are difficult to imagine.

A coach brings out the latent talent of athletes and helps them to achieve emotional gratification and social growth. A coach holds an influential and prestigious position in the eyes of the athletes. Coaches do not merely prepare players for public entertainment, they help young people to achieve excellence in body and mind. Therefore, a good coach knows both sport and people.

No more is expected of coaches than of any other adults who help young people to become better. As in any other leadership role, there will be abrasive moments you must face. But in the end, perhaps no other moment in life is more satisfying than when you can see past the anguish and put aside the wins and losses and know that young people have profited from their experience and from your influence.

Suggested Projects

1. When a high school athletic team performs poorly, there can be a great deal of public criticism of the coach. Yet, if a high school orchestra performs poorly or a school play is mediocre, there is somehow a public acceptance of this sub-par performance. Discuss in class why critical standards for public performances of school programs seem to differ.

2. Describe your own motives for wanting to become a coach. What are the origins of these motives? What characteristics do you have that you believe are your strongest predispositions for survival in the profession?

3. Teaching and coaching differ in many respects, such as the technical preparation for each role, the nature of the competencies expected in each role, the atmosphere of the environment, the motives in each setting, the pressures involved, and the criteria by which success is evaluated. Discuss these differences. Are there any elements to the two roles that are complementary to both?

4. Discuss the idea that coaches should have pressure to win. Orient the discussion on the concept that winning teams can generate school and community spirit and a greater sense of affiliation. Debate whether certain sports should have this responsibility more than others.

5. Create a perfect coaching profile. Collect a list from everyone in class of the characteristics they have found to be the most favorable among the coaches they have had in the past. Piece together the most commonly stated traits for the hypothetically perfect coach.

6. Role-play some uncomfortable situations that will arise in the coaching profession. For example, one person assumes the role of a coach and another the role of a booster who is questioning the coach's strategy, or a parent demanding that their son or daughter get more playing time, or another teacher wondering why you lost to Rival High School.

7. Learn the legal meaning of negligence, tort, reasonable and prudent behavior, assumption of risk, and battery. Apply their meanings to the coaching profession. Suggest ways that coaches can reduce their legal vulnerability (see Figone, 1989b, for reference).

References

Caroon, A. V. (1980). *Social Psychology of Sport.* Ithaca, NY: Mouvement Publications.

Chaumeton, N. R., and Duda, J. L. (1988). Is it How You Play the Game or Whether You Win or Lose? The Effect of Competitive Level and Situation on Coaching Behaviors. *Journal of Sport Psychology, 11,* 157–174.

Cherniss, C. (1980). *Staff Burnout: Job Stress in the Human Services.* Beverly Hills, CA: Sage.

Claxton, D. B. (1988). A Systematic Observation of More and Less Successful High School Tennis Coaches. *Journal of Teaching Physical Education, 7,* 302–310.

Applications

Coakley, J. J. (1986). *Sport in Society* (3rd ed.). St. Louis: C. V. Mosby.

Dwyer, J. J. M., and Fischer, D. G. (1988). Psychometric Properties of the Coach's Version of the Leadership Scale for Sports. *Perceptual and Motor Skills, 67,* 795–798.

Ellis, M. J. (1988). *The Business of Physical Education: Future of the Profession.* Champaign, IL: Human Kinetics Publishers.

Figone, A. J. (1989a). Preventing Professional Stagnation in Teacher Coaches. *The Physical Educator, 46*(1), 9–12.

Figone, A. J. (1989b). Seven Major Legal Duties of a Coach. *Journal of Physical Education, Recreation, and Dance, 60*(7), 71–75.

Fouss, D. E., and Troppmann, R. J. (1981). *Effective Coaching: A Psychological Approach.* New York: John Wiley & Sons.

Garland, D. J., and Barry, J. R. (1988). The Effects of Personality and Perceived Leader Behaviors on Performance in Collegiate Football. *The Psychological Record, 38,* 237–247.

Gilbert, M. (1989). *On Social Facts.* New York: Routledge.

Gill, D. L. (1986). *Psychological Dynamics of Sport.* Champaign, IL: Human Kinetics Publishers.

Gordon, S. (1988). Decision Styles and Coaching Effectiveness in University Soccer. *Canadian Journal of Sport Sciences, 13*(1), 56–65.

Gould, D., Hodge, K., Peterson, K., and Giannini, J. (1989). An Exploratory Examination of Strategies Used by Elite Coaches to Enhance Self-Efficacy in Athletes. *Journal of Sport and Exercise Psychology, 11,* 128–140.

Griffey, D. C., Housner, L. D., and Williams, D. (1984). Coaches' Use of Nonliteral Language: Metaphor as a Means of Effective Teaching. In M. Piëron and G. Graham (Eds.), *Sport Pedagogy: The 1984 Olympic Scientific Congress Proceedings* (Vol. 6, pp. 131–137). Champaign, IL: Human Kinetics Publishers.

Hennessy, J. T. (1989). A Successful Philosophy of Coaching. *The Physical Educator, 46*(2), 58–61.

Humphrey, J. H. (1987). *Stress in Coaching.* Springfield, IL: Charles C. Thomas.

Jones, B. J., Wells, L. J., Peters, P. E., and Johnson, D. J. (1989). *Guide to Effective Coaching: Principles and Practices.* Dubuque, IA: Wm. C. Brown.

Keller, I. A. (1982). *The Interscholastic Coach.* Englewood Cliffs, NJ: Prentice-Hall.

Lackey, D. (1977). Why Do High School Coaches Quit? *Journal of Physical Education and Recreation, 48*(4), 22–23.

Lackey, D. (1986). The High School Coach: A Pressure Position. *Journal of Physical Education, Recreation, and Dance, 57*(3), 28–32.

Lacy, A. C., and Darst, P. W. (1985). Systematic Observation of Behaviors of Winning High School Head Football Coaches. *Journal of Teaching in Physical Education, 4,* 256–270.

Locke, L. F., and Massengale, J. D. (1978). Role Conflict in Teacher/Coaches. *Research Quarterly for Exercise and Sport, 49*(2), 162–174.

Mancini, V. H., and Agnew, M. (1978). An Analysis of Teaching and Coaching Behaviors. In W. F. Straub (Ed.), *Sport Psychology: An Analysis of Athletic Behavior* (pp. 402–409). Ithaca, NY: Mouvement Publications.

Markland, R., and Martinek, T. J. (1988). Descriptive Analysis of Coach Augmented Feedback Given to High School Varsity Female Volleyball Players. *Journal of Teaching in Physical Education, 7,* 289–301.

Massengale, J. D. (1981). Researching Role Conflict. *Journal of Physical Education, Recreation, and Dance, 52*(9), 23ff.

McClelland, D. C. (1975). *Power: The Inner Experience.* New York: Irvington.

McKenzie, T. L. (1984). Analysis of the Practice Behavior of Elite Athletes. In M. Piěron and G. Graham (Eds.), *Sport Pedagogy: The 1984 Olympic Scientific Congress Proceedings* (Vol. 6, pp. 117–121). Champaign, IL: Human Kinetics Publishers.

National Federation Handbook 1989/90. (1989). Kansas City, MO: National Federation of State High School Associations.

Ogilvie, B. C., and Tutko, T. A. (1966). *Problem Athletes and How to Handle Them.* London: Pelham Books.

Sabock, R. J. (1985). *The Coach* (3rd ed.). Champaign, IL: Human Kinetic's Publishers.

Sage, G. H. (1987). The Social World of High School Athletic Coaches: Multiple Role Demands and the Consequences. *Sociology of Sport Journal, 4*(3), 218–228.

Schliesman, E. S. (1987). Relationship between the Congruence of Preferred and Actual Leader Behavior and Subordinate Satisfaction with Leadership. *Journal of Sport Behavior, 10*(3), 157–166.

Seagrave, J. O. (1981). Role Preferences among Perspective Education Teacher/Coaches: Its Relevance to Education. In V. Crafts (Ed.), *Proceedings of the National Association for Physical Education in Higher Education* (Vol. 2). Champaign, IL: Human Kinetics Publishers.

Sherman, M. A., and Hassan, J. S. (1984). Behavioral Studies of Youth Sport Coaches. In M. Piěron and G. Graham (Eds.), *Sport Pedagogy: The 1984 Olympic Scientific Congress Proceedings* (Vol. 6, pp. 103–108). Champaign, IL: Human Kinetics Publishers.

Sinclair, D. A., and Vealey, R. S. (1989). Effects of Coaches' Expectations and Feedback on the Self-Perceptions of Athletes. *Journal of Sport Behavior, 12,* 77–91.

Sisley, B. L., and Capel, S. A. (1985). Oregon Coaches Background Survey: Background of Coaches in Oregon High Schools 1984–1985. Unpublished manuscript, University of Oregon, Department of Physical Education and Human Movement Studies, Eugene. Cited in M. J. Ellis [1988], *The Business of Physical Education: Future of the Profession.* Champaign, IL: Human Kinetics Publishers.

Stillwell, J. L. (1979). Why PE Majors Want to Coach. *Journal of Physical Education and Recreation, 49*(9), 40.

Wandzilak, T., and Ansorge, C. J. (1988). Comparison between Selected Practice and Game Behaviors of Youth Sport Soccer Coaches. *Journal of Sport Behavior, 11,* 78–88.

Weiss, M. R., and Friedrichs, W. D. (1986). The Influence of Leader Behaviors, Coach Attributes, and Institutional Variables on Performance and Satisfaction of Collegiate Basketball Teams. *Journal of Sport Psychology, 8,* 332–346.

Chapter 13

Special Populations: Considerations for the Handicapped

Who Are the Handicapped?
The Legislation for Handicapped Students
Mainstreaming
The Least Restrictive Environment
The Individualized Education Program
Inclusion or Exclusion?
The Clumsy Child
Summary
To the Reader
Suggested Projects
References

Perhaps as much as 12 percent of the school-aged population has a handicapping condition that interferes with functioning in an educational setting.

Federal laws mandate that these students must be accorded the same educational opportunities as all other students and must be provided with individualized instructional programs as needed.

As a result of these programs and with increased societal understanding of disabling conditions, new opportunities for participation in physical education, sports, and recreation have become common for the handicapped.

The objective is for a full integration of disabled persons into every facet of life experiences.

A major objective underlying all systems of education is to provide the skills necessary for a self-reliant existence in society. As indicated in chapter 2, the endeavor can broadly be thought of as "preparation for life." This overall objective holds true for all students, regardless of individual abilities, and this includes students in need of special attention. Opportunities for full participation in every school experience must be available to everyone. It is not only a moral obligation shared by all educational disciplines; it is also a law.

Physical education fits the "life readiness" objective by providing useable skills for independent leisure activities. In addition, it can potentially help handicapped persons to become more independent, to live a more well-rounded life, and to enjoy life more. To achieve such goals, it is sometimes necessary to develop special physical education programs for students with special needs, or at least to modify existing programs. Such arrangements have historically been called adapted physical education, or more recently, special physical education. These programs (1) have been created or changed to make them suitable for students with special needs and (2) will help handicapped students adjust to their particular handicapping conditions.

WHO ARE THE HANDICAPPED?

Handicapped persons are those who have a physical or mental impairment that substantially limits one or more major life activities. In an educational context, *handicapped* means being "unable to receive reasonable benefit from ordinary education" because of one or more of the following conditions: long-term physical impairment or illness, significant limited intellectual capacity, significant identifiable emotional or behavior disorder, identifiable perceptual or communicative disorder, or speech disorder. Educational definitions of handicapped students vary from state to state, although all agree fundamentally.

Handicap is a broad term and a relative term. Sometimes no distinction can be made for saying one person is handicapped while another is not. Furthermore, the term popularly implies that a person has limited capabilities. But many people prove otherwise. For example, country singer Mel Tillis has a speech impediment, except when he sings. There is a Hollywood stunt woman who is deaf, another who has only one eye. The unofficial record for aligning a scrambled Rubik's Cube was accomplished by a youngster classified as mentally retarded. Tom Dempsey was born with only half a right foot, yet in 1970 he set a National Football League field goal record of sixty-three yards. Pete Gray played the outfield for the St. Louis Browns in 1945, despite having lost an arm at the shoulder in a childhood accident. Monty Stratton and Burt Shepherd pitched for the Philadelphia Athletics and Washington Senators, respectively, during the 1930s and in 1945, both with an artificial leg. In 1989, Jim Abbott, born without a right hand, began a major league career with the California Angels. In the 1960 Olympics, Wilma Rudolph, despite having both birth defects and polio, won gold medals in the 100-, 200-, and 400-yard relays. In the 1984 Olympics, Neroll Fairhall from New Zealand, confined to a wheelchair, competed with able-bodied athletes in archery. In 1981, Phil Carpenter and George Murray, two wheelchair athletes, pushed across the United States—Los Angeles to New York—in 155 days. That same year, Terry Fox, a below-the-knee amputee from cancer, ran across most of Canada to raise donations for cancer research and died from his ailment before he could complete his journey.

While such persons are, by definition, handicapped, they are clearly not handicapped in other important ways. Helen Keller once said it: "Never mind what handicapped people can't do, look at what they *can* do."

THE LEGISLATION FOR HANDICAPPED STUDENTS

In the 1970s, an evolving sensitivity to the needs of handicapped persons led to the enactment of national legislation, which mandated that all schools offer appropriate educational experiences for every student, regardless of any disability. Two laws had particular impact. One was the now well-known *Public Law 94–142,* passed in 1975 but not put into effect until 1977, otherwise referred to as the Education for All Handicapped Children Act. The essence of the act is that:

> The term "special education" means specially designed instruction, at no cost to parents or guardians, to meet the unique needs of a handicapped child, including classroom instruction, instruction in physical education, home instruction, and instruction in hospitals and institutions.

The law requires that no individual shall be denied an equal education because of a handicap. Significantly, it was the first federal legislation ever to acknowledge and require physical education as an important and valuable addition to the total education of all students.

A second federal law that directly affected physical education (and athletics) is Section 504 of the Rehabilitation Act (*Public Law 93–112*), passed in 1973 but also not implemented until 1977. It obligates schools

The law requires that no individual shall be denied an equal education because of a handicap.
Courtesy of Special Population Programs, University of Wisconsin at La Crosse.

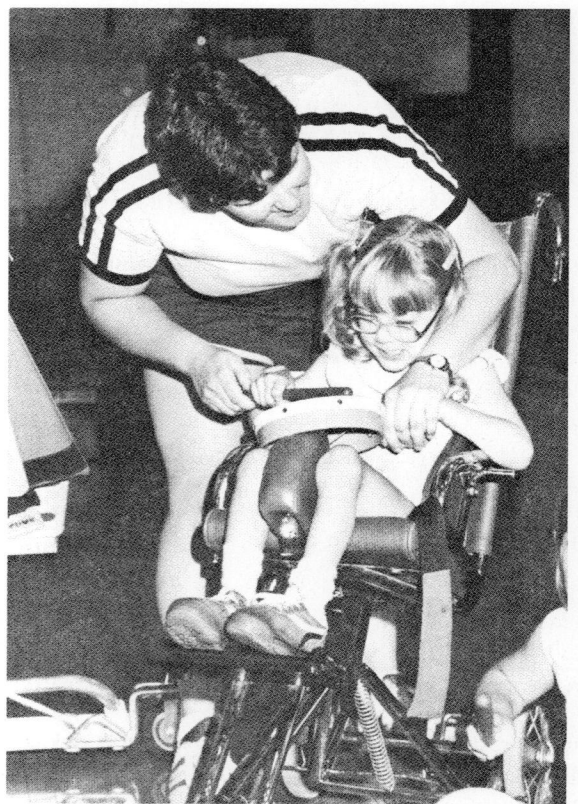

to offer handicapped students the same variety of physical education activities as the regular school population, including equal chances to participate in club, intramural, and interscholastic activities. Also, this law led to the structural changes in buildings (i.e., construction of ramps and special toilet facilities) to make them accommodating to all handicapped persons.

Prior to 1977, less than one-fifth of the nation's public schools offered any physical education at all to handicapped students (NACH, 1977). Thereafter, compliance with the federal legislation was at first very slow (Joiner and Sabatino, 1981), especially in high schools (Shapiro, 1981). The mandates were too costly for many school systems, and the federal funds appropriated to cover the costs have been unpredictably available—sometimes liberal sums of money are allocated; more often the funds are drastically cut.

Notwithstanding this, there have been at least the following three positive outcomes from the federal laws:

1. Existing special physical education programs were expanded. In some cases the existing "programs" were nothing more than space allotted for games (table tennis, shuffleboard, and the like). But the laws required a full spectrum of regular physical activities for the handicapped.
2. Programs were created where none previously existed. A major problem, however, was that additional and appropriately trained teachers were usually needed.
3. Perhaps most importantly, the laws compelled the schools to address the philosophical issues of educating the handicapped. It was rather like having to be reminded that the main focus of education is, after all, education for everyone. Nothing more, but nothing less.

MAINSTREAMING

One overall effect of the federal legislation was to encourage the movement of handicapped students out of segregated classes and into regular programs. The intent was to include them to the maximum degree possible with their nonhandicapped peers. Special classes or separate schooling is now permitted only in cases where a student is not able to fully function in a regular setting.

The practice of providing an integrated environment, handicapped with nonhandicapped, is called *mainstreaming*. It literally means the incorporation of handicapped students into the "mainstream" of educational life. The handicapped are not only to be included but also integrated into regular programs.

Effective mainstreaming in physical education requires some creative strategies. Following are some examples:

1. The activities might be modified to equalize competition, such as allowing a visually handicapped youngster to kick a stationary ball in kickball, or giving a lower-limb amputee a shorter distance to run in a race.
2. Substitution or interchange of roles could occur, such as permitting an able-bodied person to run for a handicapped person in softball, or allowing a visually impaired person to run with a sighted partner.
3. To equalize competition, the nonhandicapped might be asked to assume the condition of a disabled player, for example by being blindfolded or by hopping on one foot for a running race.

Applications

The practice of providing an integrated environment, handicapped with nonhandicapped, is called mainstreaming.

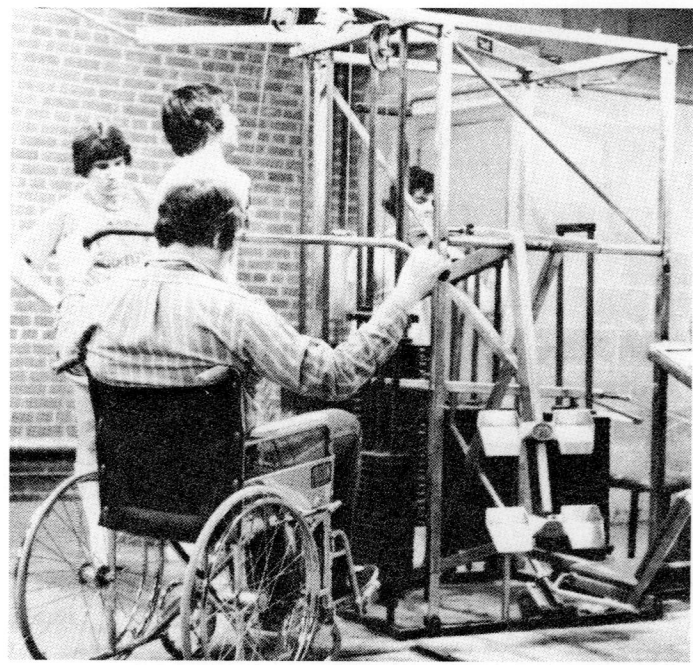

4. Playing areas could be reduced to accommodate persons with limited mobility. Tennis, badminton, or volleyball could be played in a narrower-than-normal court.

5. Elimination-type games should be avoided or modified to keep participants in the activity. For example, in dodgeball anyone who is hit might become a thrower instead of being eliminated.

THE LEAST RESTRICTIVE ENVIRONMENT

The actual mandate in Public Law 94–142 is that handicapped children must receive special education and related services in the *least restrictive environment* commensurate with their needs. Therefore, rather than imposing unconditional full integration, the intent is to provide the best match between a student and a specific learning program. It means that the student should be "restricted" as little as possible and, to the maximum possible extent, should be included in regular programs. Such arrangements should bring students closest to their learning potential,

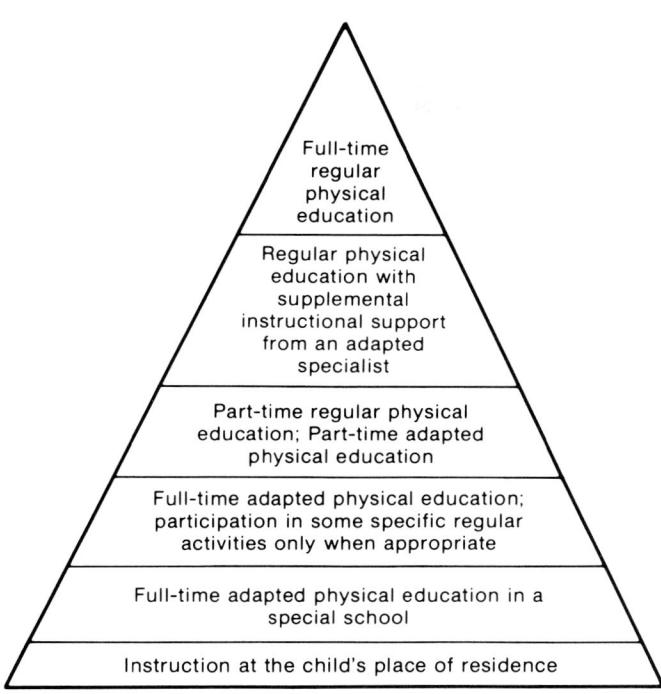

Figure 13.1 Placement possibilities for the least restrictive environment.

while still providing for their unique educational needs. Figure 13.1 shows the theoretical continuum this concept might encompass in physical education. Placing a handicapped student as high as practicable in this pyramid would provide the least restrictive environment.

THE INDIVIDUALIZED EDUCATION PROGRAM

Prior to a student's placement, an *individualized education program* (IEP) must be developed and written. The IEP is a detailed plan of instructional objectives and special services specifically designed for each student. It is normally written by a committee of all individuals who are closely involved with the student, including teachers, school administrators, support personnel (physicians, therapists, psychologists, or social workers), and the parents. The plan cannot be implemented until the parents have given approval, and at any time they can request a revision of the plan or withdraw their child from an ongoing program.

To be complete, the IEP must include:

1. A statement of the present levels of performance of the student.
2. A statement of annual goals, including short-term educational objectives.
3. A statement of the specific educational services to be provided and the extent to which the student should be able to participate in regular programs.
4. The projected date for initiation and anticipated duration of such services.
5. Appropriate objective criteria and evaluation procedures to determine whether the instructional objectives are being achieved.

An IEP is not a guarantee that a handicapped student will progress at a certain rate or even that there will be any progress at all. It is simply an organized strategy for providing the student with the most practical environment possible and with realistic educational objectives.

INCLUSION OR EXCLUSION?

Considerable debate still surrounds mainstreaming. It remains the single most controversial issue regarding the education of handicapped students (Myles and Simpson, 1989). Proponents of mainstreaming have suggested that its primary advantage may be the development of peer relationships between disabled and able-bodied students. The relationships would then eliminate the stigma of physical impairment or lower mental ability, and would give handicapped students a feeling of equality and importance.

Mainstreaming seeks an interaction in which the disabled do not feel pitied, scorned, different, deviant, morally inferior, or even specially favored. In physical education or in sport, it implies that disabled and able-bodied persons can interact as individuals, teammates, or competitors in ways that minimize or avoid potentially disadvantageous or stigmatizing consequences of impairment.

But placing able-bodied and disabled students together does not automatically or necessarily lead to genuine integration (Nixon II, 1989). In fact, appraisals of mainstreaming mostly show that handicapped students, particularly in the elementary years, have social difficulties in their schools (Gresham and Reschly, 1986). Peer acceptance of handicapped

Special Populations: Considerations for the Handicapped

Handicapped athletes demonstrate the same intensive desire and level of training as able-bodied athletes.
Courtesy of the National Association of Sports for Cerebral Palsy.

students is not readily occurring, and this becomes manifest as social deficits for the handicapped (Bryan, Pearl, and Fallon, 1989). In turn, the social deficits are now actually considered as a learning disability (Gresham and Elliot, 1989). Additionally, in mainstreamed settings the handicapped tend to get less instructional attention than their nonhandicapped peers (Gagnon, Tousignant, and Martel, 1989). This in turn may accent an already existing low self-esteem and lead to low achievement (Bursuck, 1989). And finally, all this compounds into lower levels of participation, which is especially critical in physical education where nonparticipation is aggravated by the fact that the handicapped often lack the physical skills, positive self-concepts, and positive attitudes toward activity that are necessary for successful participation (Politino and Smith, 1989).

The verdict is that integrating handicapped students into regular physical education classes does not produce instinctive social acceptance from peers. However, in cases where a supportive atmosphere exists with appropriate instructional attention, the handicapped are observed to enjoy their experience, which leads to increased levels of participation (Drummer et. al., 1987), which further leads to enhanced potentials for accepting attitudes from other class members (Stewart, 1988).

And in another related setting, physically disabled persons have increasingly been able to attain open acceptance and athletic excellence in competitive sport. Witness, for example, wheelchair basketball and marathon runs, the International Games for the Disabled, and even the regular Olympics, where handicapped athletes demonstrate the same intensive desire, levels of training, and performance accomplishments as the able-bodied (Montelione and Davis, 1986).

Handicapped persons are now also visibly participating in recreational activities for the sheer joy of involvement, ranging from bowling to basketball, from swimming to skydiving, from mountain climbing to cross-country running. Sports participation helps the able-bodied to see past the disability of the athlete and to recognize instead the ability and commitment of the person participating. And involvement in recreational activity may help to erase a stereotype. If so, then "success" and achievement can be measured intrinsically for the handicapped participant and externally as social recognition.

THE CLUMSY CHILD

Some students may not necessarily be defined as handicapped but may have motor difficulties that identify them as "awkward" or "clumsy." They may have limitations in strength, coordination, or vitality that adversely affect their motor performance, and possibly their academic performance as well. Whether the student is considered to be learning disabled, mildly retarded, or of normal intelligence, the clumsy child is characterized by awkward locomotion patterns, poor hand-eye and foot-eye coordination, and slowness in learning motor skills. Such a student is often relegated to a low social position, being excluded from normal sports and games, and by the time he or she reaches adulthood, may have lost the desire to participate in any activity.

Some individuals do not develop mature sensory input and reflex systems and as a result may never reach normal performance levels. Other individuals may eventually develop normally functioning sensory input and reflex systems, but their neurological maturation is slow, and they are therefore considered to be "developmentally delayed." For these students, a program of "motor therapy" has promise in helping them through the awkward times to become a motorically integrated, normally functioning adult (Sherrill, 1986).

Cues of developmental delays are important to identify, for they will signal the need for appropriately designed compensatory activities. Standardized tests are readily available, although simple observation will also reveal difficulties. Some of the cues include:

1. Reflex patterns that hinder efficient movement, such as running, hopping, or jumping stiff-legged, or failure to use opposition when throwing.
2. Equilibrium difficulties evidenced in inability to hold static balance positions, difficulty in shifting directions quickly, or not being able to walk heel-to-toe.
3. Poor kinesthetic information shown through uneven or inaccurate positioning of the limbs, or flaccid muscle tone.
4. Tactile difficulties that prevent the person from carrying out a sequence of movement activities, or locomotor patterns that are stumbly.
5. Disparity between the two eyes, preventing normal depth perception, evidenced in going down steps one at a time, or difficulty in climbing on an apparatus, or missing a thrown ball.

The sensory input system develops during the first few years of life. By the fourth year, the input base has normally stabilized and perceptual-motor integration starts to occur and to continue in refinement through the seventh year, thereafter to show improvements in precision (Pyfer, 1988). When there is evidence of developmental delays, particularly when detected early, programs for skill acquisition and generalization can be specifically designed to promote more normal motor gains.

SUMMARY

It is generally estimated that about 12 percent of the school-aged population (ages 6–19) in America has some manner of identifiable handicapping condition (Sherrill, 1986). Under the law, free and appropriate public education must be provided to handicapped students, including instruction in physical education. Whenever possible, this instruction must take place in regular physical education classes. If the student's needs cannot be met by the regular classes, an IEP must be developed to attend to the special needs of that student.

The effects of these laws and other efforts have been to guarantee equal opportunities in all of life's activities to every handicapped person, regardless of type or severity of the individual's condition or the individual's station in life. Through mainstreaming and placement in the least restrictive environment in the schools and through programs of sport for disabled athletes, handicapped persons now have widened opportunities for participation in physical education, recreation, and sport activities. Emphasis has been placed on the individual's abilities and potential, enabling each handicapped person to become as independent as possible and to enjoy a high-quality, challenging, and rewarding life of physical activity.

Crucial factors contributing to the success of these endeavors are (a) positive and accepting attitudes, (b) social consciousness and responsiveness to the needs of those less fortunate, (c) the commitment of professional personnel from different disciplines in providing active programs in vigorous physical, recreational, and sport programs, and (d) the acceptance by the general population of implementing mainstreaming and other equal-opportunity programs (Stein, 1986).

Physical activity is no longer limited to the able-bodied. Some individuals use wheelchairs, some make the best of limited sensory input, some compensate for missing limbs, perceptual-motor deficits, or abnormal reflex activity and muscle tone. The important matter is that disabled persons with a broad spectrum of differences can achieve the same enjoyment from participation as the able-bodied. It begins in the schools, not only by law but by moral obligation. And within the schools, the physical, intellectual, and spiritual qualities of each individual can be made manifest.

To the Reader

One of the more worrisome factors cited by beginning teachers is how to handle handicapped students mainstreamed into their classes (Templin and Schempp, 1989). Even among experienced teachers, there often is a feeling that a mainstreamed student will interrupt the status quo of the class or pose a threat to the instructional proficiency of the teacher (Friend and Bauwens, 1988). Often, mainstreaming poses more strain on the teacher than the student (Icabone and Gallery, 1982).

Teachers who are most adept at providing the individualized instruction needed by handicapped persons are those who have the best instructional skills in the first place (McDaniel and DiBella-McCarthy, 1989). Also, they quite frequently have had prior contact with the handicapped in their student teaching experience or through volunteer programs (Strickman, Cumblad, and Leyser, 1988). Therefore, for persons who envision themselves in careers that may bring them into regular affiliation with handicapped persons, the following are recommended:

1. *Academic background.* Obtaining teaching certification in most states requires the taking of at least one course in education for special populations. If this is not a requirement in your state or for your career choice, it is nevertheless suggested.

2. *Field experience.* Opportunities for field experience in existing special programs for the handicapped are often readily available. This valuable experience can range from observational involvement to actual "hands-on" participation as aids to a teacher or therapist. One of the benefits of a field experience is the chance to become familiar with the diagnostic tools that are used to differentiate between normal and unusual motor patterns.

A broad academic and experiential background is of great benefit for anyone who will work with handicapped persons. To comprehend the nature of just a single disability, such as mental retardation, is in itself an in-depth undertaking. Multiply that by the complexity and diversity of other handicapping conditions, and the task is monumental. Consequently, every course and every field experience will add to the understanding of how humans function in a variety of situations and will strengthen one's confidence for entry into the professional world.

Suggested Projects

1. Many special education programs welcome volunteer assistance. They can be located at campus child-study centers, day-care centers, hospitals, churches, private centers, or schools. Arrange to assist in a program, perhaps even through an independent study for academic credit.
2. Find out what diagnostic tools are available for assessing deviancy in motor performance. Obtain at least one test. Administer the test to class members. Compare the results with the norms given for the test.
3. Have all class members assume a handicapping condition (such as immobilizing one arm or wearing a blindfold). Select a motor skill and teach that skill to the role-playing students.
4. Visit a special education class, preferably a physical education class. Or, visit a live-in center for disabled persons. Write a few paragraphs about your visit.
5. Have a handicapped person speak to your class, in particular about social life and career aspirations and how the person has compensated for his or her disability.

References

Bryan, T., Pearl, R., and Fallon, P. (1989). Conformity to Peer Pressure by Students with Learning Disabilities: A Replication. *Journal of Learning Disabilities, 22,* 458–459.

Bursuck, W. (1989). A Comparison of Students with Learning Disabilities to Low Achieving Students on Three Dimensions of Social Competence. *Journal of Learning Disabilities, 22,* 188–194.

Drummer, G. W., Ewing, M. E., Habeck, R. V., and Overton, S. R. (1987). Attributions of Athletes with Cerebral Palsy. *Adapted Physical Education Quarterly, 4,* 278–292.

Friend, M., and Bauwens, J. (1988). Managing Resistance: An Essential Consulting Skill for Learning Disabilities Teachers. *Journal of Learning Disabilities, 21,* 556–561.

Gagnon, J., Tousignant, M., and Martel, D. (1989). Academic Learning Time in Physical Education Classes for Mentally Handicapped Students. *Adapted Physical Activity Quarterly, 6,* 280–289.

Gresham, F. M., and Elliot, S. N. (1989). Social Skills Deficits as a Primary Learning Disability. *Journal of Learning Disabilities, 22,* 120–124.

Gresham, F. M., and Reschly, D. J. (1986). Social Skill Deficits and Low Peer Acceptance of Mainstreamed Learning Disabled Children. *Learning Disability Quarterly, 91*(1), 23–32.

Icabone, D. G., and Gallery, M. E. (1982). Caught in the Mainstream: The Severely and Profoundly Retarded Learner and the Least Restrictive Environment. *Rehabilitation Literature, 43,* 66–71.

Joiner, L. M., and Sabatino, D. A. (1981). A Policy Study of P. L. 94–142. *Exceptional Children, 48,* 24–33.

McDaniel, E. A., and DiBella-McCarthy, H. (1989). Enhancing Teacher Efficacy in Special Education. *Teaching Exceptional Children, 21*(4), 34–38.

Montelione, T. L., and Davis, R. (1986). Physically Disabled Athletes Successfully Compete. In C. Sherrill (Ed.). *Sport and Disabled Athletes* (pp. 225–230). Champaign, IL: Human Kinetics Publishers.

Myles, B. S., and Simpson, R. L. (1989). Regular Educators' Modification Preferences for Mainstreaming Mildly Handicapped Children. *The Journal of Special Education, 22,* 479–489.

National Advisory Committee on the Handicapped. (1977). The IEP and Non-Academic Services. *American Education, 13*(9), 23–25.

Nixon II, H. L. (1989). Integration of Disabled People in Mainstreaming Sports: Case Study of a Partially Sighted Child. *Adapted Physical Activity Quarterly, 6*(1), 17–31.

Politino, V., and Smith, S. (1989). Attitude toward Physical Activity and Self-Concept of Emotionally Disturbed and Normal Children. *Adapted Physical Activity Quarterly, 6,* 371–378.

Pyfer, J. L. (1988). Teachers, Don't Let Your Students Grow Up to Be Clumsy Adults. *Journal of Physical Education, Recreation, and Dance, 59*(1), 38–42.

Shapiro, H. (1981). Implementing P. L. 94–142 in the High School: A Successful In-Service Training Model. *Education, 102,* 47–52.

Sherrill, C. (1986). *Adapted Physical Education and Recreation: A Multidisciplinary Approach* (3rd ed.). Dubuque, IA: Wm. C. Brown.

Stein, J. U. (1986). International Perspective: Physical Education and Sport for Participants with Handicapping Conditions. In C. Sherrill (Ed.), *Sport and Disabled Athletes* (pp. 51–64). Champaign, IL: Human Kinetics Publishers.

Stewart, C. C. (1988). Modification of Student Attitudes toward Disabled Peers. *Adapted Physical Activity Quarterly, 5,* 44–48.

Strickman, D., Cumblad, C., and Leyser, Y. (1988). Mainstreaming Volunteers: The Learning about Handicaps Program. *The Clearing House, 61(8),* 351–355.

Templin, T. J., and Schempp, P. G. (1989). *Socialization into Physical Education: Learning to Teach.* Indianapolis: Benchmark Press.

Chapter 14

Careers: Jobs Worth Doing

Careers in Education

Careers in Sport

Careers in the Health and Leisure Industries

Careers in Sports Medicine

Other Options

Summary

To the Reader

Suggested Projects

References

Some careers, most notably in teaching and coaching, have been long-standing and venerable employment areas for graduates, and will continue to be in the future.

In addition, new vocational avenues have given broad perspective to the potential career applications of the human movement sciences.

Within this expanded vocational world, certain career themes can be identified and the jobs typical of those themes can be delineated.

Thus, traditional career disciplines now combine with recently developed vocational themes to provide a wider selection of jobs than ever before.

Applications

THE discipline originally known as physical education has evolved from a general area of study that contained a convergent base of information to a series of somewhat independent subdisciplines, each with its own body of knowledge. Previously the field had a rather singular vocational focus. In earlier days a degree was a ticket to a career in teaching, with little difficulty in obtaining such a job and little thought or opportunity to do anything else.

This time-honored career path is still in prominence and continues to be the most common vocational direction taken by graduates. And in truth, never has our nation needed more from its teachers than now. Declining test scores, high dropout rates, functional illiteracy, financially weakened curriculums, rising juvenile crime rates, substance abuse, AIDS, value disorientation, and human alienation are among the problems that challenge society and the schools. Physical education can make its greatest societal contribution through its potential for positive influence on America's youth. The field must never lose sight of its fundamental mission to use organized activity and health information for the principal objective of improving the quality of life for all people and of instilling active self-management of wellness.

Within these foundational objectives, a number of specific areas of study have become subdisciplines that span a wide variety of specializations. They have grown inward, building a vast knowledge base that relates in particular to their own area but also to a more comprehensive understanding of how human beings function. This expansion of scholarly information about human movement has given attention to new descriptions of how the knowledge can be used in vocational settings. For example, job opportunities relating to exercise physiology now include wellness centers, medical clinics, therapy centers, and other areas of the health industry. A biomechanics background not only describes optimal performance criteria for athletes, it also applies to the expanding world of ergonomics. Motor control gives the understanding of how skills are acquired, and this is of use for jobs in sports medicine.

There has been a certain fragmentation to this growth of specialized knowledge. In framing their own domain, each division of human movement science has become increasingly independent, no longer as academically related to the whole as it once was. But the overlap is still there, for every subdiscipline is attempting in their own way to making a better, healthier, more enjoyable, and more self-perceptive life for all people. There are common goals to all areas of study, and they have in turn opened the floodgates to new vocational ingenuity.

Some of these career paths are described in the following pages. But there is a qualified caution to be given to this, for the vocational world, like the academic world, is also in constant flow. Even as these lines are being written events are changing, and the job market that is apparent today may not be tomorrow. Moreover, vocational avenues that become available tomorrow may not even have been thought of today. Perhaps the greatest expansion of job opportunities is yet to appear.

CAREERS IN EDUCATION

Overall, the undergraduate degree is most closely associated with careers in education. Physical education teachers work at various levels, from kindergarten to college and university settings. Coaching responsibilities are often affiliated with these teaching jobs. In some cases, usually at larger institutions, it is possible to be hired exclusively as a coach.

Teaching at the Elementary Level

A physical education teacher in the elementary grades will meet many classes in a normal day, but each class is relatively short, sometimes lasting only thirty minutes. The composition of the classes will vary considerably from grade to grade, and consequently the activities and the teaching style will need to be adjusted accordingly.

Often the teacher must work with limited facilities. Considerable ingenuity may be required to devise learning activities using minimal equipment and space; sometimes it is even necessary to conduct programs in multipurpose rooms, a vacant cafeteria, or even in regular classrooms.

In addition to teaching, the job often includes other responsibilities, such as organizing "field days," coordinating special lessons with the classroom teachers, and possibly giving lessons in health to the students in their regular classrooms. Coaching is not usually available in the elementary grades, although sometimes a coaching position at a high school in the same district is offered in conjunction with a teaching position in an elementary school.

Teaching at the Secondary Level

Secondary school is generally considered to be the years beyond elementary school, including junior high school or middle school. The age range of the students is twelve to eighteen years.

Most high schools have adequate facilities. At some of the larger schools, the physical education teachers will be able to concentrate, to some degree, on teaching in areas of particular expertise. At the smaller schools, there may be only one or two teachers, who will be expected to teach all the activities offered. Mostly, the activities will be "sports-type" with an emphasis on recreational activities that can be enjoyed throughout life, such as golf, tennis, or swimming, although there are often other unique offerings such as camping, martial arts, aerobics, or weight training.

Teachers will generally teach during all but one of the class periods in a day (six class periods are common for a high school day). Sometimes the position will include classroom teaching, often in health, but not uncommonly in an area unrelated to physical education.

Teaching in Higher Education

At this level, more emphasis is given to specialization. Normally the teaching concentrates on a few activities. Classroom teaching is sometimes part of the job, usually in courses on wellness-related areas. In colleges and universities that offer major programs, even more specialization is possible. Faculty members are expected to have a comprehensive knowledge of one or two areas, such as exercise physiology, biomechanics, motor control, and so forth. Most positions in major programs will focus on classroom and laboratory instruction, with minimal responsibilities for teaching activities. It is often expected, if not openly stated, that professors should engage in productive research. Tenure (a guarantee of a permanent position) is often granted or denied principally on the quantity and quality of the research produced.

Four levels of appointment exist: instructor, assistant professor, associate professor, and professor. Promotions in rank are based on years of service, instructional competence, and research or writing accomplishments.

Coaching Positions

A teaching/coaching contract is most likely to be secured at the high school level. Sometimes the position calls for coaching more than one sport. College teaching and coaching positions for someone with only a bachelor's degree can sometimes be found at smaller schools. In high school, occasionally the teaching duties will be reduced to compensate for the coaching responsibilities, and in some rare cases, a reduced schedule is offered instead of extra pay for coaching.

Some higher education institutions will offer assistant coaching positions to graduate students, usually for one year, often without pay, but with a full or partial tuition waiver. In other cases, the positions may be part of a graduate teaching assistantship that includes a stipend or tuition waiver.

Special Physical Education

This position involves organizing and administering programs of physical activity for handicapped students. Duties may include giving and interpreting diagnostic tests and formulating individualized education programs suited to each student's needs and capabilities.

The special physical education teacher works closely with all other people who have contact with the handicapped students. In some situations, the specialist will conduct the activity programs in an area that is designated for that purpose. In some other cases, the specialist will be itinerant; that is, the specialist travels to several schools in a district, administering programs at each school.

General Qualifications and Outlook for Careers in Education

For most jobs in elementary and secondary schools, an undergraduate degree will be sufficient. A master's degree will command a higher starting salary, but in these days of tightened school budgets, the degree may not necessarily be an advantage to job hunters. To obtain a college position without a master's degree is unusual, although possible. A doctorate will be essential to advance beyond the rank of instructor.

About half the states require an objective "competency" test that must be passed to obtain certification at the elementary or secondary level. Certification acquired in one state will usually reciprocate to other states, although the transfer will often require the taking of one or two localized courses (a history of the state is common).

The market for teachers is highly competitive. Every opening attracts many well-qualified applicants, especially in desirable living areas of the country. However, the overall projections generally are for the number of available positions and the supply of teachers to balance out somewhere around 1995. In theory, every certified teacher will then have a job available somewhere. Further predictions are that the greatest number of jobs for physical education will be in the Great Lakes region and the Middle Atlantic states (Ellis, 1988).

In the coaching profession, a great deal of turnover occurs. More assistant coaching positions are available than head coaching jobs. In more than half the states, a coaching position can be obtained without a related offering for a teaching position. The passage of Title IX dramatically increased the number of coaching jobs in women's athletics. However, the number of women actually entering the profession did not show a proportionate increase, and in fact, the percentage of coaching positions being held by women is showing a decline (Knoppers, 1987). This leads to the conclusion that qualified women coaches may have a job-search advantage.

CAREERS IN SPORT

Sport is big business. It's also small business and medium-sized business. And wherever there is business, there is a need for people to manage the business. Whether at the professional level or at a local recreation center, when sport is presented to a market, a sports program manager will be needed.

Athletic Administration

College and university athletic programs are run by a director of athletics, who often performs that job exclusively, without teaching or coaching responsibilities. At the high school level, the athletic director usually carries a full teaching load as well, or if the teaching schedule is reduced, there generally is no additional salary for directing the program.

The major responsibilities of the athletic director are to organize and administer the athletic program, including all budgetary matters. But the job also implies marketing and promoting the program, which translates into spending considerable time on the telephone, attending socials, making public appearances and speeches, and shaking many hands, both for goodwill and, most critically, to raise money.

The athletic director also attends to the morale, welfare, and motivation of the personnel in the athletic department. One of the unpleasant parts of the job is dealing with problem coaches; ultimately the matter of what to do with a losing coach will surface.

A supporting position is that of sports information director, which is almost exclusively a college and university appointment. The primary responsibility is to promote the athletic programs by informing the media of all news and activities within the athletic department, sometimes at press conferences. The sports information director is also a liaison between the athletic department and alumni and booster clubs. Additionally, the job includes keeping records and statistical data on all teams, coordinating all athletic department publications, designing media guides and programs, writing advertisements and commercials, and organizing special events such as half-time presentations or promotion nights.

Also at the college and university level, there is a director of intramurals (or director of campus recreation) who administers tournaments and other recreational opportunities for the students. This includes scheduling facility use, securing officials, keeping records, promoting the programs, and handling the budget. These place heavy demands on

The Sports Information Director promotes a school's athletic programs by informing the media of news and activities within the athletic department.
Photo by Tom Cherrey.

one's time in the late afternoon and early evening hours; on some campuses, the intramural program can run past midnight.

At the high school level, the intramural program will usually be handled by a teacher who assumes the responsibility at the end of the day, with no compensatory reduction in the normal teaching load. In higher education, the position is most often a job in itself, with no affiliated teaching responsibilities.

Corporate and Community Recreation Management

These jobs generally involve organizing and directing sports and activity programs at resorts, public and private sports clubs, Y's, other community centers, and in corporate settings. Some jobs may require the director to teach sports skills or fitness activities to the clients, or to coordinate social events and engage in fund-raising.

The management duties in corporate fitness centers typically include the hiring and supervising of instructional personnel. Because some programs, particularly in executive fitness, may involve stress tests, medical supervision is imperative. Often, the program director will also conduct classes.

Other Sport-Related Jobs

In addition to careers that fit the category of sports management, other job potentials could be available in (1) sports journalism, including television and radio sportscasting, sportswriting, publishing, video production and programming; (2) sports marketing, including advertising, sporting goods sales, and special event organization; and (3) sports entrepreneurship, including financial and legal consultation, and private investment.

Overall Qualifications and Outlook

For many of the positions described above, an undergraduate degree is a basic qualification, and course work in management and finance will be an advantage. For some jobs, such as at camps, fitness clinics, or weight-loss clinics, a degree may not be a formal qualification, but the person with a degree will have an edge over others who do not.

It is common to find athletic directors who have a background in business, and many institutions actively seek such a candidate. An advanced degree is often a bonus, but experience as a competitive athlete and a coach is a substantial prerequisite.

As of this writing, a master's degree is not mandatory to become a director of campus recreation, but the degree may become a requirement in the future, along with specific certification, obtained by passing a national examination given by the National Intramural-Recreational Sports Association.

Overall, jobs in sports management are not as plentiful as teaching jobs, and the market is competitive. Often it is possible, however, to start as an assistant, particularly in athletics and intramurals. Corporate management jobs require experience in teaching and lower-level management responsibilities, and some corporations will only consider persons who have certification from the American College of Sports Medicine (a postgraduate national certification that focuses on cardiac fitness and assessment skills, including stress testing).

CAREERS IN THE HEALTH AND LEISURE INDUSTRIES

For half a century, there was an automatic combination of study areas into a curricular package universally called health, physical education, and recreation. The delivery system was pitched mostly toward schools and community-supported recreation. Now the three areas have splintered into rather self-contained disciplines, each with its own distinctive body of knowledge, and the places of operation now include a complex of medical and corporate, public and private, and large and small enterprises that make up health and leisure industries. But they all continue to be linked by the common goals of promoting healthy life-styles and the enjoyable use of leisure.

The Health Enhancement Industry

Americans have become interested in their own health promotion. Concern with diet, fitness, stress management, the early detection of disease, and other related areas have produced a nation of attentive consumers. To satisfy this interest, services have become established in hospitals, health centers, fitness centers, weight-loss clinics, and other health-related settings. Counseling centers and advertising also fit into what can collectively be called the health enhancement industry.

Many of the establishments are profit oriented. Some are supported by government. Many exist in business and corporate settings, where it has become clear that programs given for employees have the payback benefit of reduced health care expenses, lower worker absenteeism, higher worker morale, and increased productivity. Some companies even offer financial incentives for staying healthy.

The people needed to staff these organizations could come from a variety of the health professions, including medicine. But this is an open market for persons with a background in the contemporary versions of health, physical education, and recreation.

The jobs performed could vary considerably, although most will involve some manner of assessment of the participant's current level of fitness or state of health, followed by a prescription for positive changes along with the provision of on-site programs to implement the changes. Specific responsibilities might include directing group exercises (especially aerobics and weight training), teaching specific sports skills, conducting graded stress tests, or writing out exercise prescriptions. Some establishments will offer an educational focus so that their clients may learn of the basis to health maintenance. Life-style modification may also include counseling for stress management, smoking cessation, alcohol control, or weight reduction.

The settings for such services can be markedly different. Some large corporations will have multimillion-dollar facilities with all manner of state-of-the-art fitness and recreation equipment. Smaller companies may simply offer aerobics classes in a local high school gymnasium. Some health spas might offer their facilities only, with no instructional or group activities. Others will provide a full schedule of organized fitness activities and instruction in a variety of sports skills. Some will give graded exercise tests as part of their programs, along with health-promotion classes in areas such as diet and weight control.

A number of not-so-obvious jobs are available in the travel, tourism, and hospitality business.
Photo by Tom Cherrey.

The Leisure Industry

At one time, it was predicted that the workweek would decrease (perhaps to as little as thirty hours) to the point where people had so much free time that they would not know what to do with it (Linder, 1970). That has not happened, and there may not be much more of a decline from the present workweek of approximately thirty-eight hours (Sorkin, 1988). But what has happened is that people are using the free time they have for increased participation (and investment) in recreational pursuits. The obvious implications of this relate to the augmentation of leisure and recreation services that need to be provided to the public.

Services in the leisure industry, like health enhancement, are varied. Obvious locations are community recreation centers where year-round programs are offered for all ages, including the elderly. YMCAs and YWCAs also provide sports classes, and organized programs can be found at private clubs, retirement communities, and housing complexes.

The not-so-obvious jobs can be discovered in travel, tourism, and hospitality businesses. They include planning and conducting activity programs at vacation resorts or on cruise liners. Other activity-related careers may be available through state and national park services, or with private enterprises such as the Outward Bound types of organizations.

The total employment pool of the leisure industry is sizable, with perhaps nearly five million people involved with the tour and hospitality business alone (Ellis, 1988). Of course, the percentage of this total actually involved in providing activity services is small, but as the dollar invested into the industry continues to grow (as it is projected to do), the absolute number of jobs should increase.

Overall Qualifications and Outlook

Virtually every community in the United States with a population of at least 10,000 now has a municipal recreation department (Sessoms, 1987). In addition there are now an estimated 25,000 private sport and athletic clubs in America (Desensi and Koehler, 1989), with an annual growth expected to be up to 10 percent per year through the mid-1990s (Lambrecht, 1987), which may in turn produce an additional 50,000 jobs in the industry (Veal, 1987).

Most entry-level jobs are at the instructional level, generally involving the teaching of sports activities. Opportunities in community and private recreation are more numerous than corporate settings, where fitness programs have not expanded as rapidly as was originally predicted. Such corporate settings are rarely found outside of larger population centers.

In the health enhancement industry, jobs may be preferentially awarded to persons with a strong background in exercise physiology. In some cases, a master's degree will be a bonus.

Two abilities that will be supporting qualifications for jobs are (1) a varietal aptitude for teaching sports skills, which will be beneficial for appointments in the leisure industry, and (2) an exercise physiology background, particularly if it includes ability in graded stress testing and exercise prescription, which will have application in the health enhancement business.

CAREERS IN SPORTS MEDICINE

Sports medicine is primarily concerned with athletic welfare, particularly regarding sports injuries. It encompasses the diagnosis, treatment, rehabilitation, and prevention of injuries. In broad perspective, sports medicine includes other interest areas (exercise physiology, biomechanics, sport psychology, and so forth), all of which are focused on preparation for athletic competition and reduction of the potential for harm.

Part of an athletic trainer's job is to administer emergency first aid.
Photo by Tom Cherrey.

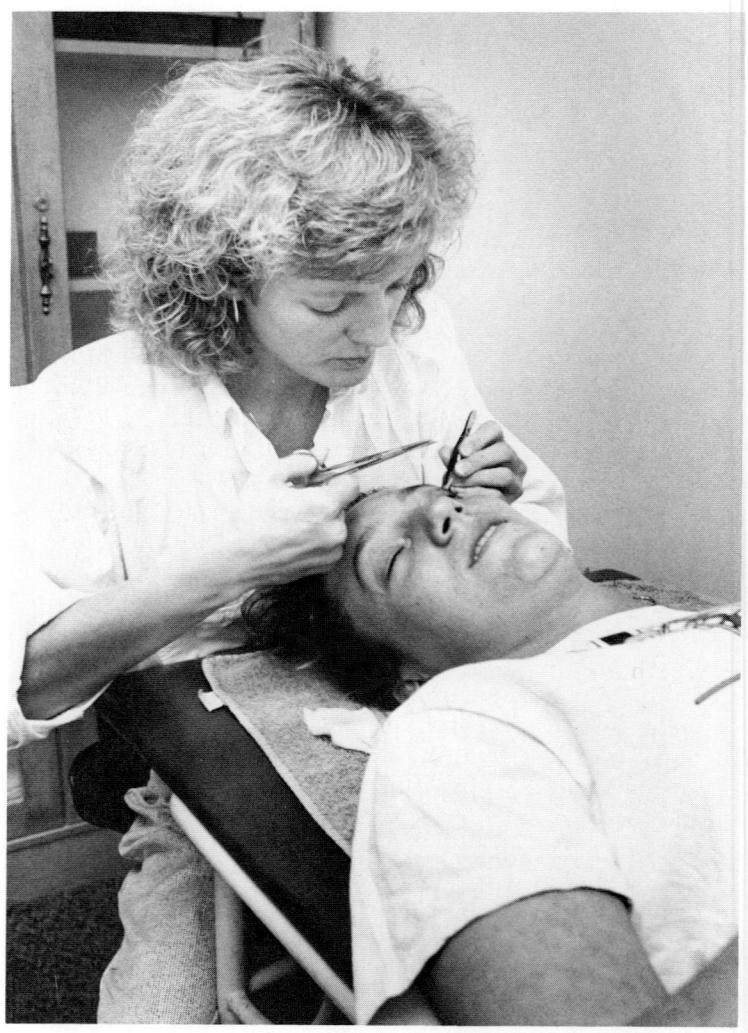

Athletic Training

An athletic trainer works within the athletic setting to implement prevention-of-injury programs, provide immediate treatment of injuries, and rehabilitate injured athletes. Among other things, the trainer administers first aid, applies bandages and strapping to reduce the potential for injury, administers therapeutic techniques under the supervision of a physician, assists with physical examinations, establishes and administers preventive conditioning programs for athletes, provides nutritional advice and supervises diets, selects and fits equipment, and oversees the safety of facilities and equipment.

The athletic trainer is primarily trying to prevent injuries; therefore, much of the job is devoted to the application of physical support systems to athletes, such as tape, braces, and so on. However, the trainer literally needs the broad knowledge and good common sense of a general practitioner to be able to deal with the variety of concerns and immediate-care-of-injury situations that arise on the job.

Physical Therapy

The distinguishing feature of the physical therapy profession is rehabilitation. Therapists do not usually diagnose or evaluate athletic injuries, but rather work more exclusively to design and implement rehabilitation exercise programs. Often these programs are prescribed by a doctor and then administered in a hospital. However, there is a trend away from the hospital setting to private practice (Magistro, 1989), where assessment of injuries has now become a more common service (Dennis, 1987).

The marked differences between an athletic trainer and a physical therapist are: A therapist essentially has a job of regular hours, while a trainer must devote extended days to covering games; and the therapist does not provide the emergency medical care a trainer does in cases of athletic injuries, nor does the therapist engage to as much of an extent in preventive care. The therapist works primarily with muscular and skeletal problems, whereas the athletic trainer is called on to deal with internal injuries as well. Therapists see clients on a one-to-one basis, usually for a time-limited appointment in a relatively quiet setting. In contrast, anyone who has been in an athletic training room just before teams are about to practice knows how electric, not to mention hectic, the atmosphere can be.

Exercise Technology

These positions involve the administration and analysis of stress and fitness tests for hospitals, medical clinics, health clubs, or fitness centers. In medical settings, the position usually emphasizes stress testing; whereas, in health clubs or fitness centers, the job may also include giving fitness assessments, body composition analyses, tests of respiratory function, and motor performance tests. In all cases, the tests are followed by a prescription for an exercise program. In the medical scenes, the program will be specific, usually designed to overcome a certain health condition. Cardiac rehabilitation centers are noticeable locations. In health maintenance centers, the exercise prescriptions will be more general, often including related recommendations for other influencing factors, such as diet.

Other Sports Medicine Positions

Some careers under the broad category of sports medicine do not directly involve a background in medicine or physiology. For example, biomechanics professionals analyze human movement for companies that manufacture sports equipment or for corporations interested in improving the efficiency and safety of their employees. Elsewhere, sport psychologists analyze and treat behavioral and emotional problems that affect athletic performance. Other positions may involve the assessment and remediation of developmental disorders, or the study of exercise within the realm of wellness. But in truth, such positions are unusual. Most of these opportunities emerge from college and university teaching positions that provide the base for work in research labs and as a consultant.

Overall Qualifications and Outlook

Most positions in sports medicine require highly specialized training. National certification standards must be met for athletic trainers, physical therapists, and exercise technologists working in medical clinics. These standards dictate the academic and practical experiences necessary for sanction to work in those fields.

The job market for athletic trainers and physical therapists is wide open. Acquiring certification in these fields is a virtual assurance of a job. Athletic training was once an all-male profession, but now the market has become particularly inviting for women. It would seem logical to predict that jobs for athletic trainers are ready for an incredible increase in number, especially in the high schools, where there is only one certified trainer for every 5,500 athletes (Stopka and Kaiser, 1988). Legal liabilities will assuredly coerce more and more high schools into hiring trainers. And in physical therapy, the availability of professional positions is expected to stay ahead of the supply of certified therapists through the 1990s (Scully and Barnes, 1989). Overall, sports medicine offers a highly promising avenue for the acquisition of a professional career.

OTHER OPTIONS

Some potential careers are not obviously apparent but may be found outside of traditional arenas. Anyplace where humans are in motion, there could be a career for someone who has studied human motion. In this regard, career options may be limited only by one's imagination.

Many new vocational areas have recently appeared or have been created. They ebb and sway in keeping with public need or with trends in certain professions. For example, sport management became a vocational vogue when private and corporate fitness centers began their phenomenal growth. Similarly, special physical education was once an expanding discipline, but governmental restrictions in funding never provided the jobs that were anticipated. Recently, wellness-related jobs have appeared in considerable number, but will the supply of qualified persons eventually exceed the demand?

There is some convenience to devising a list of potential careers, and indeed such a list is provided in table 14.1. But such a listing is useful mostly for stimulating one's thoughts about the variety of potential jobs that could be available. It does not really define the particular nature of the job that is listed. And some practicality must be injected into the thought process as well. It may be intriguing, for example, to think of oneself as a trainer for a professional team, without recognizing that a thousand other aspiring athletic trainers have the same lofty goal.

Table 14.1 Potential Careers in the Human Movement Sciences

Education	
Preschools	Junior/Community Colleges
Elementary School	College and University
Junior High/Middle School	Foreign Schools
High School	Military Schools
Special Physical Education	Church Schools

Coaching	
Interscholastic Programs	Community Sport Programs
Intercollegiate Programs	Military Sport Programs
Sports Academies	Sport Camps

Applications

Table 14.1 *Continued.*

Health and Leisure Industries

Health/Fitness Centers	Community Recreation Centers
Weight Loss Clinics	YMCA/YWCA
Diet Counseling Centers	Camps
City/County Health Centers	Geriatric Programs
Stress Management Programs	Country Clubs/Resorts
Military Fitness	Travel and Tourism
Business/Corporate Fitness	Retirement Communities
Police and Fire Departments	Housing Complexes
Industrial Recreation Programs	State/National Park Service
Wellness Centers	Outward Bound/NOLS
Public or Private Sports Clubs	Cruise Liners

Sports Medicine

Athletic Training	Dance Therapy
Physical Therapy	Recreation Therapy
Sports Injury/Rehabilitation Centers	Occupational Therapy
Exercise Technology	Paramedical Centers
Exercise Prescription	Assessment/Remediation of Developmental Disorders
Medical Clinics/Hospitals	
Cardiac Rehabilitation Centers	Human Movement Analysis for Manufacturers
Pediatric Centers	
Nursing Homes	Ergonomics
Research	Sport Psychology/Counseling
Schools of Allied Health	Sports Nutrition
	Trauma Centers

Sports Management

Athletic Administration	Retirement Communities
Physical Education Programs	Resorts/Country Clubs
Director of Campus Recreation	Facilities Management
Director of Intramurals	Sports Events Organization
Sports Information Director	Penetentiaries
Corporate Fitness Programs	Professional Sports
Community Recreation Centers	Athletic Finance
Health/Fitness Centers	Commercial Sport Clubs

Other Sport-Related Careers

Sports Journalism	Sport Facilities Design
Sports Photography	Sport Clothing Design
TV/Radio Sportscasting	Direct Sales
Video Production	Sport Equipment Design
Sports Program Director	Officiating
Sport Art	Sport Law
Sports Marketing	Financial Legal Consultant

Or a career in ergonomics whereby one would study the efficiency of human work patterns may sound like an appealing and lucrative job, but competition for such a position will come from others who have graduated from programs in human engineering.

On the other hand, something is to be said for the motivational power of a determined career objective. Given a vocational target, or at least a cluster of desirable job settings for one's personal interests, energies can become directionalized. Then, the years of academic preparation and the early vocational apprenticeships that may at first be necessary will ultimately coalesce into the target career. Said differently, a determined person sees a career goal clearly, aims for it, and gets it.

SUMMARY

Not so long ago, when someone obtained a degree in physical education, they got a teaching job that included coaching. End of career choice.

That avenue is still the most lasting physical education vocation and is still taken by many people. But now other options add to the appeal of the discipline. New applications for the sciences of human movement have emerged from the expansion of the study areas that make up the profession. Perhaps even more careers, not yet envisioned, are still on the horizon. It's the best of both worlds. The traditional careers still exist, and intriguing new careers are emerging.

To the Reader

The pursuit of a career might be divided into three phases: *awareness, exploration,* and *preparation.* In the career awareness phase, all the potential jobs that deal with human movement are identified, including some that may at first seem only remotely related. In the second phase—career exploration—the choices are narrowed, and the characteristics of each one are investigated. The preparation phase is the acquisition of actual job skills that relate to the fields of choice.

From this three-phase viewpoint, the exploration segment probably receives the least attention. Exploration means not only narrowing the choices down to those that fit your interests but also actively identifying the particulars that make up the real occupations. One direct way to accumulate such information is to identify a possible career and then seek on-the-job specifications about the nature of that career. For example, even though teaching has been an openly viable profession for much of your life (and it may seem that you know all about it), conversations with teachers might reveal some peculiarities about the job that you may not have previously recognized. Your intention is to gain some "inside information" about the job by asking questions such as: What do you really do in your job? Is there anything you wish you would have had more preparation for when you began your career? What do you find intolerable? What do you see as the future of the profession? Most people, in any profession, are fairly analytical about their career choice once they are on the job.

Ask your source for permission to go through at least half a day with them to see first-hand what the job entails. You may be surprised, for example, to find how much time an athletic director spends by necessity in political posturing, or how much attention a health club director gives to financial matters, or how many ankles an athletic trainer tapes. But more than that, you will have gained insights and realistic information that will add to your decision-making process about career choices.

Suggested Projects

1. Invite several faculty members who teach in different subdisciplines (such as biomechanics, exercise physiology, etc.) to your class. Have them discuss, either individually or as a panel, the job potentials in their respective fields.
2. Visit the placement service on your campus and leaf through the announcements of job openings. Can you identify major categories of jobs, such as education or the leisure industry, that seem to have the greatest availability?
3. Assume you are a career counselor in a high school. A student comes to you who is considering attending college to major in physical education. What factors will you discuss with this student who is contemplating that career choice?
4. A friend of yours is thinking of becoming a sport psychologist. How would you help your friend to decide whether or not to go ahead with this idea?
5. Compile a list of agencies, resources, and other contacts that you can use to help you secure a job in a specified field.
6. Write your own definition of an ideal career. Include such factors as the nature of the work, whether it is service oriented, whether you must work with other people, whether you want to be your own boss, what time of the day you would work, and anything else you can think of. Do any existing careers in the human movement sciences fit your description?

References

Dennis, J. K. (1987). What Physiotherapists in Private Practice Do: The Effect of Sex and Training on Clinical Behavior. *Australian Journal of Physiotherapy,* 33, 245–252.

Desensi, J. T., and Koehler, L. S. (1989). Sport and Fitness Management Opportunities for Women. *Journal of Health, Physical Education, and Recreation,* 60(3), 55–57.

Ellis, M. J. (1988). *The Business of Physical Education: Future of the Profession.* Champaign, IL: Human Kinetics Publishers.

Knoppers, A. (1987). Gender and the Coaching Profession. *Quest,* 39(1), 9–22.

Lambrecht, K. (1987). An Analysis of the Competencies of Sports and Athletic Club Managers. *Journal of Sport Management,* 1(2), 116–128.

Linder, S. B. (1970). *The Harried Leisure Class.* New York: Columbia University Press.

Magistro, C. M. (1989). Clinical Decision Making in Physical Therapy: A Practitioner's Perspective. *Physical Therapy,* 69, 525–534.

Scully, R. M., and Barnes, M. R. (1989). *Physical Therapy.* Hagerstown, MD: J. B. Lippincott.

Sessoms, H. D. (1987). Reassessing the Role of Public Leisure Services. In J. J. Bannon (Ed.), *Current Issues in Leisure Services: Looking Ahead in a Time of Transition.* Washington, DC: International City Management. (pp. 168–177).

Sorkin, A. L. (1988). *Monetary and Fiscal Policy and Business Cycles in the Modern Era.* Lexington, MA: Lexington Books.

Stopka, C., and Kaiser, D. (1988). Certified Athletic Trainers in our Secondary Schools: The Need and the Solution. *Athletic Training,* 23, 322–324.

Veal, A. J. (1987). *Leisure and the Future.* London: Allen and Unwin.

Chapter 15

Career Development: Getting Ready for the Real World

The Academic World and the Vocational World

Narrowing the Focus

Vocational Values

General Vocational Themes

Specific Job Requirements

The Value of Field Experiences

Summary

To the Reader

Suggested Projects

References

The appropriate pathway to acquiring background preparation for a career begins with noting interest areas and recognizing personality characteristics.

Clusters of jobs can be categorized by the nature of their work environment, and an individual's personality traits can be matched with the job categories.

Upon this match, the specific requirements of qualification for job clusters can be identified.

This leads to plans of action that will provide the required and supplemental background experiences of preparation for a given career.

IT'S a tough job being a student. The uncountable assignments, the overwhelming amount of information that must be assimilated, the endless evening hours that slip into early morning hours trying to cram one more fact into an already crowded brain—sometimes it seems that to be a student requires the sacrifice of two things: free time and sleep.

It is a considerable investment of time and energy, to say nothing of money, to acquire the background essential for entry into the professional world. Along with this commitment, you may occasionally feel—perhaps already have felt—insecure about the path to take. Of course, the completion of a required list of classes is necessary for the degree. But beyond that, will other experiences and course work enhance career readiness? Is there anything one can do to make oneself more marketable?

THE ACADEMIC WORLD AND THE VOCATIONAL WORLD

The general purpose of academic preparation is to provide a broad-based background for a career. A more focused goal is to offer specific courses of study and experiences related to the various specialties within a given field.

The core courses of a curriculum—those required by a department—provide the foundation for a career. They are broad in scope and are designed to establish a solid base for any further study within the discipline. For example, a first course in human physiology (or exercise physiology) serves to build an extensive background about how human systems operate and therein acts as a supporting course for other studies of human function.

These general background courses are required of all majors and are usually fulfilled during the first and second years of college. They are based on the identifiable concepts and principles that constitute the academic discipline of the profession and are derived from certain global philosophies and the specific bodies of knowledge within each subdiscipline. The sum total of these concepts and information illuminates the dimensions, phenomena, and outcomes of human movement. This core preparation is designed to equip students with information that is applicable to all physical education careers.

Some occupations, however, require preparation and/or certification that is unique to that field. The particular academic and experiential requirements for athletic training, for example, are markedly different from those for sports management. While the core curriculum offers the foundation for both an athletic trainer and a manager of a sports facility,

Career Development: Getting Ready for the Real World

The core courses of a curriculum provide the foundation for a career.
University of Denver file photo.

the academic background should be as centered as possible on the courses that will bolster one's qualifications for a given career. In this regard, the academic world can be more closely matched with the vocational world.

NARROWING THE FOCUS

There's a sign that can be found in career counselors' offices: "There are 35,000 careers to follow. Which one do you want to know about?"

The current diversification of potential occupations poses a significant dilemma for someone who has not clearly focused on a particular specialty. If you entered college in the "undecided" category, you are part of a growing body of students that may now approximate 40 percent of incoming freshmen nationally (Rentz and Saddlemire, 1988). And if you are typical, your anxiety level and feelings of insecurity about your

Having elected a major field of study—physical education, sport sciences, human movement, or exercise science—one still has to choose from among a multitude of directions that can be taken within that major.
Photo by Tom Cherrey.

future are higher than those of students who have declared a major (Newman, Fuqua, and Seaworth, 1989), but you are nevertheless a reasonably happy and well-adjusted student (Lucas and Epperson, 1988). If you *have* elected a major field of study—physical education or sport sciences or human movement or exercise science or whatever the designation is at your school—you still have decisions to make about the multitude of directions that can be taken within that major.

When uncertainty exists, begin by identifying a range of possible careers, cluster them around some logical principle, then find what actions lead to the appropriate background. If, for example, you would like a career in teaching and coaching, the required curriculum for certification is determined by the state, and your path to that end is well laid out. But even so, there may be some other unrequired experiences and course work that, in addition to the regular curriculum, will help you to stand out from the rest of the crowd when you apply for your first job.

Or suppose you envision yourself working in a profession that deals with the care and treatment of athletic injuries. Again, certification standards will direct you into a rather specific collection of courses and experiences that must be completed for sanction into the job market. Beyond that, certain field experiences may be the factor that will get you the job you want.

Or, perhaps a career in sports management is an appeal. Additional course work in finance, management, or marketing may be valuable assets in your background.

In all cases, the final decision of a specific preparatory pathway will emerge when you have identified the cluster of potential careers that is appealing and then narrowed the choices to those that can fit into a general scheme of academic foundation that will support all of the possibilities. This will engender a certain lineup of study that will give you the best return for your investment. The origin of all this is based on (1) what your interests are, (2) what your skills and abilities are, and (3) the cluster of occupational areas that fit the other two.

VOCATIONAL VALUES

Often the terms *interests* and *values* are used interchangeably. It is generally assumed that interests are preferences for those things someone values. And so it is further assumed that vocational interests would be closely related to someone's life values. Implicit in this assumption is the central idea that interests and values would stimulate vocational preferences, and indeed this does seem to be generally true (Borgen, 1986).

As a psychological construct, *values* could be considered to fit two categories. The first are values regarding desirable and undesirable modes of conduct; for example, being ambitious, honest, loyal, and so on. These are called *instrumental values*. The second kind of values pertains to desirable end-states of existence, such as having a comfortable life, happiness, a pleasant place to live, and so on. They are called *terminal values* (Rokeach, 1973). The two are often interrelated. For instance, a health club manager may have high instrumental values of being hardworking, organized, and efficient. These traits will lead to the terminal values that come from a smoothly run facility.

From another perspective, however, the two value systems may not be so complementary. An aspiring teacher may have the instrumental values of enjoying intellectual stimulation, creative endeavors, and a reasonable degree of independence. All these are possible through that profession. Yet the teacher may also have a high terminal value for affluent living. A conflict thus arises, for to become wealthy by teaching is simply not possible.

This dichotomy is often reflected in tests of vocational aptitude. The Strong-Campbell Interest Inventory is the most widely used vocational preference instrument in America (Raskin, 1987). Results of the test consistently show that being a college professor ranks high as a desirable career. In contrast, being a real estate agent ranks among the least desirable careers. Yet in any given month, there are more people taking the qualifying examination for a real estate license than there are people acquiring a teaching degree in an entire year.[1] Presumably one of the reasons for this is that becoming a teacher involves four years of study, whereas one can become a real estate agent after only a few months of preparation. However, it might also be that the terminal values, in this case the potential for a large income, take precedence over instrumental values. This may be an important consideration when the terminal values are not obtainable through a desirable profession; frequently the instrumental values will be subordinated to the terminal values. For example, some evidence indicates that physicians in general practice are less content with their career choice than physical therapists are (Scully, 1989), but they persist in their choice because of the financial returns.

Viewed differently, instrumental values can simply outweigh terminal values. Athletic trainers, for instance, will not become wealthy through their profession. But their satisfaction with their career choice is very high, and the burnout rate in their profession is very low (Capel, 1986).

GENERAL VOCATIONAL THEMES

To provide a theoretical structure for how occupational choices are made, vocational psychologists often rely on a description of events that lead to job preferences. One widely recognized theory (Holland, 1985) offers two basic assumptions:

1. As a result of a person's heredity and experiences, that person will develop interest in, and preferences for, certain activities that lead to the development of related occupational skills. These interests then further influence the development of other aspects of the individual's personality. For example, a physical education teacher presumably had an original interest in motor activity, with a correlated development of ability in performance leading to further participation in activity, which in turn influenced that person's personality development, in part because of the social contacts that were made through participation and in part because sports magnified and satisfied certain predispositions.

---

[1] Data obtained from the Jones Real Estate College in Denver, Colorado, and the *Chronical of Higher Education*.

An interest in physical activity may be maintained through teaching and/or coaching.
University of Denver file photo.

2. For each interest and preference, there exists somewhere a compatible occupation. The physical education teacher who wanted to continue an interest in activity found that through teaching and coaching, this interest could be maintained. Other people, because of similar interests, have also chosen the same career, and thus they help to create and perpetuate the working atmosphere.

According to this theory, a career choice is an outgrowth of a preference for certain life activities. Participation in those activities emphasizes certain personality characteristics, which in turn reinforces the interests, which prompts a vocational choice that allows for exercising the skills and abilities developed through participation.

The second part of this theory categorizes certain vocational types. It describes six vocational clusters, each one essentially summarizing what is known about the people who are in a given occupational category. They are described here, along with a few suggested careers for each type of person:

- *Realistic personality.* Typically, these are people who prefer to deal more with things than with ideas. They perceive themselves as having mechanical and athletic ability. They prefer to be involved with concrete rather than abstract situations and may avoid settings that require verbal or interpersonal skills. They tend to be conventional in thought and have qualities of persistence, maturity, stability, and practicality. Potential careers might be in research, athletic training, physical therapy, exercise technology, or other technical fields.
- *Investigative personality.* These persons are analytical, abstract, and intellectually self-confident. They have high mathematical and scientific ability, but tend to shy away from interpersonal relationships. They are cautious, curious, and independent, with good capabilities for inventive thinking. Potential careers might be in research and sports medicine, along with certain administrative positions, or technical fields that require mathematical and scientific ability.
- *Artistic personality.* This type tends to rely more on feelings and imagination. They perceive themselves as expressive, original, intuitive, nonconforming, introspective, independent, and artistic. They value aesthetic qualities and tend to place less importance on material matters. They have artistic rather than mathematical aptitudes and prefer free and unstructured situations that allow for their creative self-expression. Obvious careers may be in teaching, along with leisure and recreation, sports journalism, and other creative fields.
- *Social personality.* These are people who have high interest in other people and are sensitive to the needs of others. They prefer situations calling for the interpersonal skills required to support other people and to help them improve in any regard. They value social and ethical concerns and view themselves as being humanistic, empathetic, cheerful, impulsive, scholarly, and verbally oriented. They are clearly inclined toward careers in teaching, coaching, leisure and recreation, sports information, and any of the helping vocations.
- *Enterprising personality.* Persons who are adventurous, dominant, and persuasive are in this category. They are drawn to power and leadership roles. They perceive themselves as aggressive, popular, self-confident, social, possessing leadership and speaking abilities,

and lacking scientific aptitude. They use their social and verbal skills to obtain status or goals. Enterprising types might be found in sports management and administration, industrial and corporate fitness centers, outdoor "adventure-type" jobs, and in other leadership roles.

Conventional personality. This type tends to be practical, organized, and enjoys working in well-structured situations. They feel most comfortable with environments that ask for handling numerical data, keeping records, or using computers. They value business and economic achievement and view themselves as being orderly conformists with high clerical skills. They are generally conscientious, efficient, practical, and self-controlled. Potential careers could be in research, sports management, manufacture and sale of sports equipment, or sports-related business jobs.

While no individual is all one type, people tend to affiliate with, enjoy being around, and have the characteristics of one, two, or sometimes three of the types. Work environments likewise tend to attract the personality types that fit the demands of the job. Thus, when personality and the work environment are closely matched, success in the job, at least in theory, is more probable.

SPECIFIC JOB REQUIREMENTS

Defining what the real world on the job will be like is essential before one can prepare for it appropriately. What people *do* in their professions determines what they need preparation for. Effectively translating the academic world to the work world begins with knowing the work world. But sometimes defining a job will result in a list of only those things that are definable. For example, it is said that for any administrative job a person needs a "master's degree in common sense." But common sense is a reasoning capacity that is mostly developed through experience and not suddenly acquired from a particular course. Similarly, an analysis of teaching would show a great deal of time being spent in some form of communication, yet communication skills are seldom offered as a distinct course, or even as part of a course, in a standard curriculum.

Sometimes, however, jobs have very defined preparational requirements. Sports medicine careers are most noticeable in this regard. Qualifying for certain positions can occur only when a candidate has been certified by a national association. Athletic training, for example, requires certification from the National Athletic Trainers Association (NATA). As of this writing, that includes: (1) a bachelor's degree,

Certification as an athletic trainer includes on-site experience under the direct supervision of a National Athletic Trainers Association trainer.
Photo by Tom Cherrey.

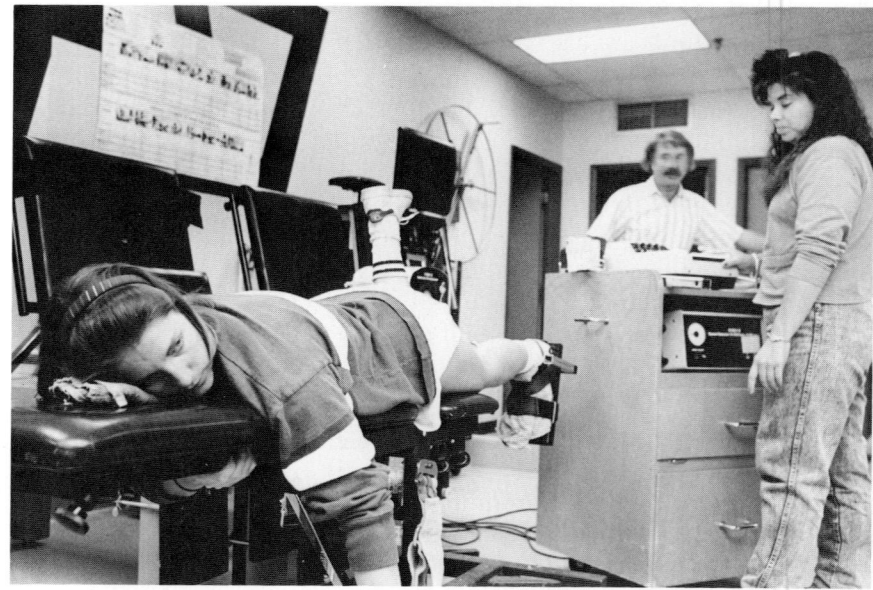

(2) current Red Cross first aid and CPR certification, and (3) at least fifteen hundred hours of experience under the direct supervision of an NATA-certified athletic trainer or successful completion of an NATA-approved athletic training education program. This is followed by an examination that includes written, oral, and simulation sections, given at specified times and locations by the NATA. Lowest scores on this exam, incidentally, occur on the oral section (Draper, 1989), thus suggesting that the preparation hours should include more oral examinations in the classes.

In physical therapy, licensure is regulated by state law and obtained from each state, although a national certifying exam is a prerequisite. Course preparation for this exam generally encompasses two years beyond the bachelor's degree.

Some positions in exercise technology will require certification from the American College of Sports Medicine. Four levels of certification are available: Fitness Instructor, Exercise Test Technologist, Exercise Specialist, and Exercise Program Director.

Other professions may, in the future, have specific certification requirements. For instance, no national coaching certification system currently is in place, and in most states, there are no specific requirements to be met. But both the National Federation Interscholastic Coaches Association and the National High School Athletic Coaches Association have recommended a national standard for certifying coaches. In addition, coaches apparently are also in favor of some sort of certification system (Kimiecik, 1988).

In another regard, the National Association for Sport and Physical Education has recommended a standard curriculum for preparing all students for careers in fitness, and the American Association of Fitness Directors in Business and Industry has suggested a curriculum for students interested in careers in corporate fitness. Accordingly, a specific career pathway may need to adhere to the specifications dictated by a certifying agency, or if no certification is needed, the curriculum should at least stay within the guidelines provided by nationally recognized professional associations.

THE VALUE OF FIELD EXPERIENCES

One especially valuable way to prepare for a job is to actually get into the marketplace while still in school. Internships are an excellent way to gain on-site career experience and learn more about the vocational area, besides making contacts that may be important for the future. Internships are usually part-time work assignments and generally last for one academic term. They tend to be project-oriented and usually carry credit, sometimes even pay. And they can be arranged to fit around a campus class schedule.

Sometimes a cooperative educational experience can be arranged whereby the time given is longer or more extensive than an internship and the responsibilities of the job are more formalized. If your school does not have an internship or co-op program in place, other field studies can be arranged by channeling the experience through an independent study or simply by diligently searching for a suitable volunteer field arrangement. Even summer jobs can build one's skill base for future employment. In the long run, career-related field experiences turn out to be the factor that carries the most positive influence for job acquisition (Stevens, 1986).

SUMMARY

In the final view, becoming prepared for a given profession might be summed up as (1) first identifying your skills and interests, then (2) determining a cluster of jobs that suit those skills and interests, and (3) mapping out the courses and experiences that will maximize your marketability. In most cases, the appropriate background is built into the major curriculum, and/or is determined by certification requirements. But extra attention to appropriate field experiences and other, related course work will enhance your qualifications for easy entry into a chosen career.

To the Reader

It may be that the final considerations for a career choice come down to the following seven factors (Conway, 1981):

1. *Monetary reward.* Money is a strong inducement to people who fit into the enterprising occupational group of the Holland theory discussed earlier in this chapter. If money is a high terminal value for you, then you simply must recognize that high salaries for jobs in the human movement sciences are rare.

2. *Type of Work.* Some people prefer working primarily with data, others with people, and still others with things. Most people entering the broad fields of physical education prefer working with people and therefore fit into the artistic and social occupational categories of the Holland theory.

    The Holland system is of help in the selection of a career because it emphasizes that personal interests and personality characteristics are important considerations. Furthermore, people who change jobs later in their careers often have started out in an occupational group that was not the best match for their characteristics. Their change usually brings them into a group that is in closer alignment with their primary interests and personality traits (NOICC, 1986).

3. *Level of responsibility.* Decisions about the degree of responsibility one is willing to assume are usually established only after being on the job and may change with time. Often, they also change in nature. For example, education promotions lead to administrative positions, which require less of what someone may have originally enjoyed about the field (teaching) and more of what they did not like (budgeting, scheduling, answering parents' concerns, and similar tasks).

4. *Work environment.* The job environment is very important for someone who needs to satisfy strong instrumental values. Since physical education and its outgrowth professions tend to attract people who have an affinity for working with people rather than things, and presumably this is also related to instrumental needs, the work environment is a major consideration.

5. *Social needs and desires.* Certain careers do not allow much leisure time. Coaching is a prime example; and most administrative positions also demand long hours on the job. If free time is important to you, then the range of jobs you might consider is narrowed. Teaching has the distinct advantage of providing large blocks of free time (summer vacation) when one can travel, study, or work in a different environment. Furthermore, while the demands of teaching are more than might be originally realized, the after-hours work can be accomplished at home at a relaxed pace. Other jobs may require that all the work be accomplished on-site. A director of campus recreation must devote many evening hours to the job, and an athletic trainer must be available for games held after school and on weekends. In these cases, the extra work required is on-the-job-site work.
6. *Prestige.* The need for ego satisfaction is in part met by the prestige associated with certain careers. Jobs associated with human physical activity can vary widely in terms of their societal status, but this may be of secondary importance if the job matches your instrumental values with your occupational personality type.
7. *Security.* Job security can be a serious consideration. In teaching, the professional future is relatively assured once tenure is acquired. Security with coaching is tenuous at best. Likewise, jobs that rely on funding are less stable. Positions in industry, or even in leisure and recreation, might suddenly be affected by changes in allocated money.

In the final analysis, perhaps the best guide is your feelings—your general sense of what you believe you would like to do for a living. Some careers seem to be "alive" in your mind with a general spirit of conscious perception about their desirability. The most telling factor in making a career choice might be that when it's right, you know it's right.

Suggested Projects

1. Write a two-page autobiography summarizing factors that you view to have been influential at certain points of your life. How do you think they may have affected your contemplation of a career at this time?
2. Prepare a brief outline of all the jobs you have had to this point in your life. Then analyze the pattern of the jobs (and your satisfaction with each) on the basis of the Holland theory of career formulations.
3. Talk to some experienced counselors about their theories of career development and how they put them to use in their own lives.

4. Interview someone currently employed in the vocational area that is of your preference. Ask that person what the most unexpected parts of their job were when they first began their career, and have them suggest a series of academic and/or field experiences that will best prepare you for entry into that career.
5. Develop an individual plan of action that you can use over the next two or three years to assure that you will acquire the proper background preparation for your career preferences.
6. Devise a plan of action that you can put into use between now and the start of the next term. Include the following:
   a. Define your career plan. (What do you want to do upon graduation?)
   b. Gather information. (Spend at least 10 hours investigating the job possibilities that fit your career plan.)
   c. Clarify your values. (Does the information you gathered about the possibilities seem to fit your vocational value system?)
   d. Identify alternatives. (What other routes are possible within your career plans?)
   e. Estimate probable outcomes. (What likely career directions does this lead you to?)
   f. Start action. (Determine a list of activities that focus on your estimated probable career choices that you can begin before the start of the next term.)

References

Borgen, F. H. (1986). New Approaches to the Assessment of Interests. In W. B. Walsh and S. H. Osipow (Eds.), *Advances in Vocational Psychology. Vol. 1. The Assessment of Interests.* Hillsdale, NJ: Lawrence Erlbaum Associates.

Capel, S. A. (1986). Psychological and Organizational Factors Related to Burnout in Athletic Trainers. *Athletic Training, 21,* 322–327.

Conway, K. (1981). Seven Factors in Setting Career Goals. *Journal of College Placement, 42*(1), 53–55.

Draper, D. O. (1989). Students' Learning Styles Compared with Their Performance on the NATA Certification Exam. *Athletic Training, 24,* 234–235ff.

Holland, J. L. (1985). *Making Vocational Choices: A Theory of Vocational Personalities and Work Environments.* (2nd ed.). Englewood Cliffs, NJ: Prentice-Hall.

Kimiecik, J. C. (1988). Who Needs Coaches' Education? Us Coaches Do. *The Physician and Sportsmedicine, 16*(11), 124–136.

Lucas, M., and Epperson, D. (1988). Personality Types in Vocationally Undecided Students. *Journal of College Student Development, 29,* 460–466.

National Occupational Information Coordinating Committee (1986). *Using Labor Market Information in Career Exploration and Decision Making: A Resource Guide.* Garrett Park, MD: Garrett Park Press.

Newman, J. L., Fuqua, D. R., and Seaworth, T. B. (1989). The Role of Anxiety in Career Indecision: Implications for Diagnosis and Treatment. *The Career Development Quarterly, 37,* 221–231.

Raskin, P. M. (1987). *Vocational Counseling: A Guide for the Practitioner.* New York: Teachers College Press.

Rentz, A. L. and Saddlemire, G. L. (1988). *Student Affairs Functions in Higher Education.* Springfield, IL: Charles C. Thomas.

Rokeach, M. (1973). *The Nature of Human Values.* New York: The Free Press.

Scully, R. M., and Barnes, M. R. (1989). *Physical Therapy.* Hagerstown, MD: J. B. Lippincott Company.

Stevens, N. D. (1986). *Dynamics of Job-Seeking Behavior.* Springfield, IL: Charles C. Thomas.

Chapter 16

The Future: Not Exactly Like the Present

The Changing Marketplace
Providing a Better Product
New Preparation Needs
Readiness for Tomorrow
Summary
To the Reader
Suggested Projects
References

To predict the future, it is necessary to rely on a projection of present-day trends.

In this regard, certain societal trends can be seen to have the effect of changing the marketplace for the future vocational delivery of services for enhancing human well-being.

This changing marketplace in turn influences the manner in which persons entering the professions of human movement should prepare for their careers.

The end product is an anticipation of certain future changes with a readiness for adapting to the events to come.

Future. That which is to come.

Future shock. An inability to cope with rapid changes that have not been properly anticipated.

Futurology. Studying the probable form of future conditions by making assumptions based on known facts.

THE evolution of technical and social development in the world today has accelerated. Change once occurred slowly over long periods; now it is compressed into brief moments. Virtually every human endeavor has undergone wave after wave of imagination, invention, and innovation, all increasing the tempo of change itself. Newness constantly intrudes in everyday existence, flowing through the present at an ever accelerating pace, with less time for each new event. We are left to wonder if the future is really happening only one day at a time.

Predicting the future is like looking into an opaque mirror. There are reflections of the present and cloudy images beyond. It is often said that the future contains elements of necessity, of volition, and a random element. We may know, to some extent, what we need for tomorrow and have some control over getting it, but there can be no rigorous forecasting of the random element. This random element makes it necessary to restrain any predictions with "perhaps" and "possibly" and "likely" and other qualifiers that allow for variability.

To forecast the future, we are relentlessly bound to a present-day frame of reference. What is happening now is all that can be known, and all that can be anticipated with any reasonable degree of certainty is the continuation of present trends. Thus, it is usually necessary to analyze the present, and this analysis often extends into the past in order to detect the trends predominant enough to continue into the future. By projecting trends, we can assume that the future will move in certain directions, and in anticipation we can make plans of readiness. But not just linear plans that are tied to trends. We also need alternative plans that allow for the randomness of tomorrow. We need contingency preparation—ready plans of action that reduce the time it takes to adapt to change. We become armed, then, with skills that fit the continuation of trends and also with the versatility to adapt to the haphazard nature of the future.

THE CHANGING MARKETPLACE

There will always be children and young adults in schools needing the services of a physical education teacher. And there will always be coaching jobs. And if forecasts are correct, the availability of these jobs will improve. All this is buoyed by the attitude of parents, for more than 85 percent of them believe that physical education should be a required part of the curriculum (Stewart and Green, 1987). Administrators are also highly supportive of physical education (Wandzilak et. al., 1988), and there are favorable attitudes emerging from both high school students

The Future: Not Exactly Like the Present 273

Many forces shape the future job market.
University of Denver file photo.

(Rice, 1988) and college students (Mowatt, DePauw, and Hulac, 1988). Furthermore, competitive athletics continues to strengthen its solid endorsement as a school-sponsored program (Lewis, 1989).

But there are large forces at work in society that are reshaping the total job market. For one thing, the American population is getting older. The so-called baby boom opened up a wealth of teaching jobs in the 1950s and 1960s. Now that population has reached its prime working years, and is approaching retirement. Additionally, people are retiring earlier in life. This trend for early retirement, the growing numbers of people reaching a mature age, and their increasing longevity, should dramatically increase the number of health maintenance positions available in work with older age groups.

Another strong social force is the steady rise that has been occurring in the amount of "disposable" income that Americans have (essentially, the money left over after the bills are paid). This is paralleled by an increased spending on leisure activities. If we assume that disposable income will continue to rise, then another assumption follows that spending on leisure will increase as well.

An affiliated influence is the growing public awareness of health-related life-styles. Increased media attention and magazine articles on health issues have alerted the public to the benefits of an active self-management of one's own welfare. Also, physical education programs at all levels have begun emphasizing wellness, and all these factors together have put more people on the bike paths and jogging trails and in the fitness centers.

The combined effect of (1) more disposable income being spent on leisure and recreation and (2) a growing public interest in the pursuit of a healthy life has been to produce a clientele who are seeking organized ways to achieve their leisure and fitness goals. And they are willing to pay for this service. They are willing to spend more of their disposable income for the service of organized self-enhancing activities, and the opportunities for extending these services represents a strong potential job market. The jobs will appear in the private sector, where increasing numbers of clients will pay for well-managed aerobics and other fitness programs. And they will appear in the corporate market, where more companies, realizing the cost savings in medical expenses and better productivity as the results, will provide more fitness programs for their workers (Ellis, 1988).

The working population now has more free time for recreation. Even if the workweek remains steady, without the decline that has occurred since the 1960s, it is apparent that the public is viewing recreation and fitness with increasing importance, and therefore the public is consciously finding the time it needs to play, to exercise, and to enjoy an otherwise active leisure.

The whole picture points to a need for more leisure suppliers. This ranges from large-scale tour wholesalers, cruise-line companies, and resort complexes, to the smaller face-to-face services of teaching pros, community recreation leaders, fitness instructors, and so forth. In between are the multitude of middle organizations that serve local needs, such as recreation and parks districts, weight-control centers, health maintenance clubs, and so on, all of which see countless numbers of clients every day. All need personnel, from the management to the instructional level.

In sum, the population being served today is changing. Previously, organized activity programs were delivered mostly through school systems. Today, the clientele has broadened to include interested people of all ages.

More leisure time and money point to a need for more leisure suppliers.
University of Denver file photo.

PROVIDING A BETTER PRODUCT

On top of all this, the delivery of services to the expanded market is now expected to be of high quality. There are two reasons for this. The first is legal. In the past, it was typical for a health club or leisure service to hire instructional personnel who were unqualified. To get hired, it was merely necessary to have an interest in activity and some motor ability. But poorly conducted programs began to result in consumer dissatisfaction, and more importantly, in accidents and injuries incurred from harmful fitness programs. Lawsuits followed. Some health clubs went out of business. The public became wary. So health and fitness centers began to hire properly trained personnel so that they could gain consumer satisfaction and provide protection against the potential for lawsuits.

The second reason for providing a better product is found in the information about wellness that is now being given to the public. Television, radio, newspapers, and popular magazines all carry information about issues of health and fitness. Best-seller book lists often include wellness-oriented publications. As a result, the public is generally more knowledgeable, or at least more aware, of matters that can affect their

In general, the public has become more knowledgeable about wellness and therefore has higher expectations than in the past.
University of Denver file photo.

well-being. Given this, when the public now pays for a service that is designed to improve one's state of wellness or add to one's leisure skills, the expectations are for the service to be of good quality. Just as the service rendered by other professionals (ranging from medicine to auto repair) is expected to satisfy a need, the service given by the health and leisure industries must likewise comply to a high standard.

NEW PREPARATION NEEDS

What all this means is that alternate directions may need to be taken by the field in general. Courses in finance, marketing, management, and program evaluation now become of increasing worth as the job of delivering services becomes as much of an entrepreneurship as an information-dispensing system. The understanding of human behavior and motivational techniques may be useful tools for every student's readiness for entry into professions where the unpredictability of the human mind may affect the consequences.

Change in the marketplace often takes place faster than change in educational curriculums. In part this is due to the generally conservative nature of educational systems and the inherent need of college professors to maintain stability and predictability (Glatthorn, 1988). Curriculums may be getting better at divesting the absolute scientific information that comes from exercise physiology, biomechanics, and so forth, but they are not yet so good at preparing students for understanding the ubiquitous nature of human behavior (Bain, 1988). Nor does the curriculum usually endow one with the communication skills that are necessary for virtually every job in the human movement sciences. And how about computer literacy? Or logic? Or ethics? And a very pressing question: Are we becoming knowledgeable about the legal cautions that must accompany a profession that has widened its job world?

Change is a challenge in itself. Attempting to understand change is even more compelling. And trying to predict change is an enigma. But there is no doubt that the professional curriculums and the students in them must be prepared to encounter a work world that is in constant metamorphosis.

READINESS FOR TOMORROW

Notwithstanding the shortcomings that are inherent in trying to predict the future, some foresight can nevertheless help one to:

1. *Establish a framework for decision making.* Decisions made today almost unavoidably affect the future. You have made a decision to enter, or at least to consider, one of the professions concerned with human movement. You have projected your interests into the future via decisions about a present course of study.

2. *Identify opportunities.* Based on present trends, certain jobs may have a more promising outlook than others. And previously nonexistent opportunities may arise. Predicting the changes in the job market will likewise predict where the opportunities will be.

3. *Increase the degree of choice.* By identifying a range of possible career avenues, it becomes more possible to prepare for a cluster of jobs, which in turn will lead to more adaptable qualifications that can be applied to new careers that will emerge within this cluster.
4. *Emphasize the present.* Projections of future events invariably impress on one the importance of the present. Preparation for the future must begin with a plan for the courses of study that will allow for the unpredictability of change. The future may not be absolutely foreseen, but the future makes the laws for today.

SUMMARY

A part of physical education will remain in the future very much as it is today. Colleges and universities will continue to prepare teachers who will then deliver the service of organized activities and wellness programs to young people through the school systems. It is a highly regarded service, with valid objectives that transcend time.

Another part of physical education has become reconceptualized. The marketplace now includes adult clients who want high-quality services of health maintenance and leisure provisions. So physical education has become exercise science, or leisure studies, or sports management, or all the other alterations within the original discipline that must now answer to and predict the changes in the marketplace.

To the Reader

There are two ways of looking at the future. One is to seek the *desirable* future, or what we would like to happen. The other is to judge the *probable* future, or what is likely to happen. Sometimes the two are difficult to separate among the range of possibilities. Our acceptance of probable future events is based in part on how they correspond to what we want to happen.

We are forever beset with the problem that the future, as an unknown quantity, is not available for study. There are no facts about the future simply because the facts have not yet occurred. However, the very absence of fixed data can be seen as an advantage, for it suggests that we must be open-minded about what might happen instead of narrowly expecting that predicted events will happen. Thus, a forward-thinking person looks ahead not with the idea that things can be guaranteed but with a sense of versatility and readiness for the yet-unknown changes that will occur.

If we are living, as is so often said, in a time of rapid change, then we must expect that all established knowledge is vulnerable to being outdated. It might be said that there is no absolute knowledge because at some time in the future new information may make it change. It is more important to be imaginative and insightful about the future than it is to be absolute. We can never know enough to plan ahead with certainty, but we can look forward with a sense of exhilaration and a spirit of adventure.

Suggested Projects

1. Review your local newspaper for at least one week, and collect as much additional material as you can to try to determine societal trends that may affect the future job market in the field of your vocational choice.
2. Outline a brief talk on "tomorrow's jobs," using whatever information sources you can to make the predictions. As a prime reference, check your placement service or library for a copy of the *Occupational Outlook Handbook,* which is the most comprehensive publication available on job prospects for tomorrow.
3. Sketch the development of contemporary thought about physical activity. How will this carry into the next century?
4. Evaluate the future impact of increasing technological invasion into everyday life. How will this affect the use of leisure time?
5. What changes do you envision for sport in the future? What changes would you like to occur?
6. Suppose a society outlawed all sport and recreational activity. Estimate the sociological problems that would accompany this.
7. Take a position for or against the idea that tomorrow will be better than today.
8. Assume you have complete control over all events of the world for the next ten years. What will you do?

References

Bain, L. L. (1988). Beginning the Journey: Agenda for 2001. *Quest, 40*(2), 96–106.

Ellis, M. J. (1988). *The Business of Physical Education: Future of the Profession.* Champaign, IL: Human Kinetics Books.

Glatthorn, A. A. (1988). A Curriculum for the Twenty-First Century. *The Clearing House, 62*(1), 7–10.

Applications

Lewis, A. C. (1989). The Not So Extracurriculum. *Phi Delta Kappan, 70*(9), K1–K8.

Mowatt, M., DePauw, K. P., and Hulac, G. M. (1988). Attitudes toward Physical Education among College Students. *The Physical Educator, 45,* 103–108.

Rice, P. L. (1988). Attitudes of High School Students toward Physical Education Activities, Teachers, and Personal Health. *The Physical Educator, 45,* 94–99.

Stewart, M. J., and Green, S. R. (1987). Parental Attitudes toward Physical Education. *The Physical Educator, 44,* 344–348.

Wandzilak, T., Ansorge, C. J., Scheer, J., Bahls, V. M., Loper, D. A., Petrakis, E., O'Donnell, D. J., and Owens-Nauslar, J. (1988). Administrators' View of Physical Education for the 1990s. *The Clearing House, 64*(4), 180–182.

Glossary

Academic discipline An organized body of knowledge, specific to a particular area of study, with formal courses of learning.

Action research Nonlaboratory research, usually conducted by observation, with real-life situations as the setting; for example, when a teacher observes first-hand the effects of particular teaching methods.

Adapted physical education A program of physical education created or changed to make it suitable for handicapped persons.

Aerobic exercise Any exercise that can be prolonged without incurring an oxygen debt.

American Alliance for Health, Physical Education, Recreation and Dance (AAHPERD) The largest professional association in America that includes members from physical education, sports and athletics, health and safety education, recreation and leisure, and dance.

American College of Sports Medicine The largest and most influential sports medicine group in the world. It offers certification programs for individuals interested in fitness and exercise science.

Anaerobic exercise Exercise of intensity to produce an oxygen debt, wherein the demand for oxygen exceeds the supply.

Athletics Organized, vigorous, competitive sports, with specific rules governing their structure; usually meaning interscholastic, intercollegiate, or professional sports.

Athletic trainer A person who works within an athletic community to implement prevention-of-injury programs, provide immediate treatment of injuries, and rehabilitate injured athletes.

Awkward child A child who has coordination problems that make effectively performing most typical motor skills difficult.

Behaviorism As applied to teaching, a method relying upon a stimulus-response view of learning; that is, given a set of circumstances, the response of people to those circumstances is predictable.

Biomechanics An area of study in physical education that describes the movements of the human body through the use of laws of physics and principles of mechanics.

Cardiac rehabilitation An exercise-based program designed to restore organic function to people who have suffered cardiac debilitation.

Cause-and-effect In research, the notion that every event has a cause, and knowing the relationship makes it possible to control events by influencing the factors that cause them.

Corporate fitness Organized programs designed to improve the fitness of employees in corporate settings.

Dance Rhythmical and patterned succession of bodily movements, usually to the accompaniment of music.

Dance therapy A program of dance designed usually as remedial therapy to bring people to full and normal organic and/or cognitive function.

Director of Athletics A professional position that involves the organization and administration of the interscholastic or intercollegiate athletic program.

Director of Intramurals (or Director of Campus Recreation) A professional position involving the organization and administration of intramural programs; in higher education, often including other campus activities.

Education for All Handicapped Children Act (Public Law 94–142) This federal law mandates that school systems shall not deny an equal education to any individual because of a handicap.

Ergonomics The science concerned with the interactions of humans with their work and/or technological environment.

Exercise physiology Study of how the body, from a functional standpoint, responds and adjusts to exercise.

Exercise prescription A specific program of individually prescribed exercise, usually aimed at the prevention of or recovery from heart disease.

Exercise technology. A branch of the physical education profession that generally involves the administration and analysis of exercise stress tests to ascertain responses to heightened physiological states.

Handicap Any identifiable condition that limits one or more normal life activities for the afflicted person.

Handicapped person Any person who, in an educational setting, is unable to receive reasonable benefit from regular programs.

Health The general condition of the body, usually meaning an ability to function in a state of well-being, and often expressed as having physical, mental, and social dimensions.

Health enhancement Programs designed to promote wellness or to improve the general condition of the body.

Humanism An educational philosophy founded on the concept that learning is more meaningful when it is self-discovered through exploration rather than being taught by another.

Individualized education program (IEP) A detailed plan of instructional objectives and special services individually designed for a handicapped student.

Industrial recreation Programs of recreation offered to regular workers and executives in industry, often focusing on the promotion of physical fitness.

Information processing Generally, the transformation of external stimuli into memory or a response.

Interdisciplinary Study that incorporates information and/or interests from more than one academic discipline.

Kinematics A science of describing motion in terms of position, velocity, and acceleration.

Kinesiology The scientific study of movement founded on an understanding of human anatomy; often literally taken to mean the sum total of all that is known about the mechanical dynamics of human movement.

Kinetics A science of describing motion by determining the force, or cause, of the motion.

Learning In a dictionary sense, it means to gain knowledge, comprehension, or mastery through experience or study. As generally used in education, it implies a relatively permanent change in behavior.

Least restrictive environment Placement of a handicapped student in an environment that to the maximum extent possible includes regular programs.

Leisure Freedom from necessary occupation; spare time.

Mainstreaming The incorporation of handicapped students into the "mainstream" of regular educational life.

Mental practice The use of mental imagery to visualize the performance of motor skills, without accompanying overt physical execution in the normal sense of "practice."

Mind-body harmony In general, a now widely accepted recognition that the mind and body are not separate entities, but rather an integrated and mutually influential whole.

Motor control An area of study, aligned with motor learning, that endeavors to ascertain how the brain formulates plans for the control of motor movement.

Motor learning An area of study in physical education that is directly concerned with the conditions that facilitate the acquisition and/or improvement of motor skills.

Motor programs Neural patterns, stored as memory, that control general motor movements for given situations.

Motor skills Any definable physical activity, often suggesting those of an athletic bent. It also implies an ability to use the body in motion to efficiently accomplish objectives.

Movement education A teaching-and-learning technique that encourages students to experiment with motor movement to discover potentially effective ways of performing.

Occupational therapy Originally, specific work-related rehabilitation programs; now more widely used to include any constructive program for handicapping conditions.

Physical education The sum of all the physical, mental, emotional, and social outcomes that occur from an organized program of physical activity. The profession of physical education includes the academic knowledge, the unique areas of study and research techniques, and the vocational opportunities that are possible. In all cases, the central focus is on human movement.

Physical fitness A difficult-to-define concept that invariably suggests some higher level of functional capacity for the whole body, but also meaning the body's present state of being.

Physical therapist A person who attends to designing and/or implementing programs of rehabilitation for injuries, usually to athletes.

Play Spontaneous activities, with no predetermined ending and no tangible outcome, victory, or reward except for the activities themselves.

Public Law 94–142 *See* Education for All Handicapped Children Act.

Recreation Identifiable activities, often of a sport-like nature, that are voluntarily undertaken during time in which one is not required to work.

Rehabilitation Act (Public Law 93–112) Federal legislation mandating that schools must provide handicapped students with the same variety of physical education activities as the regular population.

Research A systematic way of answering questions or discovering information, using the most scientific and objective techniques possible.

Sociology of sport An area of study in physical education that investigates the structure and role of organized sports in society and the effects on the participants.

Special physical education Programs of physical education for students who, by definition, have a handicapping condition.

Sport A competitive physical activity that involves specific administrative organization and that has limits set in formal and definitive rules governing the behavior of the participants.

Sport psychology An area of study that centers on the use of psychological techniques to improve athletic performance and/or to help athletes overcome any personal problems that may interfere with their performance.

Sport science Study and research of a scientific nature that is applied toward understanding human movement in sport performance.

Sports Information Director A person who promotes an athletic program, usually at a college or university.

Sports management A course of study or career in managing organizations or establishments of sporting endeavor.

Sports medicine A branch of physical education originally referring to the application of medicine to the diagnosis, treatment, rehabilitation, and prevention of sports-related ills and injuries.

Stress test A test of a person's physiological responses to a controlled intensity of physical exercise.

Therapeutic recreation Programs using recreation as therapy for the ill, disabled, handicapped, or aged.

Title IX A federal law requiring all schools to provide equal sports opportunities for females and males.

Wellness An active approach to the life management of all factors that influence one's state of health.

Index

action research, 62
adapted physical education. *See* SPECIAL PHYSICAL EDUCATION
altered states of consciousness (in sport), 153–54
American Alliance for Health, Physical Education, Recreation and Dance (AAHPERD), 44
American College of Sports Medicine, 264
Anderson, William G., 44
Aristotle, 35
athletic coaching. *See* COACHING
athletics
   defined, 20
   origins of competition in, 36–38
   See also SPORT
athletic trainer
   duties of the, 166–67, 246–47
   importance of the, 165–66
athletic training
   careers in, 24, 248
   certification requirements for, 263–64
   defined, 22
   functions of, 246–47
   qualifications for, 171

Basedow, Johann, 40
battle of the systems, 44
Beck, Charles, 43
Beecher, Catherine, 43
behaviorism, 185–86
biomechanics
   applications of, 101–5
   compared to kinesiology, 95
   computers in, 99–101
   defined, 95
   kinematics, kinetics, and optimization in, 100–101
   qualitative applications of, 98–99
   quantitative analysis in, 99–100
   scientific basis of, 95–97
   used to define movement, 97
Boston conference, 44

career choices
   expanding variety of, 236–37
   factors influencing, 13, 266–67
career development
   new preparation needs in, 277
   phases of, 251–52
   value of field experiences in, 265
career opportunities, 235–52
   in coaching, 238–39
   in education, 237–39
   in health and leisure industries, 242–45
   in recreation, 241–45
   in special physical education, 239
   in sports management, 240–42
   in sports medicine, 245–48
careers
   narrowing the choices of, 257–59
   preparation for, 255–67
   vocational themes in, 260–63
   vocational values in, 259–60
clumsy child, 228–29
coaches
   factors in success of, 205–6
   personality characteristics of, 204–5
   role expectations of, 201–4
   typical working day of, 200–201
coaching, 199–214
   career opportunities in, 238–39
   compared to teaching, 213–14
   evaluating one's potential for, 211–12
   reasons for entering, 206–8
   reasons for leaving, 208–9
   teaching/coaching conflicts, 209–11
computers, in physical education, 99–101, 105

dance
   defined, 22
dance therapy, 169
data, in research, 57–58
de Coubertin, Baron, 44
Director of Athletics, 240
Director of Campus Recreation, 240–41
Director of Intramurals, 240–41

education-through-the-physical, 8–9, 45
exercise
 benefits of, 79–80, 86–87
 prescription, 84–86
exercise physiology, 23, 70–88
 defined, 70
 electrocardiogram uses in, 71–72
 study of cardiac risk factors in, 80–83
 study of energy sources in, 73–75
 study of muscle in, 72–73
 subcellular study in, 76
 wellness as objective of, 77–78
exercise technology, 247–48
 qualifications for positions in, 264

Fitz, George, 70
Follen, Charles, 43
Franklin, Benjamin, 42

Guts Muths, Johan, 40–41

handicapped students
 definition of, 220
 legislation for, 221–23
health
 careers in, 242–45
 defined, 22
 industry of, 26, 242–45
Henry, Franklin, 23
Hetherington, Clark, 45
history of physical education, 32–49
 Civil War to the turn of the century, 43–44
 during the Roman Empire, 38–39
 in early United States, 42–43
 in Europe, 39–42
 Greek origins, 32–38
 twentieth century America, 44–47
Homer, 32–33
humanism, 185–86
hypothesis, in research, 57

individualized education program, 225–26

Jahn, Friedrich Ludwig, 41

kinesiology
 compared to biomechanics, 95

learning
 concepts of, 110–13
 conclusions about, 114–15
 defined, 111–12
 dimensions of, 110
 stages of, 113
least restrictive environment, 224–25
leisure
 careers in, 241–45
 growing nature of, 24–25, 244–45
 industry of, 26
Lewis, Dio, 43
Ling, Per Henrick, 41

mainstreaming, 223–24
 effects of, 226–28
mental practice, 115
mind-body harmony, 6, 8–9, 10, 35–36, 38, 39, 41
motor control, 23, 109–21
 brain mechanisms of, 117–19, 120, 143–44
 defined, 110
 information processing in, 115–16
 motor programs as part of, 116–17
 neuromotor integration in, 117–19
 relationship to motor learning, 110, 120–21
 role of sensory feedback in, 119–20
motor learning, 23, 110–16
 conclusions about learning from, 114–15
 defined, 110
 information processing in, 115–16
 learning and performance as components of, 110–12
 mental practice in, 115
 relationship to motor control, 110, 120–21
motor skills
 effects of emotions on, 142–47
 effects of practice arrangements in acquiring, 114–15
 stages in learning of, 113
movement
 as an educational medium, 8–9
 as basis of physical education, 7
 control of, 116–20, 143–44
 descriptions of, 116–20, 143–44
 understanding of, 26
movement education, 186

Nachtegall, Franz, 41
natural athlete, 62–63
Newton, Isaac, 95
 laws of motion, 95–96

occupational therapy, 169
Olympic Games, 36–38, 44

peak experiences, 10, 153
physical activity
  public participation in, 6
physical education
  as a socializing process, 130-31
  careers in, 26-27, 28, 235-52
  changing marketplace of, 272-74
  concepts of, 8-10
  defined, 7
  future of, 271-78
  history of, 32-49
  interdisciplinary nature of, 23
  meaning of, 7, 27-28
  movement as basis of, 7
  need to provide a better product through, 275-76
  new preparation needs in, 277
  new terms for, 7-8
  profession of, 20, 24-26, 28
  qualifications for entering the profession of, 10-13
  reasons for entering the profession, 10-11, 13
  reasons for name changes, 8
  relationship to medicine, 26-27
  relationship to other areas, 20-22
  research in, 62-65
  science in, 23-24, 75-76, 95-97, 99-100
  technology in, 26
physical educators
  personality characteristics of, 12
physical fitness
  defined, 22
physical therapist
  duties of the, 167-69
physical therapy
  as a profession, 167-68
  career potentials in, 169, 248
  compared to occupational therapy, 169
  compared to recreational therapy, 169
  defined, 22
  licensure requirements for, 264
physiology of exercise. See EXERCISE PHYSIOLOGY
Plato, 35
play
  defined, 21
psychology of sport. See SPORT PSYCHOLOGY

recreation
  careers in, 241-45
  defined, 21
  public participation in, 25, 45-46, 241-45
recreation therapy, 169
research, 55-66
  action, 62
  characteristics of, 57-58
  data in, 57-58
  defined, 56
  examples of, 62-65
  hypothesis in, 57

impact on physical education of, 62-66
interpretation of data in, 58-59
meaning of, 56
validity in, 57
value of, 59
RISKO, 80-83
Round Hill School, 43
Rousseau, Jean-Jacques, 40

Salzmann, Christian, 40
Sargent, Dudley, 43-44
sociology of sport, 24, 125-37
  applied to educational settings, 130-32
  as a study of equity and discrimination, 133-34
  as a study of the future of sport, 134-35
  defined, 126
  focus of, 126-28
  future of, 136
  sport as a socializing process in, 128-30
Socrates, 35
special physical education
  careers in, 239
  defined, 220
  developmental delays, 228-29
  individualized education program in, 225-26
  least restrictive environment in, 224-25
  mainstreaming in, 223-24, 226-28
  preparation for teaching in, 230-31
Spiess, Adolph, 41
sport
  altered states of consciousness in, 153-54
  and social values, 127-28
  as a socializing process, 128-30
  beginnings of, 36-38
  defined, 20
  equity and discrimination in, 133-34
  in educational settings, 131-32
  future of, 134-35
sport psychology, 24, 141-55
  as a study of altered states of consciousness, 153-54
  as a study of arousal levels, 144-47
  defined, 143
  functions of professionals in, 154
  intervention strategies in, 147-48
  mental practice in, 151-53
  qualifications to enter the field of, 154-55
  study of emotion in, 143-44
Sports Information Director, 240
sports management, 240-42, 249-50
sports medicine, 24, 39, 76, 159-71
  applied to preparation for competition, 161-63
  areas included in, 160-61
  as a study of environmental stress, 163-65
  athletic trainer's use of, 165-67
  careers in, 245-48
  defined, 22
  use of therapeutic modalities in, 167-69

teaching, 179–92
    career opportunities in, 237–39
    components of the job, 178–80
    evolution of methods in, 185–86
    factors that relate to obtaining a job in, 192
    financial considerations of, 188–89
    importance of class management in, 181–82
    profiles of effective, 182–85
    reasons for career choices in, 186–88
    state of the market, 189–90, 239
Turner movement, 41

validity, in research, 57

wellness
    defined, 22
    objectives of, 77–78
Williams, Jesse Feiring, 45
Wood, Thomas, 44–45